TOWARDS EM

WITHDRAWN

TOWARDS EMANCIPATION

German Women Writers
of the Nineteenth Century

Carol Diethe

Berghahn Books
New York • Oxford

First published in 1998 by

Berghahn Books

© 1998 Carol Diethe

Library of Congress Cataloging-in-Publication Data
Diethe, Carol, 1943–
   Towards emancipation : German women writers of the
nineteenth century / Carol Diethe.
      p.   cm.
   Includes bibliographical references and index.
   ISBN 1-57181-932-0 (alk. paper). -- ISBN 1-57181-933-9
(pbk. : alk. paper)
   1. German literature -- 19th century -- History and criticism.
   2. German literature -- Women authors -- History and
criticism.
   3. Women authors -- Germany -- Biography. 4. Women --
Germany -- Social conditions. 5. Feminism and literature --
Germany.   I. Title.
PT345.D54 1998
830.9'9287'09034--dc21   97-31869
                                                       CIP

British Library Cataloguing in Publication Data

A catalogue record for this book is available
from the British Library.

For my father, Geoffrey Parker

CONTENTS

ILLUSTRATIONS

1. Hermann Grimm, *Bettina von Arnim in front of her Goethe Memorial*, Etching from a Painting of 1939. Reproduced with kind permission of the Freies Deutsches Hochstift – Frankfurter Goethe-Museum.

2. Luise Seidler, *Ottilie von Goethe*. Reproduced with kind permission of the Stiftung Weimarer Klassik.

3. *Malwida von Meysenbug*. Reproduced with kind permission of the Richard-Wagner-Museum, Bayreuth.

4. *Ida Hahn-Hahn*. Lithograph from *Europa*, 1842 (shelfmark PP 4793C), signed by Hahn-Hahn with the words 'Only someone who fights, struggles and strives – lives'. Reproduced with kind permission of the British Library.

5. *Hedwig Dohm*. Reproduced with kind permission of the Bild-archiv preußischer Kulturbesitz.

6. *Louise Andreas-Salomé*. Reproduced with kind permission of the Stiftung Weimarer Klassik.

ACKNOWLEDGEMENTS

I would like to thank St John's College, Oxford for providing me with a visiting scholarship during the summer of 1996, and particularly Ritchie Robertson, who gave me advice on the first draft of the book. I would also like to thank the Stiftung Weimarer Klassik for providing me with a grant from the Thyssen Stiftung which enabled me to visit Weimar, February-March 1997.

Note: without wishing to show disrespect, some women are referred to by their first names because that was current practice at the time (e.g., Rahel) or in order to distinguish them from famous male relatives (e.g., Johanna and Adele Schopenhauer), or simply because it seems natural to do so, though in general, the full name is given as often as possible. Titles of works are given in German; a translation of the title is added if the work exists in translation. All translations from German are my own unless an English-language translation of the work has been cited. The primary texts of a writer, together with selected secondary sources, can be found under the writer's name in the bibliography. There is also a list of general sources in the final section of the bibliography.

Carol Diethe, 1998

INTRODUCTION

Germany: the Historical Context

The Embryonic Nation State of Germany

To speak of Germany at the beginning of the nineteenth century is to refer to a people united by a common language and culture. As a result of the Napoleonic re-ordering of the map of Europe, especially after the defeat of Prussia at Jena in 1806, and after the settlement at the Vienna Congress in 1815, the conglomeration of German territories had been transformed into the German Federation (*Deutscher Bund*) with a still unwieldy total of thirty-nine states. In spite of this streamlining, trade (and travel) was still difficult between German territories, remaining so until the customs unions (1828, 1834 and 1867) facilitated border crossings. In a way, the history of the rise of the German national state in the nineteenth century was the history of the rise of Prussia, which, when unification came in 1871, was larger than the rest of Germany taken together, excluding Austria. In 1848, Friedrich Wilhelm IV made it clear that the new Germany would not be a democratic state. It would subsequently be Bismarck's task 'to ensure that Germany was merged in Prussia, not Prussia in Germany';[1] he unswervingly brought about the preferred Prussian and authoritarian solution of founding the second German Reich, forged in the defeat of France in 1870/1871. Germany thereby acquired Alsace and Lorraine, and extended from the Benelux countries in the west to East Prussia in the east,

---

[1]   G. Barraclough, ed., *The Times Concise Atlas of History*, London, 1982, p. 114.

with the northern and southern borders where they still are today. The overwhelming majority of people spoke German, with the exception of a thin wedge of territory in West Prussia, where Polish was spoken.

Female Education

The Stein/Hardenberg reforms in Prussia, set in motion in 1807, had made provision for children of both sexes to receive state education up to the age of fourteen, though parents were not compelled to send girls to school and many wealthy parents of daughters chose to employ tutors. Berlin University was founded by Wilhelm von Humboldt in 1810, and the reform of *Gymnasien* took place in 1812. These were boys' grammar schools which educated boys for the *Abitur*, then, as now, the only route to university. Though state primary education for both sexes was enshrined in the laws of the Reich in 1871, the law-making provision for both sexes to receive state education for thirteen years was not promulgated until 1908. Since in Germany, children attend school from the age of six, 'thirteen years' meant until the age of nineteen. In practice, this meant that girls at last had the legal right to prepare for the *Abitur* at school, though many had done so through private tutors in order to enter any university which would take them. German universities had been bastions of male privilege, and only began to allow women to sit their examinations from 1900 onwards, though some universities were already allowing women to 'sit in' at lectures as *Hörerinnen*. Prior to that, German women who wanted an academic qualification (something which had not been seen as a remote possibility until the latter part of the nineteenth century) had to study for their degree outside Germany, usually at the German-speaking Swiss universities of Zurich and Bern. Such women (one thinks of Lily Braun and Helene Stöcker) often became radical activists in the feminist movement.

Religious Persuasion

An acknowledgement of the importance of religious faith can be detected in nearly all the creative writing of German women during the nineteenth century. Women were expected to be religious, and usually expected it of themselves; they also gained recognition from within society if they set an example in this area. In the case of converted Jews, this could become problematic, since they might be left with no faith at all, as happened with Fanny Lewald and Hedwig Dohm. Their writing shows a refreshing challenge to religious assumptions. For the most part, women writers operated from a position of genuine faith, and have not been given credit for their success in exposing the hypocrisy of the 'holier than thou' pietism which, by mid-century, swept all before it. A clear-headed critique of religious bigotry is demonstrated in the work of the Protestant Eugenie Marlitt and the Catholic Marie Ebner-Eschenbach as well as the (probably) atheist Gabriele Reuter. Some writers, such as the Catholic Helene Böhlau, went out of their way to preach tolerance, in her case towards the Jews; she herself embraced Islam in order to marry her husband, whose wife refused to divorce him. Lou Andreas-Salomé's loss of faith appears to have been a defining moment in her life, as was Ida Hahn-Hahn's conversion to Catholicism. Furthermore, the Church offered women the equivalent of a career at a time when there were very few openings for women outside marriage and governessing.

In Britain, Dissenters had been roused from their cosy eighteenth-century congregations to respond to the anxieties of a populace reeling from the effects of war and industrialism with 'a gospel of assurance';[2] gradually in the rest of Europe, evangelical fervour swept though all churches. The new pietists in Germany founded numerous foreign mission societies in the first decades of the nineteenth century along the lines of the immensely influential Evangelische Missionsgesellschaft (Protestant Mission Society), itself founded in Basle in 1815. The mission received support, at first, from Württemberg before the impetus became so great that missionary societies were formed in other states of Germany, such as Saxony, where Ludwig von Gerlach founded a mission in 1829, with the deliberate aim of countering the liberal tendencies in the theology faculty at Halle University. However, the most reactionary of the newly 'awakened' was Ernst Wilhelm Hengstenberg, who became the 'grand organiser and strategist of the political forces'[3] within the Prussian state church in his capacity as Professor at Berlin University. Here he set himself against the mild and tolerant Schleiermacher, viewing the latter's emphasis on feeling as a wrong-headed search for eternal truths when what was necessary was acceptance of dogma and 'an emotional reliance on the inscrutable will of God'.[4] Part of the missionary activity of 'the awakened' was directed at the conversion of the Jews, whose legal

---

[2] Ian Sellers, *Nineteenth-Century Nonconformity*, London, 1977, p. 1.
[3] Robert M. Bigler, *The Politics of German Protestantism: The Rise of the Protestant Church Elite in Prussia, 1815–1848*, Berkeley, Los Angeles and London, 1972, p. 88.
[4] Ibid., p. 132.

circumstances are discussed in Chapter One. Much of the phil-
anthropic work of the mission societies was done by women.[5]

Whilst the pietists such as the Moravian Brothers had been
characterised as 'quiet people', the new pietists forecast hell-
fire and brimstone awaiting those who were not, like them,
'awakened'. The emphasis was on Bible reading, good works and
obedience. Hengstenberg was the key figure in persuading scores
of 'awakened' priests to move over to a new, rigid form of
Lutheran orthodoxy, though not everyone could accept his 'rabid
support of the alliance between throne and altar'.[6] The new pietist
movement set itself in opposition to rationalist Lutheranism,
which had cherished an admiration for the democratic potential of
the French Revolution. It attracted some of the most influential
nobles in the land, leading Groh to comment: '[t]his awakening
might be called the "Von-Awakening", to symbolise its noble
lineage.'[7] Undoubtedly, the Junkers saw their interests served by
the conservative dogma.[8] Friedrich Wilhelm IV, who came to the
throne in 1840, was deeply influenced by the new pietism, though
he maintained a determined show of even-handedness towards
his subjects of different convictions. The new pietism made some
of the humbler churches fashionable, and indeed, the incongruity
of the richly attired elite queueing to enter the dimly lit Bethlehem
churches struck contemporary Berliners as odd.[9]

The new pietism was rejected by the free-thinkers, whose
latitudinarianism began to spread in Germany around mid-
century. The Society of Protestant Friends (not to be confused with
Quakers) first met in 1840 at Gnadau in Saxony; the group grew
and spread rapidly, with numerous offshoots calling themselves
Lichtfreunde or 'Friends of Light'. In 1847, the Prussian king
allowed the *Lichtfreunde* to secede from the state church in an
attempt to 'smother the group with freedom by calling it a sect'.[10]
The main tenets of belief were 'God, virtue and immortality';[11] the
Lichtfreunde also welcomed Jews to religious meetings whether they
were baptised or not. They turned increasingly towards radicalism
during the build-up to the 1848 revolution. Another popular
radical group in the 1840s was the 'German Catholics', who

---

[5]   John E. Groh, *Nineteenth Century German Protestantism: The Church as Social
      Model*, Washington, 1982, p. 134.
[6]   Ibid., p. 156.
[7]   Ibid., p. 124.
[8]   Bigler, *The Politics of German Protestantism*, p. 155
[9]   Ibid.,p. 130.
[10] Groh, *Nineteenth Century German Protestantism*, p. 199.
[11] Ibid., p. 198.

allowed priests to marry and were in general rationalist; by 1859 they had merged with the *Lichtfreunde*, and are not to be confused with Roman Catholics, towards whom the predominantly Protestant state of Prussia had been traditionally tolerant. However, the Napoleonic wars engendered a certain degree of anti-Catholic feeling, as did Bismarck's *Kulturkampf* of the 1870s.

The Social Context

Finding a Female Voice

The nineteenth century began with varied attempts by women to 'find their voice' in the literary world. Letter-writing had been cultivated during the eighteenth century, but even women whose education would have merited the publication of their correspondence often did not consent to publication out of modesty, and not many letters by women found their way into print.[12] With the growth of the salon culture, this was to change. One reason for the changes, according to Konrad Feilchenfeldt,[13] was that the salons, where letters would often be read aloud as a shared cultural pursuit, bore the imprint of Jewish culture, which promoted home life. Wealthy Jewish families also often encouraged all forms of cultural activity. The most important nineteenth-century letter-writer, certainly in terms of influence, was Rahel Varnhagen, though she was preceded by Caroline Schlegel-Schelling, whose letters represent, according to Reinhard Nickisch, 'the crown of female letter-writing'.[14] Caroline's social skills, of which letter-writing was just one, kept the group of early Romantics in Jena in a cohesive, integrated circle. Autobiography also became a popular form of self-expression as the century progressed. This could take the form of diary entries, but also – after Johanna Schopenhauer's early travelogues – frequently appeared as the record of a journey. Sometimes, as with Ida von Hahn-Hahn, the purpose of the journey itself was the travelogue which would be written when it was over. Journals, or 'public' diaries, were enormously popular with women writers throughout

---

[12] Reinhard M. G. Nickisch, 'Briefkultur und sozialgeschichtliche Bedeutung des Frauenbriefes im 18. Jahrhundert', in C. H. Beck, *Deutsche Literatur von Frauen, I: Vom Mittelalter bis zum Ende des 18. Jahrhunderts*, ed. by Gisela Brinkler-Gabler, Munich, 1988, pp. 389–409, p. 392.

[13] Konrad Feilchenfeldt, 'Salons und literarische Zirkel im späten 18. und frühen 19. Jahrhundert', in Beck, *Deutsche Literatur von Frauen*, pp. 410–420, p. 412.

[14] Nickisch, 'Briefkultur und sozialgeschichtliche Bedeutung des Frauenbriefes im 18. Jahrhundert', p. 406.

the nineteenth century.[15] Sadly, a journal was all the young Marie
Bashkirtseff was able to write in her short life.[16] Listing Louise
Aston, Fanny Lewald, Malwida von Meysenbug and Marie Ebner-
Eschenbach, Kay Goodman states that the social restrictions which
had, earlier in the century, prevented women from writing directly
about themselves, were ameliorated to the point that women could
now write about their experiences, including unpleasant ones such
as the pain of repression, in the first person.[17]

'Sense' and Sexuality

During the nineteenth century, women were having large families
with little recourse to information on birth control and mainly
without chloroform (available, in theory at least, only from the
1860s), something which makes the debate about a woman's
independence curiously distorted, without the additional factor
of the marriage of convenience, which forced so many women to
marry, and bear children to, men they did not love. No wonder
their perception of their own sexuality was frequently distorted,
even without the further complication of male opinions of female
sexuality, which simply overlooked any sexual desire women
might have and spoke instead in terms of their moral
responsibility. Women tended to accept these male norms and to
relay them in their writing. The perception among German
women writers that they themselves did not match up to the
idealised norm set for them by men could explain the frequency
with which women writers express their own unease by
portraying their female characters as driven by inner conflicts,
whilst the social values which cripple women's flair and libido are
not challenged. Only in women's letters to each other do social
conventions occasionally break down, though even in expressly
private letters we find that women writers are still hidebound by
convention when discussing intimate topics; notions of good form
were exacerbated by the sheer lack of a vocabulary with which to
describe their own bodies.[18] The over-arching impression

---

[15] Gustav René Hocke, *Das europäische Tagebuch*, Wiesbaden 1963, p. 221 n. 4,
   includes Bettina von Arnim, Marie von Ebner-Eschenbach, Fanny Lewald and
   Adele Schopenhauer in his list of prominent women writers of journals.

[16] See Marie Bashkirtseff, *Journal de Marie Bashkirtseff*, 2 vols, Paris, 1903.

[17] Kay Goodman, 'Die große Kunst, nach innen zu weinen. Autobiographien
   deutscher Frauen im späten 19. und frühen 20. Jahrhundert', in *Die Frau als
   Heldin und Autorin. Neue kritische Ansätze zur deutschen Literatur*, ed. by Wolfgang
   Paulsen, Berne and Munich, 1979, pp. 125–135, p. 133.

[18] The fact that linguistic prudery in all aspects of life reached a crescendo in the
   nineteenth century (compared to the relative frankness of, say, Rabelais), is
   pointed out by Jean Claude Bologne, *Histoire de la Pudeur*, Paris, 1986, p. 268.

conveyed by early nineteenth-century women writers is that they accepted and internalised the Rousseau-inspired view of woman as repository of moral rectitude, close to nature and the emotions and therefore able to guide rational man in matters of the heart. This was the Rousseau of *Julie, ou la nouvelle Héloise* (*Julie, or the New Éloise*) (1761) rather than the Rousseau of the chapter entitled 'Sophie' in *Emile* (1762), the latter being a section of writing which demonstrates all Rousseau's inconsistencies towards the female sex and which disqualifies him (or ought to) from stating what constitutes woman's nature.

Rousseau's pedagogy did, however, gain enormous credence in Germany, and there were a number of women writers who sought to follow his precepts in their own pamphlets on how to educate the young girl.[19] The upshot was that the passions came to be looked on with deep suspicion: a woman of good sense was expected to suppress any passionate sexual desires. Part of the explanation for this lies in male fears of female sexuality, which, during the Enlightenment, became rationalised into the ideal of the morally pure wife.[20] The denial of woman's sexual desire during the nineteenth century has become a cliché, but its origins lie in the marriage of convenience, in which the wife's suppression of passion was probably often merely a reflection of her actual feelings towards her husband. Given the simple fact that a woman had not married the man she loved, sexual intercourse, inextricably linked to child-bearing in the minds of both women and men and affirmed by doctors, was a duty which one must suppose had very little to do with the type of *jouissance* of which it is possible to speak now, when women have control over their own fertility. No doubt there were many happy marriages throughout the nineteenth century in which sexual intercourse was a natural and pleasurable activity; but there were countless cases, most frequently amongst the bourgeoisie and

---

[19] In the eighteenth century, Sophie von la Roche's *Geschichte des Fräulein von Sternheim* (1771) was enormously popular as was Marianne Ehrmann's essay *Philosophie eines Weibes* (1784); nineteenth-century tracts include Amalia Holst's *Über die Bestimmung des Weibes zur höheren Geistesbildung* (1802), Caroline Rudolphi's *Gemälde weiblicher Erziehung* (1807); Betty Gleim's *Erziehung und Unterricht des weiblichen Geschlechts* (1810) and *Über die Bildung der Frauen und die Behauptung ihrer Würde* (1814); Caroline de la Motte Fouqué's *Briefe über Zweck und Richtung weiblicher Bildung* (1811) and *Die Frauen in der großen Welt* (1827), all discussed in Part One of Birgit Wägenbauer's *Die Pathologie der Liebe. Literarische Weiblichkeitsentwürfe um 1800*, Berlin, 1996.

[20] Bärbel Becker-Cantarino, 'Priesterin und Lichtbringerin. Zur Ideologie des weiblichen Charakters in der Frühromantik', in Paulsen ed., *Die Frau als Heldin und Autorin*, pp. 111–124, p. 116.

aristocracy, where women were either in love with a man other than their husband all their married life, or were indifferent to their husbands; frustrated sexuality was thus frequently a problem, though it went unrecognised.[21] All too often, 'true love' involved renunciation; this is a constant theme in the literature of the writers discussed in this book. What is surprising is that they do not challenge the need for such renunciation. The patriarchal codes whereby women were married off for reasons of finance or lineage were accepted as unfortunate but necessary.

Birgit Wägenbauer has recently argued that a way out of the dilemma lay through illness. Paying particular attention to the fictional work of two writers at the beginning of the nineteenth century, Fanny Tarnow and Caroline de la Motte-Fouqué, she highlights the notion of illness as a reassuring place of refuge from the dilemmas facing women whose only hope of actual romantic love (as opposed to dutiful obedience in their capacity as wives and mothers) lay in fantasy: '[t]he permanence of suffering ensures a feminine identity and this possesses the same status [*Stellenwert*] as love'.[22] Naturally, sickness was a very effective way of escaping from unwelcome sexual demands on the part of a husband, but the characters in the novels escape into illness much too regularly for that to be the sole determinant. As Wägenbauer puts it, women writers such as Caroline de la Motte Fouqué endowed their heroines with a veritable *Wille zum Leid*,[23] though one should never forget that illness was indeed a frequent visitor to women, whose function as child-bearers made them prone to gynaecological problems as well as other physical and mental disorders. Nevertheless, throughout the century, it will be seen that women writers select a fatal illness as a means of disposing of women characters who are in danger of stepping beyond the norm.

The conclusion we can draw is that for women whose instincts and drives were being repressed, illness was an escape route. Small wonder that the medical profession took this to heart as the century progressed: there was a very great deal of money to be made in finding a cure. Indeed, things became worse rather than better, since the cures themselves were calculated to induce or increase depression. A woman suffering from neurasthenia ('nerves') would attract much medical debate,[24] most of it fruitless.

---

[21] Wulf Köpke, 'Die emanzipierte Frau in der Goethezeit und ihre Darstellung in der Literatur' in Paulsen ed., *Die Frau als Heldin und Autorin*, pp. 96–110, p. 100.

[22] Birgit Wägenbauer, *Die Pathologie der Liebe. Literarische Weiblichkeitsentwürfe um 1800*, Berlin, 1996, p. 273.

[23] Ibid., p. 273.

[24] For example, Albert Moll, *Das nervöse Weib*, Berlin, 1898.

By the end of the century, health was very much a political issue and one which had a direct impact on women's lives. Though respectable women could not talk openly about sexuality, it was the topic of much medical speculation which would ultimately evolve into the new science of sexology. This science found spurious evidence to confirm woman's innate modesty[25] whilst confirming her destiny as a breeder.[26] Inured to obeying men, women obeyed the doctor, invariably male since women were excluded from the profession until after the turn of the century. Nietzsche in his *Zur Genealogie der Moral (On the Genealogy of Morality)* (1887), while criticising the preoccupation of many wealthy women with frippery and show (without recognising that it was often a symptom of deep malaise), nevertheless inveighed against the iniquitous Weir-Mitchell cure introduced into Germany from the United States.[27] The cure involved bed rest and refused patients any kind of intellectual stimulation on spurious medical grounds. Setting aside the question of whether Freud had anything valuable to say specifically on female sexuality, on the wider issue of repression and sublimation one could surmise that many German women writers took up writing of any genre in order to assert their personal identity and to escape from the frustration of their lives as women. It is particularly noticeable that women who were married to much older men frequently enjoyed a virtual rebirth when widowed. At least the lower orders, whatever their disadvantages, were largely immune to the crippling effects of marriages of convenience – though other factors counted, such as a woman's ability to bear children.[28]

Though male writers of the period might flirt with the portrayal of an independently minded woman, they generally adhered to the conventional portrayal of woman in her domestic place,[29] which anticipated female fidelity but permitted the male double standard. However, there are, in the Romantic period, a few isolated examples of women challenging convention and indulging in free love as a component part of the belief in the free individual: but the result was often the embarrassing birth of illegitimate children. Caroline de la Motte Fouqué's daughter by her lover, Lehnsdorff, was accepted into the family without any

---

[25] Richard von Krafft-Ebing, *Psychopathia Sexualis*, Stuttgart, 1887 [1886], p. 12.

[26] Heinrich H. Ploss, *Das Weib in der Natur und Völkerkunde*, 2 vols, Leipzig, 1884, II, p. 585.

[27] Friedrich Nietzsche, *On the Genealogy of Morality*, ed. by Keith Ansell-Pearson and trs. by Carol Diethe, Cambridge, 1994 [1887], I: 17, p. 17.

[28] Köpke, 'Die emanzipierte Frau in der Goethezeit', p. 97.

[29] Ibid., p. 108.

distinction being made amongst the children, but such tolerance was rare; the husband of a well-born woman was more likely to send her back to her father if she disgraced his name, as happened with Louise, Duchess of Saxe-Coburg and Gotha, whose husband divorced her for adultery in 1826; her two young sons, one of whom was Prince Albert, never saw her again. A similar theme is dealt with fictionally in Fontane's *Effi Briest* (1895), from which we can conclude that attitudes in this domain were slow to change. Ottilie von Goethe was a widow when the 'embarrassment' of pregnancy overtook her after an unwise affair, and she travelled to Vienna to have her baby in secret. The daughter died a year later. Mary Wollstonecraft's bid for 'free love' whilst in Revolutionary Paris also ended in the birth of a daughter (Fanny). Though these instances might invite us to surmise that educated women were casting off the Enlightenment shackles and embracing Romantic ideals of personal liberty, the end result was often the sobering fact of pregnancy. Towards the end of the nineteenth century, a new wave of sexual liberalism swept over the writing sisterhood in the aftermath of Nietzsche's iconoclasm, but the problem with regard to illegitimate offspring did not go away. One could even assert that women's sexuality only became truly liberated with the advent of the oral contraceptive pill in the early 1960s: up to that point, the possibility of an unwanted pregnancy resulting from a woman's extra-marital affair was too serious a matter to warrant the description of that woman's behaviour as 'liberal'.

Making a Match

Not all parents who married their daughters off to older men were monsters: there was a widespread belief that material ease was more important than unreliable emotional attachments. But this argument only held good while it was impossible for a woman to support herself financially. Men had a vested interest in opposing a woman's right to retain their earnings; once that right was established, there was no reason for a woman to remain in an unhappy marriage of convenience such as that suffered by Louise Aston. The demand for the chance to pursue a career went hand-in-hand with a woman's refusal to enter, or desire to escape from, the married state. Naturally, all the accoutrements of a career now had to be fought for: education, prestige and legal independence. These comments only apply to the aristocracy and the bourgeoisie; lower-class women were, as ever, busy earning their keep. Earlier in the nineteenth century, writing provided an income for women who had never contemplated actually having to do a job of work. The flowering of Johanna Schopenhauer's writing talent after the death of her husband gave her writing the status of a career in her life; it was also a compensation for her neglected artistic creativity. Her daughter Adele, however, only took up writing because she feared that she would otherwise have to keep herself by doing paid work, and the openings for such work (as a governess, for example) filled her with horror. Fanny Lewald was the first woman writer to branch out on her own and live on her writing; she was also an active early feminist. Although German feminists towards the end of the century were notorious for factional splits, they could agree on at least one thing: the necessity for proper female education so that a woman could achieve financial independence if she so desired.

In the marriage mart, status was far more important than wealth, though the two might go together. The most common difficulty found in the novels of women writers of the nineteenth century is the barrier erected between the bourgeoisie and the nobility. This could be something below the surface, such as the niggling rancour which informed Adele Schopenhauer's view of the world, even though (or perhaps because) she was the closest friend of Ottilie von Goethe, a woman with every benefit of wealth, rank and looks (though still deeply unhappy, as we shall see). It could occur in veiled or coded form, as in almost every plot imagined by Adele's mother, Johanna Schopenhauer. It could, and often did, blight a woman's chance of marital happiness in real life. The biographical details of the women writers under discussion often sound uncomfortably like the plots of novels; in fact, some real-life stories are so theatrical that life appears to mimic art. One thinks of Frau von Eybenburg, born Marianne Meyer, a friend of Henriette Herz and, like her, a member of the bourgeoisie. Forced to renounce the suitor she loved, Graf Christian Bernstorff, because his parents objected, she accepted the hand of Graf von Reuss, only to receive a letter from Bernstorff on the very morning of her wedding day informing her that he was now free to marry her if she would reconsider his offer. Marianne married Reuss, but had to accept a morganatic marriage whereby she lived excluded from the court. On the death of Reuss, Marianne was treated as an ordinary bourgeois and appealed to the king, who gave her the aristocratic title of 'von Eybenburg'. As she lay dying in Vienna, she was visited by her former love, Graf Bernstorff – the man she should have married decades previously. Unfortunately, this type of thwarted love was commonplace, as we shall see repeatedly. It can be assumed from the above that many men as well as women were made miserable by such social divisions, though the barriers were invariably accepted as insuperable.

On the matter of physical beauty, the descriptions of writers – men as well as women – tend to be brutally precise. The writings of Lavater had made people acutely aware that their moral worth might be judged by their physiognomy.[30] Many descriptions go beyond what is acceptable today, though we must remember that photography has made such descriptions largely redundant. The scales were not evenly balanced between the sexes, however. An ugly man could and often did marry a beautiful woman, sometimes half his age (as happened with Marcus Herz, husband of Henriette, and Graf von Reuss, much older than Marianne and, if we believe Henriette, 'as ugly as night'[31]). Women could be the severest judges of each other's looks: Fanny Lewald was appalled at Adele Schopenhauer's ugly face, to which she devotes a paragraph before describing her awkward and haughty bearing – she then added that she liked her company![32] Mrs Vaughan Jennings, writing in 1883, continued the tradition with her description of Dorothea Veit as having 'no pretension to beauty'.[33] What was at issue was not just that looks were greatly important to a woman in making a match; an unattractive face gave the subliminal message that a person had a bad character, whereas a pretty face spoke for itself.

The Feminist Dimension

In writing this book, I regarded the biographical, historical and cultural approach as more important than the application of feminist theory, though no doubt any approach would reach the conclusion that women in the nineteenth century accepted male evaluations of their 'different' status, which amounted to tutelage in law and sometimes actual servitude. This results in profound paradoxes, with women writers failing to draw the conclusions from their own criticisms of society: popular writers such as Ida

---

[30] Johann Kasper Lavater, *Physiognomische Fragmente*, Zurich, 1968 [1775–1778].

[31] Henriette calls him 'häßlich wie die Nacht' in *Henriette Herz. Ihr Leben und ihre Erinnerungen*, ed. by J. Fürst, Berlin, 1850, p. 145.

[32] Fanny Lewald, *Römisches Tagebuch 1845/46*, Leipzig, 1927 [1847], pp. 47–53. Fanny was particularly upset when Adele included Fanny in a reference to single women 'of our age' being at a social disadvantage in Rome. Perhaps a clue to the slight *contretemps* lies in Fanny's next remark: 'Fräulein Schopenhauer was at least twenty years older than I' (p. 48). Actually, Adele was only thirteen years older than Fanny.

[33] Mrs Vaughan Jennings, *Rahel: Her Life and Letters*, London, 1883, p. 147. Dorothea Veit, a close friend of Rahel von Varnhagen, was the daughter of Moses Mendelssohn; she divorced Veit to marry Friedrich Schlegel.

Hahn-Hahn and Eugenie Marlitt are particularly prone to pulling their punches, whilst women with free lifestyles such as Lou Salomé prescribed domestic lifestyles for other women: her comments, including disapproval of women's aspirations for career opportunities, are downright anti-feminist. Much earlier in the century, Caroline de la Motte Fouqué took a similar stance on women's desire to be professionally creative. What the lack of sisterly solidarity shows is just how far women identified with a patriarchal system which denigrated those who challenged it. In addition, many women who were radical in their youth became more conservative with age. As the feminist movement gained pace in Germany, it would be prone to factional splits, with early feminists such as Louise Otto-Peters striving for better working conditions for poor women, whereas conservative women simply wanted greater recognition of their contribution to society through their home-making skills. Many early women's groups were simply charitable societies, often linked to Church missionary activity. The women who came to style themselves 'moderate' feminists made it a policy issue to develop their Persönlichkeit ('personality' understood in a cultured sense) within the existing establishment. The call for the cultivation of woman's Persönlichkeit drew on the accepted notions of woman's biological – and therefore mental – difference. It is small wonder that women who became active in the socialist movement in the last decade of the century, such as Lily Braun, were anathema to such 'moderate' feminists. One could certainly argue that German women frequently acted against their own interests in failing to challenge a regime which repressed them.

In broad terms, the texts referred to in the present study exhibit confirmation of the more obvious statements of post-structuralist thinkers such as Lacan, who argued that woman's desire is dependent upon a phallic 'master signifier'[34] which places them permanently in the category of 'other'. Certainly, the capacity for women to obey paternalistic laws and indeed insist that their children obey them, even in the physical absence of a father, gives credence to le nom du père, the Name-of-the-Father.[35] In French, 'nom' sounds like 'non'; Lacan argues that the father's prohibition is synonymous with his name. The same paternalistic veto forms a clear thread through the works

---

[34] Jacques Lacan, 'Signification du Phallus', *Ecrits* II, Paris, 1966, p. 109f.

[35] Elizabeth Grosz, *Jacques Lacan: A Feminist Introduction*, London, 1990, p. 47: '[t]he imaginary father usually takes on the symbolic function of law, but in any case these laws and prohibitions must be culturally represented or embodied for the child by some authority figure'.

discussed in this book, so much so that in most cases one does not need a theory in order to state the obvious. What was salient in women writers in the last century was a self-conscious acceptance that women thought, and therefore wrote, differently from men. This is a reminder that Silvia Bovenschen's question '[i]s there a feminine aesthetic?'[36] has yet to be answered, and the jury is still out on the question as to whether women do actually think differently from men, and if they do, to what extent this affects their intelligence. During the nineteenth century, there was no doubt in anyone's mind that women thought differently from men: whilst rationalism was considered a male prerogative, woman's capacity for sentiment was raised to the level of ideology.

My personal stance is mainstream feminist, but there are limits to the usefulness of feminism during the era under investigation. Firstly, the survival of feudalism in Germany into the early nineteenth century indicates that many men as well as women suffered under unjust laws, though in Prussia at least, divorce was possible under the new civil code of 1794, certainly when children were not involved. However, it nearly always disadvantaged the woman, as Ute Frevert has pointed out.[37] Secondly, the class distinctions in Germany remained unremittingly unfavourable towards woman of the lower orders. Such women could often not even write their own name, let alone literature of any form. Hence, this book omits a whole section of German women in society since it merely purports to deal with women writers: and women writers belonged to the better-off classes. Usually an upper-class milieu is the chosen setting, though there are notable exceptions, with Bettina von Arnim and Marie von Ebner-Eschenbach, for example, demonstrating a large measure of noblesse oblige by making direct comments on social problems in some of their writing.

At the beginning of each chapter, a brief indication will be given of the relevant historical context, and more detailed information will emerge during a discussion of the individual writers. The selection of women discussed has had to be made according to strict criteria of date: early Romanticism is scarcely touched upon, and the writers whose main works were published in the twentieth century are also excluded. If Goethe's influence was unavoidable during the first decades of the century, Nietzsche's was just as

---

[36] Silvia Bovenschen, 'Über die Frage: Gibt es eine weibliche Ästhetik?' in *Ästhetik und Kommunikation*, 25, 1976, pp. 60–74, *passim*.

[37] Ute Frevert, *Women in German History: From Bourgeois Emancipation to Sexual Liberation* Oxford, 1993 [1986], p. 53f.

strong at the close, and both men will receive due mention, not least because Goethe's coining of the phrase the 'Eternal-Womanly' at the close of Faust Part Two (1832), to indicate woman's power to save man from his own baser impulses, though later mocked by Nietzsche, became integrated into the double standard and contributed to the ideology which viewed women as sexless angels of the home – or harlots. Other prominent men are mentioned within the context of their importance for the topic under investigation, but there is no systematic attempt to give a simultaneous portrayal of the writing of German men of the period: any standard literary history will do that, whilst barely mentioning any of the women in these pages. This neglect has been, in my opinion, very largely unjustified.

Bettine

Hermann Grimm, *Bettina von Arnim in front of her Goethe Memorial*, Etching from a Painting of 1939. Reproduced with kind permission of the *Freies Deutsches Hochstift – Frankfurter Goethe-Museum*.

1

THE ROMANTIC LEGACY

Liberal Tendencies at the Beginning of the Century

Both women and men of the lower orders were denied access to many of the most basic legal rights at the beginning of the nineteenth century. Enlightened German intellectuals deplored this and hailed the French Revolution as the harbinger of equal rights. Indeed, there were so many injustices in society that radical Germans welcomed Napoleon's occupation of German territory in 1806, because it meant that the code civile came with him. The destruction of the old Reich resulted in a number of new statutes being passed which, directly or indirectly, were bound to lead to 'at the very least some "social betterment" of the Jews'.[1] Prussia, through the Stein-Hardenberg reforms, was forced to push through a number of measures such as the abolition of serfdom.[2] Jews attained legal equality in Prussia in 1811–1812, but their position in other areas of Germany varied greatly.[3] When Napoleon was driven from Germany after his defeat at Leipzig in 1813, the conservative element in the Prussian government sought to water down the reforms, which received further, definitive,

---

[1] Reinhard Rürup, 'The Tortuous and Thorny Path to Legal Equality: "Jew Laws" and Emancipatory Legislation in Germany from the Late Eighteenth Century', in *Leo Baeck Institute Yearbook*, 3, 1986, 3–33, p. 13. I am grateful to Ritchie Robertson for drawing this article to my attention.
[2] Ernest K. Bramsted, *Germany*, New Jersey, 1972, p. 117.
[3] Mary Fulbrook, *A Concise History of Germany*, Cambridge, 1990, pp. 88–89.

obstruction from Friedrich Wilhelm IV in 1841.[4] The effect was not only to push back democratic progress but also – since they were linked – to delay the granting of civil rights to Jews, such as a Jew's right to marry a Christian;[5] this would have serious consequences for some of the Jewish women discussed in this chapter. They were to find that simple conversion was not a *passe-partout* which would wipe out anti-Semitism at one stroke. The see-saw of hope and disappointment with regard to liberal reform was characteristic in Germany: liberal hopes pinned on the French Revolution were dashed by the brutality of the Girondist terror; radical expectations of Napoleon's liberating potential, and then of the measures following the Treaty of Versailles, 1815, were cancelled out by the harsh Carlsbad decrees of 1819, and ultimately, the excitement of the 1848 Revolution would culminate in an autocratic imperialist regime under Bismarck in 1870.

The Berlin Salons and the Jewish Question

Henriette Herz 1764–1854

Henriette Herz, for decades hailed as 'the most beautiful woman in Berlin',[6] ran a salon in Berlin through the good offices of her husband, Marcus Herz, who liked to entertain on a grand footing. His wife, if left to her own devices, would probably not have been prominent in society, since she was fundamentally shy. In her salon, however, she appears to have been lively and quick-witted: men loved her, to the point where it has been suggested that her husband was jealous of her social success.[7] Henriette was the daughter of a wealthy Jewish family. Her father, a Portuguese Jew, Lemos, whose own grandfather had fled the Inquisition, was the first Jewish doctor in Berlin. Her mother had eye trouble, which made her irascible towards her daughter. Her close friend was the

---

[4] Rürup, 'The Tortuous and Thorny Path to Legal Equality', p. 25. Friedrich Wilhelm's refusal to recognise the integration of Jews into German society rendered the laws of 1812, which had laid down principles of full legal equality, ineffective.

[5] According to Claus Barsch in *Juden im Vormärz und in der Revolution von 1848*, ed. by Walter Grab and Julius Schoeps, Stuttgart and Bonn, 1983, p. 385: 'The close affinity between Judaism and democracy can be explained by the fact that the anti-Semites had also been opponents of social levelling.'

[6] Anon., *Schleiermacher und seine Lieben in Briefen der Henriette Herz*, Magdeburg, 1910, p. 5.

[7] Leo Sievers, 'Juden in Deutschland: Der Salon der Henriette Herz', *Der Stern*, 18, 1977, pp. 145–157, p. 155.

daughter of Moses Mendelssohn, Dorothea. Henriette Herz was married at the age of fifteen to Marcus Herz, a man seventeen years her senior, in an arranged marriage about which her parents were extremely pleased, since Marcus Herz was also a respected doctor and a well-regarded scholar besides. Marriages of convenience in which the husband was much older than his wife were often instigated by the most well-meaning parents. Though Henriette later regretted the lack of passion in their relationship, she respected her husband, who was generous and, in the early period of their marriage, unstinting in his efforts to educate his young wife. The betrothal had taken place when Henriette was twelve-and-a-half years old; in her reminiscences, she recalls that she bridled at being referred to as 'das Kind'[8] during her engagement (though she actually *was* still a child). Such use of the term remained widespread throughout the century, even when there was no great difference in age between husband and wife: the law placed the woman in a position of tutelage.[9]

A timbre of condescension entered into the intellectual companionship of the Herz couple, since Henriette enjoyed the work of the young Romantic writers such as Novalis, whilst Herz labelled their aesthetics 'untrue and incomprehensible',[10] and teased Henriette accordingly. He preferred the rationalism of Lessing, whom he knew personally. Such anecdotes show that Marcus Herz was on one level pleased to have a beautiful young bride whom he proceeded to educate, but was on another level quite unaware of any needs she might have for her personal creativity. He no doubt assumed that she would bow to his authority: and she did. But in her reminiscences the tone of nostalgia for a foreshortened youth is unmistakeable:

> I can call my marriage a happy relationship, if not, perhaps, a happy marriage. Marriage for my husband was not the focal point of his existence, and secondly, ours was not blessed with children ... But I can say this for myself: I made my husband as happy as any other woman could have done.[11]

Even when writing her own reminiscences, Henriette puts the interests of her husband first, as she has spent her life doing; all

---

[8] Henriette Herz, *Henriette Herz. Ihr Leben und ihre Erinnerungen*, ed. by J. Fürst, Berlin, 1850, p. 24. Husbands frequently referred to their wives in this way throughout the nineteenth century.

[9] See Carol Diethe, *Aspects of Distorted Sexual Attitudes in German Expressionist Drama*, New York, Bern, Frankfurt am Main and Paris, 1988, p. 32.

[10] Herz, *Henriette Herz. Ihr Leben und ihre Erinnerungen*, p. 95.

[11] Ibid., p. 28.

we can glean is that the marriage left her in many respects unfulfilled. Her description of her wedding day is tinged with nostalgia, most of it pure homesickness and not helped by the wintry weather, but in any case, sobriety would not have allowed any reference to sexual matters. Her remark that 'a thousand conflicting feelings swept over me'[12] sounds a note of despondency, yet nowhere does she speak out against the fact that she was catapulted into adulthood much too soon.

Since the marriage was, to her regret, childless, Henriette was able to benefit from her freedom to travel; her European grand tour after her marriage encompassed Paris, where she saw the regal Marie Antoinette in procession with the much less regal King Louis XVI a decade before the outbreak of the French Revolution. Her childlessness also meant that she could devote a good deal of her time to hospitality. She and her husband took the unruly Löw Baruch into their house in 1802–1803; later he would become the radical journalist and writer Ludwig Börne. The seventeen-year-old Baruch/Börne was so infatuated with Henriette Herz, who was twenty-one years his senior, that he considered poisoning himself. He declared his love for Henriette by letter after the death of Marcus in 1803, writing that 'he could not be content with mere friendship' for Henriette, which elicited a reply in which he was firmly put in his place: 'I must repeat what I have told you countless times, I cannot be more to you than a friend.'[13] He was tactfully sent on to Halle, where he initially studied medicine. In spite of other offers of marriage from her close friend Alexander von Dohna and from a much younger man, Immanuel Bekker (who accompanied her home from Italy in 1819), Henriette Herz chose not to remarry, though she was gratified by the offers. Indeed, in the case of Bekker, Henriette told Wilhelm von Humboldt, whose guidance she sought on the matter, that only the difference in age prevented her from accepting the offer.[14]

During the twenty years of Henriette's marriage to Marcus Herz, the house had been open to some of the most prominent thinkers and writers of the time: Friedrich Schleiermacher, Friedrich Schlegel, Alexander and Wilhelm von Humboldt, Friedrich von Gentz, Johannes von Müller, Ernst Moritz Arndt and Prinz Louis Ferdinand amongst them; Dorothea Veit, Sara and Marianne Meyer, the writer Sophie Schubart (later to marry

[12] Ibid., p. 26.
[13] Both letters were written in April 1803 and are printed in Hans Landsberg, ed., *Henriette Herz. Ihr Leben und Ihre Zeit*, Weimar, 1913, p. 239.
[14] In Landsberg, *Henriette Herz. Ihr Leben und ihre Zeit*, p. 92.

first Professor Friedrich Ernst Karl Mereau, whom she divorced in 1801, and then – briefly – Clemens Brentano) and Caroline von Dacheröden (later to marry Wilhelm von Humboldt) were all frequent guests, as was Schleiermacher from 1796 onwards. His presence as a third party with the Herz couple caused some gossip.[15] Indeed, Schleiermacher had to reassure his sister Charlotte that he was not getting too mixed up with Jews.[16] Rahel von Varnhagen was also a visitor, though Drewitz surmises – tendentiously – that Henriette must surely have envied her since she was liable to upstage Henriette on such occasions;[17] however, there is no evidence for this assertion. Although she was well able to converse on all topics current in a Berlin salon, Henriette Herz seems to have been a shy person who never quite overcame her lack of proper schooling, in spite of the best efforts of her husband to fill in the gaps, though as indicated, he tended to disapprove of the very writers she most admired. Since these writers, such as Goethe, were frequently the topic of conversation in the salons, this is not an insignificant detail. Goethe's later work would, of course, remain unknown to Marcus; Henriette survived her husband by some fifty-one years.

Probably the initial reason why men swarmed round Henriette Herz was, quite simply, her beauty, perhaps also the modesty with which it was coupled, but the reason why some of the most prominent men of the day remained friendly with her is that her intelligence was focused on how to *feel*, and this insistence on the importance of feeling was an integral part of the *Zeitgeist*. Thus, Schleiermacher repeatedly turned to Henriette for advice in his own affairs of the heart, which were complicated enough, especially when he fell in love with a married woman, Eleonore Grunow. Eleonore's moral code was so rigid that she had insisted upon marrying at the age of fifteen, simply because she had promised her husband her hand at the age of twelve. A similarly exaggerated feeling of loyalty prevented her from leaving her husband, though up till 1805, Schleiermacher had cherished hopes that she would do so.[18] It is noteworthy that Schleiermacher

---

[15] Friedrich Schlegel, for example, felt that Henriette tried to monopolise Schleiermacher, who was a 'spare part' on many occasions. See Ingeborg Drewitz, *Berliner Salons. Gesellschaft und Literatur zwischen Aufklärung und Industriezeitalter*, Berlin, 1965, p. 31. However, Schlegel was not the only one to gossip about the attachment. See (anon.) *Schleiermacher und seine Lieben in Briefen der Henriette Herz*, p. 8.

[16] Drewitz, *Berliner Salons*, p. 27f.

[17] Ibid., p. 34.

[18] (Anon.) *Schleiermacher und seine Lieben in Briefen der Henriette Herz*, p. 16.

was so certain of the right to happiness of the individual that he
was prepared to 'poach' the wife of another man, especially as
that man was generally held to be completely unworthy of his
wife. Schleiermacher's influence over Henriette was of the kind
he offered to Rahel and Bettina: with all three women he was
concerned that they 'find themselves'. He persuaded Henriette to
convert to Christianity, though for many years she did not
publicly convert out of respect for her mother; in 1817 she did
finally agree to being baptised, something which her biographer
Fürst records with a tone of not a little triumphalism.[19]

For half a century, Henriette Herz maintained correspondence
with old friends, and she made a number of journeys. In 1813 she
went to Breslau with Rahel, who by this time had begun her
relationship with her future husband, Varnhagen; Berlin was at
that moment full of stories about Napoleon and whether or not
his occupation of Prussian territory would be ended. Social life in
Berlin was severely disrupted.[20] Henriette had visited Vienna in
1811, and went on an extensive visit to Italy in 1817, the Vienna
Congress of 1814 having made it possible for Germans to resume
visits to Italy. The Veit brothers, both painters, were in Rome at
the same time, as were Dorothea Schlegel and Caroline
Humboldt. In the summer of 1818, Dorothea, Henriette and
several friends, amongst them the painter Louise Seidler, took
accommodation in Genzano, near Rome, where the group was
dominated by Dorothea, though Henriette Herz also came in for
her share of praise. According to Seidel:

> The magic of her beauty and simplicity enveloped her whole being;
> she was distinguished by her genuinely feminine goodness of heart.
> Completely modest, she seldom revealed her many talents, especially
> her great gift for languages.[21]

That same simplicity irritated some observers, such as
Varnhagen,[22] and others saw fit to comment on her *embonpoint* (a
Swedish acquaintance commented in 1825 that she was a 'big fat
woman who must formerly have been a great beauty'[23]). In 1819,
after two years' travelling, she passed through Bonn on her way
back to Berlin in order to visit Ernst Moritz Arndt, only to find
herself in the middle of a police raid on his house. This was, of

[19] J. Fürst, Editor's Introduction, *Henriette Herz. Ihr Leben und ihre Erinnerungen*,
p. 70.
[20] Landsberg, *Henriette Herz. Ihr Leben und ihre Zeit*, p. 85.
[21] Ibid., p. 92.
[22] Ibid., p. 86.
[23] Ibid., p. 95.

course, just after the proclamation of the Carlsbad decrees. Henriette's decision to convert to Christianity had therefore been a wise one, since the decrees, in curbing democracy, had had the effect of making things worse for the Jewish community. Henriette Herz was able to continue with her social life, though in straitened circumstances, until she received a small pension from Friedrich Wilhelm IV, at Alexander von Humboldt's suggestion.

The years after the death of Herz seem to have represented a downward slide for Henriette, in spite of her many friends and frequent travels. It is greatly to be lamented that a woman such as Henriette Herz found it unbecoming in a woman to turn to writing: her memoirs would have been a fascinating document of the time. The explanation for her silence has been described by Martin Davies as a direct result of salon culture: with Friedrich Schlegel as one of the regular visitors, Henriette Herz may have found it impossible to contradict his definition of woman's role. This had been set out in *Lucinde* (1799) and in the essay 'Über die Philosophie. An Dorothea'(1799). In the latter, according to Davies, Schlegel 'defines book learning as the sphere of male creation, while conversation is the proper sphere of female activity.'[24] Henriette did, however, translate Mary Wollstonecraft's *Vindication of the Rights of Woman* (1792) in 1832, as well as two lesser-known works,[25] though her name is not on them. Apart from her translations, we have only the brief memoir of her youth and a wealth of correspondence. Even allowing for the status afforded to letter-writing at this time, the literary legacy of Henriette Herz is disappointingly meagre.

Henriette appears to have been disorientated as she grew older. Clearly, she internalised the salon attitudes towards women, and this must have left its mark on her sense of self. Drewitz, stressing both Henriette's beauty as well as what she esteems to be her prudery, speaks of her bearing as that of 'a *prima donna*' during the years of her salon, and suggests that she found ageing difficult, always wearing clothes too young for her. Drewitz interprets the widowed Henriette's refusal to marry Dohna – tendentiously, again – as proof that she was 'too prudish to trust her feelings', and took refuge in a moral rectitude which appeared bigoted.[26]

---

[24] Martin Davies, 'Portraits of a Lady: Variations on Henriette Herz (1764–1847)' in *Women Writers of the Age of Goethe*, Occasional Papers in German Studies: 5, ed. by Margaret Ives, Lancaster, 1992, pp. 45–75, p. 54.

[25] According to Davies, 'Portraits of a Lady', p. 69, Henriette Herz translated Mungo Park's *Journey to the Interior of Africa in the Years 1795 and 1797* (1799) and Weld the Younger's *Travels to the United States of America* (1800).

[26] Drewitz, *Berliner Salons*, p. 30.

Drewitz's remark completely overlooks the sovereign right of Henriette Herz to do what she wanted with her own life. She did not attract the homage of the teenager Börne or the cabinet minister Dohna through coquetry, but through sympathetic friendship, something which is clear in her correspondence. Nevertheless, the letters hint at a wistfulness which belies the fact that she had something more to offer, though such ideas had to be firmly smothered. What one can assert is that the marriage of a young girl of fifteen to a man old enough to be a father figure must have had as crippling an effect on her emotions as the renunciations forced on so many of the other women mentioned in this chapter.

Rahel von Varnhagen 1771–1833

The Herz household offered abundant hospitality to those with lively intellectual or artistic ambitions, but Rahel's salon shone because of her own brilliance. Though from a wealthy family, she herself was not rich; she lived with her family in her own attic apartment at the centre of Berlin. Her first salon lasted from 1790 until 1806, when political events caused a rupture in all social life, and her second, after she had married, lasted from 1819 until 1832. Like Henriette Herz, she never attempted to publish her work, which consists of several volumes of letters and diaries. Neither woman attempted to write creative work, but sought instead to inspire other writers. Gerd Mattenklott has sharply criticised the culture in which women like Rahel Varnhagen and Henriette Herz had their horizons limited; he argues that they knew perfectly well that as Jewesses, their own creative attempts would not have been tolerated:

> They could make a virtue of this limitation [*Einschränkung*]: the salon; they could reflect it in writing: the letter. They could not overcome it.[27]

What I shall attempt to deal with in this section is the double disadvantage under which Rahel laboured, that of being a *woman* and a Jew. Deborah Herz regards the argument that Rahel was held back by her Jewishness as overdone:

> She [Rahel] was at the center of salon society and her life was a dramatic example of how far and how quickly a Jewish woman could travel away from tradition, family, and the Jewish community.[28]

---

[27] Gert Mattenklott, *Jüdische Intelligenz in deutschen Briefen 1619–1988*, Frankfurt am Main, 1988, p. 89.

[28] Deborah Herz, 'Hannah Arendt's Rahel Varnhagen', in *German Women in the Nineteenth Century: A Social History*, ed. by John C. Fout, New York and London, 1984, pp. 72–87, p. 74.

Deborah Herz proceeds to write off Hannah Arendt's appreciation of Rahel as an example of Arendt's own obsession with the Jewish past,[29] but the facts relating to Jewish exclusion from civil rights speak for themselves: the struggle of Jews in the ghetto had been one of simple survival. Only wealthy Jews such as Moses Mendelssohn were beginning to be able to show cultural leadership. Thus it should be said that, for all her inspirational qualities, Rahel retained an inferiority complex common to many Jews. 'Rahel's life was bound by this inferiority',[30] writes Arendt. This inferiority was no doubt bolstered by the general hostility towards Jews in society at large, but also by anti-Semitism closer to home. Caroline von Humboldt behaved with reserve towards Rahel because she was Jewish, though as has been seen, she was a close (if not intimate) friend to Henriette Herz. Possibly this was only to please her husband. Another visitor to the salon who held pronounced anti-Semitic views was Clemens Brentano,[31] though his sister Bettina spoke nothing but praise of Rahel, and was deeply influenced by her example of independence of mind.

It is a mark of Rahel's success that although she was neither beautiful nor rich (Arendt writes dismissively that 'nature went to no great trouble with Rahel'[32]), and was Jewish to boot, her house was the place in which to be seen if you were an aspiring intellectual at the turn of the century; amongst the guests were Georg Wilhelm Friedrich Hegel, Leopold Ranke, Prince Louis Ferdinand of Prussia, Heinrich Heine, Achim and Bettina von Arnim, Clemens Brentano, Jean Paul, Ludwig Tieck, Friedrich von Fouqué, Alexander von Humboldt, Friedrich Schleiermacher, Johann Gottlieb Fichte and Friedrich Schlegel.[33] Not to be compared with the formal and exclusive court, nor the aristocratic circles of high society (from which, incidentally, Rahel was firmly excluded, so that invitations were one-sided), and worlds away from the military, diplomatic or commercial pulse, Rahel Varnhagen, like Henriette Herz but more systematically,

---

[29] Herz, 'Hannah Arendt's Rahel Varnhagen', p. 73.

[30] Hannah Arendt, *Rahel Varnhagen. The Life of a Jewess*, London 1957, p. 5.

[31] Walter Grab states: 'Brentano, who was one of Rahel's regular guests, spread traditional Christian hatred of Jews by his animosity towards the growing capitalist trade and money market ... it is incomprehensible how Rahel could have been on a friendly footing with that type of fierce anti-Semite'. In Grab and Schoeps, eds, *Juden im Vormärz*, p. 380.

[32] Arendt, *Rahel Varnhagen*, p. 3.

[33] Edith Waldstein, 'Identity as Conflict and Conversation in Rahel Varnhagen (1771-1833)' in *Out of Line/Ausgefallen: The Paradox of Marginality in the Writings of Nineteenth-Century German Women*, ed. by Ruth-Ellen Boetcher Joeres and Marianne Burkhard, Amsterdam, 1989, pp. 95-113, p. 98.

provided something quite different: the nucleus for a new aesthetics. Ultimately, this would crystallise into a Goethe cult, since Rahel Varnhagen was one of the first to appreciate his work fully, though she only met him once, in 1829. Ironically, the Sage of Weimar was himself somewhat eclipsed after his death in 1832 by the Rahel cult which gripped the reading public of Berlin after her own death in 1833; this was largely because her widower, Varnhagen, published her letters posthumously (and not always accurately) in his immensely popular *Rahel. Ein Buch des Andenkens für ihre Freunde* (1833), which was so sought after that it was expanded to three volumes in 1834. It was soon to become known as *Das Buch Rahel*, and was particularly popular with women, as Kay Goodman has pointed out.[34]

People were fascinated by the personality of Rahel which emerged in her published writing, consisting of diary entries and voluminous correspondence. At all events, *Das Buch Rahel* was more important as a social phenomenon than as a literary document. Some of what Rahel wrote had epigrammatic quality, but at other times she laid her soul bare to those she loved and trusted; it made the readers consider their own lives and examine their own inner thoughts. As with that other catalytic converter, Nietzsche, people extracted from the Rahel in Varnhagen's book the Rahel they wished to find. Naturally, Varnhagen only printed what he considered suitable for public consumption. In particular, Varnhagen censored the correspondence between Rahel and the libertine Pauline Wiesel, who, in spite of her promiscuous lifestyle, remained Rahel's closest woman friend.[35] Varnhagen had been shocked when, in 1815, Pauline made a pass at him when he visited her in Paris at Rahel's instigation; Rahel just found the incident amusing.[36] Subsequently, Varnhagen was to collaborate with that other forger of letters, Bettina, whose own star began to rise at this point, so that a Bettina cult superseded the Rahel cult.[37] Varnhagen was of use to Bettina in introducing

---

[34] Kay Goodman, 'The Impact of Rahel Varnhagen on Women in the Nineteenth Century' in *Gestaltet und gestaltend. Frauen in der deutschen Literatur*, ed. by Marianne Burkhard, Amsterdam, 1980, pp. 125–153, p. 128.

[35] Varnhagen cunningly paid the penniless Pauline a ducat for every letter Rahel had sent her (there were fifty-five in all) so that he could censor the affectionate and frank correspondence between the two women. See Marlis Gerhardt, ed., *Rahel Varnhagen/Pauline Wiesel. 'Ein jeder machte seine Frau aus mir, wie er sie liebte und verlangte'. Ein Briefwechsel*, Darmstadt, 1989, p. 118.

[36] Gerhardt, ed., *Varnhagen/Wiesel. Ein Briefwechsel*, p. 115f.

[37] Konrad Feilchenfeldt, 'Die Anfänge des Kults um Rahel von Varnhagen und seine Kritiker' in Grab and Schoeps, eds, *Juden im Vormärz*, pp. 214–232, p. 228.

her to court; through Bettina, Varnhagen had access to Clemens Brentano's letters for the project upon which he had embarked: the publication of the correspondence between Clemens Brentano and Arnim.[38]

Varnhagen was fourteen years younger than his wife, whom he first met in 1808. This was not the love of her life; she had been engaged to Count Finckenstein from 1796 to 1799, but he backed away from their engagement – Rahel was undesirable to his family both as a bourgeois and as a Jewess – delivering a shock to Rahel from which, arguably, she never recovered. Twelve years later, when he visited Rahel and suggested that she might like to meet his wife, she was not immune to the pain this caused.[39] In 1806 she was jilted – not too strong a term – by her fiancé Don Raphael d'Urquijo, who had wrecked their relationship through his constant and unfounded jealousy. The anguish of this episode in her life streaks through the letters of 1806, never more clearly than when she assures her correspondent that she is getting over the pain. In a letter to her brother, Ludwig Robert, then in Paris, she wrote:

> My soul is healthy. Urquijo does not hurt me any more. I regret nothing and I do not feel any different about what has happened. My inner self becomes increasingly clarified, and there is no lack of work ...[40]

Though she was obviously shocked by this personal catastrophe, her attachment to Alexander von der Marwitz – whom she met in 1809 when he was twenty-two and she was thirty-eight – would be even more intense. Marwitz was the man who was closest to Rahel Varnhagen after the fiasco with Finckenstein. According to Drewitz, he was 'the only partner she had in life who was her intellectual equal'.[41] Rahel's letters in their correspondence, which includes some prose descriptions of her dreams, are probably the best things she wrote.[42] It was only after

[38] Ibid., p. 232, n. 42.

[39] Arendt, *Rahel Varnhagen*, p. 31.

[40] Letter of 7 October 1806. Cited in Friedrich Kemp, *Rahel*, 4 vols, I, p. 370:
I: *Rahel Varnhagen im Umgang mit ihren Freunden (Briefe 1793–1833)*, Berlin, 1967.
II: *Rahel Varnhagen. Briefwechsel mit August Varnhagen von Ense*, Munich, 1967.
III: *Rahel Varnhagen. Briefwechsel mit Alexander von der Marwitz*, Munich, 1967.
IV: *Rahel Varnhagen und ihre Zeit (Briefe 1800–1833)*, Munich 1968.

[41] Drewitz, *Berliner Salons*, p. 104.

[42] See Hans Meisner, ed., *Rahel und Alexander von der Marwitz in ihren Briefen*, Gotha and Stuttgart, 1925, *passim*. For a discussion of Rahel's letters to Marwitz, see Barbara Hahn, *'Antworten Sie mir!' Rahel Levin Varnhagens Briefwechsel*, Basle and Berlin, 1990, pp.153–168, *passim*.

Marwitz's death in 1814 that Rahel agreed to marry Varnhagen. During the first years of their relationship, Rahel seems to have blown hot and cold towards Varnhagen. As she wrote to Fouqué in 1811: 'I have lived with Varnhagen all summer: first, things went badly, then very well … I love him.'[43] It is significant that a few days after this letter she wrote in far more passionate terms to Marwitz, telling him that she was disgusted with herself because her inner life had become 'wooden, shut in and dumb,'[44] hardly a recommendation for her relationship with Varnhagen. However, the gap in age between Rahel and Marwitz might have become problematic with time, so that one can only speculate about what would have happened had Marwitz not died in 1814. The matter is further complicated by the fact that an early biographer of Rahel, Ludmilla Assing, was Varnhagen's niece; in spite of her rigorous fairness, her account nevertheless tends to flatter Varnhagen, as in the following assessment:

> Varnhagen's love was like a healing balm for her deeply wounded heart, offering her peace and comfort, a happiness she had never encountered hitherto, a home [*Heimat*] for her soul.[45]

In order to marry Varnhagen it was necessary for Rahel to be baptised as a Christian, and this took place in 1814, the year they were married. It is typical of the whole climate of the Rahel cult that this conversion could be seen in pious terms as an effect of the holy spirit:

> In her, the spirit and character of an Old Testament revelation can be recognised, simultaneously filled with all that is essential to Christianity.[46]

At least, after her conversion, Rahel was safe when the Hep-Hep movement (*Hierusalem ist perdita*) led to a wave of pogroms throughout Germany in 1819.[47] However, like many other converted Jews, Rahel remained in something of a state of limbo. Arendt goes so far as to assert that for a Jew to assimilate properly into Prussia at that time would have involved becoming anti-Semitic oneself.[48] (Deborah Herz counters this with the assertion

---

[43] Letter to Fouqué dated 29 November 1811. Cited in Kemp, *Rahel*, III, p. 310.

[44] Letter of 3 December 1811. Cited in Kemp, *Rahel*, I, p. 136.

[45] Ludmilla Assing, ed., *Aus Rahels Herzensleben. Briefe und Tagebücher*, Leipzig, 1877, p. 249.

[46] *Rahels Religiosität*, Leipzig, 1836, p. 21. No author given apart from 'by one of her old friends', though the British Library suggests Varnhagen von Ense as the author.

[47] Eda Sagarra, *A Social History of Germany 1648–1914*, London, 1977, p. 316.

[48] Arendt, *Rahel Varnhagen*, p. 182.

that such statements have more to do with Arendt's own agenda of castigating rich Prussian Jews for their lack of solidarity with poorer Jews during the last century than with the difficulties facing Rahel at the time.[49]) The irony is that Rahel herself embraced her new faith with integrity; furthermore, though she was thoroughly non-political, she was stoutly nationalistic – unlike Goethe, who distrusted the sentiment, and whose judgement in all other matters she trusted and revered. She had arrived at this nationalism through her profound resentment towards the presence of Napoleon's troops in Berlin in 1806, and it was confirmed by a study of Fichte, especially his *Reden an die deutsche Nation (Addresses to the German Nation)* (1808).[50] However, she had different views on nationalism after the wave of pogroms in 1819:

> A time will come when national pride will be looked on in just the same way as selfishness and other vanity, and war as butchery. The current position is contrary to our religion.[51]

The mention of Christianity as 'our religion' indicates that Rahel, at least, was clear about which faith she professed.

The magnetic quality of Rahel's personality, coupled with the sheer brilliance of her conversation, to which all her friends bear witness, forces us to question why she was not able to launch herself as a writer in her own right, as Johanna Schopenhauer was able to do the moment she was widowed, or indeed as her friend Caroline de la Motte Fouqué had been able to do, whilst running a home and family, albeit with plenty of servants. It appears that the pressure to conform as a woman bore down on Rahel: in 1819 she wrote to her married sister, Rose Asser, who was in Holland:

> It is a human blunder that people imagine our mind [*Geist*] is different and constructed for other things, and that we can, for example, derive our entire existence from our husband or son. This requirement only arises from the presumption that a woman knows nothing higher in her whole soul than precisely those requirements and demands of her husband in the world ... we love, cherish, care about the loved ones' wishes; fit in with them, make them our highest priority and most urgent occupation; but they can never fulfil us,

---

[49] Herz, 'Hannah Arendt's Rahel Varnhagen', p. 81.

[50] Arendt in *Rahel Varnhagen* writes (p. 105): 'The old world had been shattered [in 1806], and Fichte was a "comfort and hope" to Rahel because he desired to exclude all tradition from the reconstruction of a new world'. Arendt argues that Rahel was opposed to the reform of Judaism because it would be harder to escape from a reformed Judaism and assimilate into German society than from an unreformed Judaism.

[51] Diary entry for 3 November 1919. Cited in Kemp, *Rahel*, IV, p. 203.

refresh us, rest us so that we can keep active, can carry on; nor can they give us strength and power for our whole future life.[52]

The above passage shows just how hopeless Rahel felt that any fight against conventions was, even when she herself challenged the very heart of those conventions by questioning the status of woman's different nature. It is thus ironic that most of the praise she attracted was precisely in tune with the sentiments objected to in her letter to Rose: like Henriette Herz, she was seen as the caring, motherly woman, in spite of her childlessness.

Doris Starr Guilleton has sought to show that Rahel's whole outlook on life is what we would now describe as feminist;[53] what she does not recognise is that some of the warmest praise for Rahel, such as that found in Ellen Key's biography of her, should actually be regarded with some scepticism,[54] since Key can now be viewed as a profoundly conservative thinker whose views were not unproblematic for the cause of feminism. For instance, Key gives a startlingly avant-garde assessment of Rahel's morality as a question of being true to oneself: avant-garde for both Rahel and Key, in view of the conventional image of woman as a selfless figurehead. However, Key's point is virtually negated by the thorough-going elitist comment *à la* Nietzsche which precedes it.[56] Indeed, most of Rahel's contemporaries, as well as later critics, including Key, preferred not to see the 'free spirit' in Rahel Varnhagen but rather the personification of femininity, precisely because Rahel chose to allow her influence to make itself felt through personal contact rather than through publications. Even the generation of *Vormärz* hotheads whom she inspired[57] viewed her as a perfect embodiment of feminine traits – the very type of categorisation which Rahel herself deplored; she was always anxious to distance herself from the type of domestic woman whose very superficiality was often seen as a feminine trait. Men, we recall, were held to be rational creatures, women the repositories of feeling, emotion and moral strength. Rahel

---

[52] Cited in Kemp, *Rahel*, IV, p. 188.
[53] Doris Starr Guilloton, 'Rahel Varnhagen und die Frauenfrage in der deutschen Romantik: eine Untersuchung ihrer Briefe und Tagebuchnotizen', in *Monatshefte*, 69, 4, 1977, pp. 391–403 *passim*.
[54] Ibid., p. 392.
[55] Ellen Key, *Rahel Varnhagen: A Portrait*, London and New York, 1913, p. 57.
[56] Key, *Rahel Varnhagen: A Portait*, p. 55: 'Rahel, like Goethe, like Nietzsche, was convinced of the importance of making one's choice between essentiality and what is only coarseness or caprice, accident or fashion, among our inclinations.'
[57] See Dragutin Subotic, 'Rahel Levin und das junge Deutschland. Ihr Einfluß auf die jungen Geister', PhD Diss., Munich, 1914.

Varnhagen instinctively avoided this sphere by placing herself amongst men; this did not, however, put her on an equal footing. As we have seen, her self-imposed habit of being an enabler in creative discourse rather than instigator attracted the very label of femininity which she sought to evade.

There is no doubt that Rahel's position caused her conflicts, though she attempted to affirm the position she had adopted. Liliane Weissberg has termed this strategy a form of 'psychoanalytic discourse',[58] whilst Marlis Gerhardt has interpreted her position in Lacanian terms of lack; her identity was excluded *ipso facto* from patriarchal discourse.[59] Does this negative interpretation tally with the Rahel Varnhagen of the letters? Certainly, there was a factor of choice in her actions, a sense of pride and indeed self-assertion. Perhaps the very real problems she faced were the source of the discernable energy and brilliance she brought into her dealings with others. Though she herself was an expert in the art of conversation, and fully aware of her talents, she chose to make it her function to draw out of others their opinions and ideas; in her letters she asked questions and demanded answers. Edith Waldstein has described her technique as a use of silence in a dynamic way:

> In her writing Varnhagen simulates conversation ... this involves both writing and 'listening'. At times the letters are intimate, such as when she is writing to lovers or close friends. At others they are intellectual and analytic in their discussions of books and topics of interest for both parties. Regardless of the content, however, they always evoke an air of spontaneity and encourage response.[60]

Significantly, in spite of the fact that her contemporaries chose to see her position as becomingly feminine, Rahel Varnhagen has served as an inspiration for generations of women writers of more radical stamp: Fanny Lewald read *Das Buch Rahel* in 1834 when she was twenty-three; in 1849 she made Rahel a central character in her novel *Prinz Louis Ferdinand* (see Chapter Three, n. 32), though Varnhagen, to whom the book was dedicated, found the portrayal of Rahel distorted.[61] Malwida von Meysenbug found the example of Rahel's achievements uplifting, as did Hedwig Dohm (the narrator in her largely autobiographical novel

---

[58] Liliane Weissberg, 'Writing on the Wall': The Letters of Rahel Varnhagen', *New German Critique*, 36, 1985, pp. 157–73, p. 171.

[59] Marlis Gerhardt, *Stimmen und Rhythmen. Weibliche Ästhetik und Avant-garde*, Darmstadt and Neuwied, 1986, p. 61.

[60] Waldstein, 'Identity as Conflict and Conversation in Rahel Varnhagen', p. 103.

[61] Goodman, 'The Impact of Rahel Varnhagen on Women in the Nienteenth Century', p. 141.

Schicksale einer Seele [1899] wishes that she had Rahel's talent for
writing letters). Ellen Key and Hannah Arendt both approached
Rahel's biography from their own angle; nevertheless, their
interest is further testimony to Rahel's crucial importance for the
women's movement in Germany.

The Portrayal of the 'Standard Woman' in the
Early Nineteenth Century Novel

Caroline de la Motte Fouqué 1775–1831

As so often with the women mentioned in these pages, Caroline
de la Motte Fouqué's life was lived within a coterie of prominent
male writers: Chamisso, Eichendorff, Fichte, Görres, Kleist, the
Schlegel brothers, Hoffmann and of course, her second husband,
Friedrich de la Motte Fouqué. Caroline de la Motte Fouqué's
writings combine many of the Romantic features familiar from
her male friends, such as an interest in the spiritual world, with
examples of second sight, mesmerism and other semi-occult
phenomena.[62] Her privileged social status took her into the
highest court circles, and she held her own salon in Berlin when
there, though for most of her life she lived on the country estate
where she had been born, Nennhausen, and indeed, Baron de la
Motte Fouqué took up residence there after his marriage to
Caroline in 1803. Caroline de la Motte Fouqué's own creativity
began with this marriage, which appears to have been genuinely
happy. However, after a quarter-century of marriage, she was
forced to witness her husband's depression at his waning
popularity, and sought help from their mutual friend, Varnhagen
von Ense, to set Fouqué back on his feet. More importantly, she
wanted her husband to believe in his vocation as a writer –
ironically, a vocation which she regarded as God-given in his case,
in view of his 'nature and position in life',[63] though she certainly
did not claim such a position for herself.

[62] Examples can be found in Caroline de la Motte Fouqué, *The Castle of
Scharffenstein* in *German Stories Selected from the Works of Hoffmann, de la Motte
Fouqué, Pichler, Kruse and Ohers*, ed. by R. P. Gillies, Edinburgh and London,
1826, p. 180f, where second sight is mentioned (the Duke has a dream that his
brother will overthrow him) and *Die Magie der Natur. Eine Revolutionsgeschichte*,
Berlin, Frankfurt am Main, New York and Paris, 1989 [1812], where we are
told that the Marquis is a scholar of Mesmer (p. 4).

[63] Karl August Varnhagen von Ense, *Biographische Portraits nebst Briefen von Koreff,
Clemens Brentano, Frau von Fouqué, Henri Campan und Scholz*, Leipzig, 1871, p.
150 (letter to Varnhagen dated 18 November 1829).

Caroline de la Motte Fouqué's first husband had committed suicide in 1799 after wrecking his fortune by gambling; she herself had had an affair with Count Lehndorff, who was the father of her daughter Klara. The tone of a letter to Lehndorff written by Caroline de la Motte Fouqué in 1811 reveals the disappointment she felt towards a man whom she had formerly loved; the letter also reveals that then, as now, men could walk away from their parental responsibilities:

> Klara asks and pesters me to write to you: she wants to hear from you, to know about you. Your name is never mentioned. Nobody knows anything about you ... You yourself have probably long ago repressed all fleeting surges of memory because you regard that as sensible, whereas it is probably just more comfortable. So you keep silent, and will refuse to answer this letter just as you refused to answer the letter I sent earlier, to your father's house at ... [sic]. But I am doing this for the child's sake. I am as disappointed in the friend as I am in the lover. And just as, earlier, I had to renounce all happiness, I now have to endure your lack of concern.[64]

Jean Wilde, author of the definitive biography of Caroline de la Motte Fouqué, regards the affair as part of Caroline's rejection of the conventions, in line with the Romantic ideals common amongst her circle of friends, which included Caroline Michaelis Schlegel-Schelling[65] and Dorothea Mendelssohn Veit Schlegel. Goethe, too, challenged bourgeois conventions by taking up with the commoner Christiane Vulpius and living with her for nineteen years before finally marrying her. Individuals of both sexes were undergoing storm and stress,[66] though I have already indicated in the Introduction that the consequences of such liaisons were often anything but liberating: one glance at Caroline de la Motte Fouqué's letter to Lehndorff reveals how profoundly disenchanted she was with her former lover. It is hardly surprising that resignation and renunciation are recurrent themes in her writing.

Caroline de la Motte Fouqué wrote over twenty novels and sundry short stories which made her well known in the literary

---

[64] In Varnhagen von Ense, *Biographische Portraits*, p. 129.

[65] Elke Frederiksen, 'Die Frau als Autorin zur Zeit der Romantik: Anfänge einer weiblichen literarischen Tradition', in Burkhard, ed., *Gestaltet und gestaltend*, pp. 83–108, p. 97, gives an assessment of why Caroline Schelling wrote so little (at least, in her name) as being Caroline's readiness to accommodate herself to the men around her, like Tieck and Brentano, who were not keen on the idea of women writers. Ironically, Brentano married a writer, Sophie Mereau.

[66] Jean T. Wilde, *The Romantic Realist: Caroline de la Motte Fouqué*, New York, 1955, p. 31.

world; some of them were swiftly translated into English. George
Soane, who translated *Die Vertriebenen, eine Novelle aus der Zeit der
Königin Elisabeth von England* (1823) into English as *The Outcasts* in
1824, thought that this particular novel 'had some striking scenes
and some happy sketches of character',[67] though he also thought
that the lack of knowledge of English customs was rather obvious,
and that any plot of this nature was bound to look second-rate
when compared with Scott. For her part, Caroline de la Motte
Fouqué was surprised at her own success, as we see from a letter
written to Varnhagen von Ense in 1813:

> I often have to ask myself how it can be that I receive so much public
> esteem and recognition. I have nothing in terms of brilliance or
> originality of the type which automatically attracts praise. My only
> merit lies in my application and my habit of long reflection. It means
> a great deal that people give me such positive recognition for that.[68]

Typically, the patriarchal code emerges strengthened and
endorsed even after a challenge has been mounted to it by a
woman desiring a channel for her own romantic yearnings. *Die
Frau des Falkensteins*, which contains autobiographical elements,
was written in 1806/1807, just after the publication of *Rodrich*,
though it was not published until 1810. The plot focuses on Luise
(Caroline), who marries the doom-laden Julius, Count von
Falkenstein, and eventually succumbs to the seduction of
Fernando (Lehndorff). An interesting twist in the plot is that Julius
is madly in love with his wife, and eventually dies. Luise could now
marry Fernando if she so desired. But when Julius is dead, Luise
still feels bound to him and cannot accept Fernando's argument
that they belong together. Although this cannot be taken as a pure
roman à clef, since the precise details of Caroline's relationship with
Count Lehndorff are not known, Luise is shown as the repository
of virtue for the whole aristocratic line, and as such she is able to
lay to rest the 'curse of the Falkensteins' through her virtue. As
Wilde points out, '[t]here is no doubt about it: throughout her life,
in all her writings, Caroline preaches the need for observing the
formalities, the importance of law and order'.[69]

The plot of *Der Scharffenstein, Eine Erzählung* (*The Castle of
Scharffenstein*) (1818) provides a typical example of the tragedy
which can blight lives when lovers ignore the rules of station and

---

[67] Caroline de la Motte Fouqué, *The Outcasts: A Romance*, London 1824, trs. and
ed. by George Soane. Editor's introduction, p. X.

[68] In Varnhagen von Ense, *Biographische Portraits*, p. 142 (letter of 10 February
1813).

[69] Wilde, *The Romantic Realist*, p. 239.

seek to marry above or below their own class. The novel, in letter
form, tells the story of the love affair between a young countess,
coyly known as Julia de — , and a prince. Julia, a lady-in-waiting
to the Dowager at an unnamed court ruled by a brutal Duke,
meets the Duke's younger brother Prince Charles, who has just
returned form his travels, at a fancy-dress ball. The Duke has
himself taken a fancy to the naive Julia, though there is no
suggestion that he would have married her. The Prince is
considered to be too blue-blooded for Julia, so they plan to elope.
Just before Julia is to run away with Charles, the Duke provokes a
fight with his brother by suggesting that Julia's honour is stained;
Charles, in trying to kill his brother, becomes a traitor. The Duke
thus has a pretext upon which to banish his brother Charles to the
gloomy and remote Scharffenstein Castle, where he is kept a
prisoner and declared insane. Charles lives in resigned despair, his
only outlet being his flute-playing. The hapless Julia takes herself
off to England, but – blind – returns to Germany and lives in the
vicinity of the castle, slipping out at night to listen to the magical
flute-playing, though she does not know that Charles is the flute-
player; nor does he have any idea of Julia's whereabouts.

The story has a framework in which we learn that the narrator
Julius, whose family members have distinguished themselves in the
service of the court, is an officer in the Ducal army who has been
billeted to guard Charles because the Duke has had a premonition
that Charles will escape (see n. 62, above). It is actually the Duke
who now goes mad: Julia and Charles are reunited, and Charles is
made king in place of his brother. However, there is no question of
there being a marriage between Julia and Charles, whom we finally
see living at court as close friends, all passion having been spent in
the intervening twenty years. Julia does, however, regain her sight.
To reinforce the moral, we are told that Divine Providence[70]
operates in such a way that evil can be conquered. Nevertheless,
there is authorial approval for the Dowager's reaction to Charles'
love for Julia as one of horror, resulting in her request for Julia to
give Charles up (a request overtaken by events when the two
brothers quarrel). There is a strong indication that if Julia had had
proper guidance she would have known how to prevent the
situation from occurring in the first place. In other words, when
Julia was dressed for the fancy-dress ball at which she made such a
stunning *éclat* that she turned all the men's heads, not just that of
Charles, she should have been instructed in the art of giving
signals only to men of her own station. The absence of such

---

[70] De la Motte Fouqué, *The Castle of Scharffenstein*, p. 272.

guidance, and her own subsequent ignorance of how to act *comme il faut* with admirers who are above her in rank, brings about the catastrophe of two wasted lives.

The novel abounds with romantic motifs such as significant dreams, a strange woman who can see the future, secret letters hidden in a casket which disclose truths hidden for decades, not to mention the flute, the requisite post-horn and the remote castle itself: the *locus*, not for evil deeds but for deep longing, a profound despair which is nevertheless alleviated, if not fully assuaged, by patient suffering. Thus the novel is virtually a compendium of everything that was necessary for the romantic tale, and it is significant that it was translated into English. However, one must note the complete absence of sexual satisfaction for both Charles and Julia: twenty years have made the loving couple middle-aged and there is no suggestion that their love is anything but platonic at the end of the story. Thus the question of their difference in rank, which gave the novel its *Problematik*, is conveniently side-stepped. Clearly, Caroline de la Motte Fouqué felt it to be axiomatic that society's moral code ought to be obeyed, so much so that she wrote a guide for women in which she set out the correct behaviour for a woman in society, *Die Frauen in der großen Welt. Bildungsbuch bei'm Eintritt in das gesellige Leben* (1826). The book explains how the debutante should behave in general, how society has evolved so that woman's place in it is as it is, what rules govern the conduct of the wife and mother, how and when women should seek the friendship of female friends and what awaits the older society women. Caroline de la Motte Fouqué recognises that poets and minstrels have praised the universality of woman's influence, but finds this too vague a concept to be helpful. She therefore narrows the matter down to the polarities in life, referring to language, which has two complete vocabularies, one containing words like love and forgiveness, the other words like jealousy and revenge.[71] Unfortunately, her glossary reinforces the standard pattern that women deal with the language of sentiment, men with the language of rationalism. Though the plea is always for active effort in order for a woman to play her proper role in society, the guide endorses the status quo, which awards woman a passive role. We have – not for the last time in these pages – the paradox of a creative female writer banning serious artistic productivity in the society woman:

---

[71] Caroline de la Motte Fouqué, *Die Frauen in der großen Welt. Bildungsbuch bei'm Eintritt in das gesellige Leben*, Berlin, 1926, p. 165.

Let women paint and make music in their own quarters to amuse male
and female friends and enliven social intercourse thereby, casting a
glittering web of notes and pictures over the sober, everyday world, but
they should not desire to become either productive artists or critics.[72]

This late stance by a woman who had earlier appeared to
embrace more liberal ideals was criticised by friends in the Rahel
Varnhagen circle who had hitherto been admirers of Caroline de
la Motte Fouqué's works; the denial of a woman's aptitude for
study was felt to be especially unwelcome,[73] since ideas had
moved on from the turn-of-the-century denial of woman's
creativity. There is certainly an element of inconsistency in
Caroline's disingenuous amazement at the success of her works if
she really believed that writing was not a woman's proper sphere.
The same inconsistencey can be detected in Lou Andreas-Salomé
later in the century, and it infuriated Hedwig Dohm.[74]

Should Caroline de la Motte Fouqué's writing be seen as either
hypocritical or inconsistent in view of her affair with Lehndorff?
The answer lies in the message of self-denial. We have already
seen the price such renunciation exacted in Caroline's decision to
renounce Lehndorff (n. 63, above); it is possible that his silence
was an indication that he thoroughly disagreed with her course of
action. Such renunciation is also found in Goethe's *Die
Wahlverwandtschaften* (*Elective Affinities*) (1809); it is a very
unromantic message indeed (hence the justification for Wilde's
description of Caroline as a 'Romantic realist'). It will be recalled
that Rousseau's Julie renounced her love for St Preux to become
the perfect, ultimately self-sacrificing mother. Her *caritas* is what
keeps the little community together; it was passionate sexual love
that had threatened to tear her life asunder. In the same way,
Luise in *Die Frau des Falkensteins* concludes that passion - sexuality
– is the enemy of love.[75] Out of love for the beloved, the parting
must be made. In another novel, *Edmunds Wege und Irrwege* (1815),
love – disembodied and ethereal love as opposed to physical
passion – is fully endorsed as a 'breath of life, the melody of the
world, which through strange oscillations nevertheless brings
everything back into balance.'[76] Passion brings with it a turbulence

---

[72] De la Motte Fouqué, *Die Frauen in der großen Welt*, p. 255.

[73] Vera Prill, *Caroline de la Motte-Fouqué*[sic], Berlin, 1933, p. 65.

[74] Hedwig Dohm, 'Reaktion in der Frauenbewegung', in *Die Zukunft*, 18
November 1899, pp. 279–291, p. 290f.

[75] Birgit Wägenbauer, *Die Pathologie der Liebe. Literarische Weiblichkeitsentwёrfe um
1800*, Berlin, 1996, p. 235: 'Love stands opposed to sexuality'.

[76] Caroline de la Motte Fouqué, *Edmunds Wege und Irrwege. Ein Roman aus der
nächsten Vergangenheit*, 3 vols, Leipzig, 1815, I, pp. 74–75.

which destroys a woman's equilibrium and thus separates her *from
herself*. The trick, Wägenbauer argues, was for the woman to *choose*
to renounce; in deciding to be passive, she became active, and her
action benefited the wider community. Vera Prill likewise describes
the contemporary opinions of woman's role as being essentially
conducive to harmony:

> Because women stand in immediate rapport with nature, their task is
> to oversee everything and make things organic... They are at one with
> the order of things, are connected to God and the world through
> their simple existence, and nature has given them the measure of all
> relationships whether in time or space.[77]

Such a woolly all-encompassing conception of a woman's role was
typical in the circle of the early Romantics and had been
definitively set out in Schlegel's *Lucinde* (1799); what one can
surmise is that Caroline de la Motte Fouqué must have found
that her own acceptance of male-inspired dogma on female
rectitude raised more questions than it answered. As Wägenbauer
informs us, '[t]he letters [from Caroline] to Rahel and Varnhagen
all circle round the question: who am I?'[78] As we shall see, Bettina
von Arnim would be preoccupied with the same question.

Bettina von Arnim, 1785–1859

Bettina von Arnim belonged to late Romanticism; though she was
on excellent terms with Rahel von Varnhagen, she did not share
the latter's reluctance to publish in her own right: quite the
reverse. Always headstrong, she made a significant contribution
to radical politics in the years leading up to the 1848 Revolution
in Germany, now designated as the *Vormärz*. Bettina is the one
name likely to be familiar to all readers of the present study. Her
mother, Maximiliane de la Roche, had captivated the young
Goethe, who then had to maintain a strict reserve because she was
already engaged to an Italian businessman resident in Frankfurt.
Goethe was later highly critical of 'Maxe's' mother, Sophie von la
Roche, for marrying her daughter Maxe off to a man twenty-
seven years her senior; Maxe's sister had to undergo the same
fate. Bettina Brentano was born in Frankfurt and spent her early
life there, but her childhood was ruptured when her mother died
in 1793 at the age of thirty-seven, having given birth to eight

---

[77] Prill, *Caroline de Motte-Fouqué*, p. 65.
[78] Wägenbauer, *Die Pathologie der Liebe*, p. 203.

children. Bettina and three of her sisters were sent to the Ursuline Convent in Fritzlar, but when Fritzlar was occupied by the French in 1794, Bettina and the two younger sisters were sent to their grandmother, Sophie von la Roche. The latter was well-known for her novel *Die Geschichte des Fräuleins von Sternheim* (1771), in which the virtuous Sophie von Sternheim emerges victorious from a series of tribulations; tricked into a marriage which she believes to be legal, but which she refuses to consummate (just as well, since the mariage is a sham), she wreaks a frigid revenge on her 'husband', and is ultimately able to extricate herself and marry the man she loves. When Bettina came to write, she would show little debt to her grandmother in terms of melodrama, but both women shared views on the importance of a proper education for a girl.

Bettina was surrounded by books in her grandmother's house and became an avid reader; she would always have access to books, since the library at her future marital home, the country estate Wiepersdorf, contained over five thousand books, including the complete works of Luther.[79] She was open to Catholic influence from her father and from the convent, and there is no doubt that the religious ceremonial at Fritzlar was an inspiration to her imagination. Her mother had been Protestant, as would be her husband, Achim von Arnim, whom she married in 1811. Achim von Arnim was a friend of her brother, Clemens Brentano, and both were central figures in German Romanticism. Bettina often lived with her seven children in Berlin while Arnim tried to settle matters at Wiepersdorf, which Bettina seems to have found boring, certainly in comparison to Berlin, where she was especially friendly with Rahel and her circle. Bettina met Schleiermacher in 1810. Schleiermacher, it will be recalled, engineered Henriette Herz's conversion; he brought about a similar change in Bettina, whose Catholic taste for ritual in religious matters now became overlaid with pietistic inwardness. This made her attitude towards religion a curious mixture of exoticism and simplicity.

Throughout her marriage to Arnim, Bettina made no secret of her admiration for Goethe, which went beyond the most extreme form of adulation. Encouraged by the Goethe cult pursued by Rahel in her salon, Bettina was to become Goethe's greatest fan during his lifetime, something which came to annoy him not a little, though at first he was no doubt captivated by the vivacious daughter of the woman he had once loved. In addition, Bettina

---

[79] Sabine Schormann, *Bettine von Arnim. Die Bedeutung Schleiermachers für ihr Leben und Werk*, Tübingen, 1993, p. 23ff.

had spent many hours in the company of Goethe's mother in Frankfurt, and Goethe was interested to hear Bettina's version of his mother's anecdotes. Bettina met Goethe briefly for the first time in 1807; she felt so uncertain of her reception that she asked Wieland for a letter of introduction.[80] She subsequently visited Weimar in 1811, 1821, 1824 and 1828; in 1810, she saw Goethe in Teplitz. In 1811, an unfortunate incident took place in which Bettina offended Christiane von Goethe; Goethe sided with his wife, though after Christiane's death, Bettina was able to re-establish a relationship of sorts with Goethe. Following Goethe's death in 1832, Bettina used her actual correspondence with Goethe as the basis for her highly fictional work, *Goethe's Briefwechsel mit einem Kinde* (1835).[81] This is divided into two parts, the *Briefwechsel*, consisting of real letters expanded or with highly diffuse additions, and an even more discursive *Tagebuch*, based on the diary Bettina had started to keep in 1808 to record her conversation with Goethe. Bettina was catapulted to fame on publication of the work, and held her own salon in Berlin from 1836 until 1839 largely on the strength of it; she even exhausted herself trying to translate the work into English, looking up almost every word in the dictionary. Her translation, which bore the title *Goethe's Correspondence with a Child*, flopped in Britain, though the book was well regarded in transcendentalist circles in the United States because it was held that 'the practice of revealing one's inner feelings in writing and conversation' encouraged the formation of interpersonal relationships.[82] In spite of the criticism to which the book was subjected in Germany, it was a best-seller; some critics, such as Ludwig Börne, even found virtue (such as freshness) in the very faults (such as naivety) criticised by others; in a review for the *Literatur-Blatt*, 14 December 1835, he welcomed Bettina's courageous voyage into unknown territory – with Goethe as anchor.[83]

---

[80] Birgit Weißenborn, *Bettina von Arnim und Goethe. Topographie einer Beziehung als Beispiel weiblicher Emanzipation zu Beginn des 19. Jahrhunderts*, Frankfurt am Main, Bern, New York and Paris, 1987, p. 64.

[81] Since Bettina herself used the obvious translation for this title in her own attempt to translate the work – *Goethe's Correspondence with a Child* – I have retained the German title, untranslated, to indicate that I am not referring to Bettina's unfortunate hack work, published by Longman in 1839.

[82] Konstanze Bäumer, 'Margaret Fuller (1810–1850) and Bettina von Arnim: An Encounter between American Transcendentalism and German Romanticism' in *Internationales Jahrbuch der Bettina-von-Arnim-Gesellschaft*, 4, 1990, pp. 45–69, p. 49.

[83] Reprinted in *Ludwig Börne, 1786–1837*, ed. by Alfred Estermann, Frankfurt am Main, 1986, p. 61f.

Naturally, the apparent inconsistency of a fifty-year old matron describing herself as a child, albeit in retrospect, was not lost on critics; however, the use of this term was crucial and should be understood within a culturally historic context. Schleiermacher's influence on Bettina had versed her in the vocabulary of pietism, one of the chief words of which is 'child': the pietist places him- or herself unconditionally in the lap of Jesus, as a child would surrender to its mother.[84] Later, Bettina would use the term in her political writing. The true inconsistency is that Bettina had no intention of surrendering to anyone. Moreover, Bettina's denial, in the letters, of any erudition, in order to reinforce the impression of child-like simplicity is a deliberate ruse, as Sabine Schormann indicates: 'she stylises herself as a genius who has no need of learning'.[85] However, it could be argued that beyond this very public display of herself, Bettina, in *Goethe's Briefwechsel mit einem Kinde*, is really conducting a monologue with herself in a quest for the type of self-knowledge which is the goal of the traditional form of pietism, but using the highly individualistic method common to Romanticism.[86] Schleiermacher's pietism, as opposed to the zealous neo-pietism which engulfed Germany for much of the century, was ultimately concerned with questioning beliefs. Bettina pays lip-service to God, but focuses exclusively on her romanticised relationship with Goethe. The book was anathema to those who construed individualism as a manifestation of lack of discipline; this group of critics included many women who had built their lives around conformity and warded off any challenge to social convention. For this reason, writers such as Annette von Droste-Hülshoff and Johanna and Adele Schopenhauer kept a strategic distance from Bettina, though Anna Brandes found comparisons between Adele Schopenhauer's vivid imagination and that of Bettina; they were also both admirers of Goethe, and both were musically and creatively gifted.[87] However, Adele's imaginative rendering of Romantic yearning, especially in her *Tagebuch einer Einsamen*, comes to appear tinged with sexual frustration, whereas Bettina's, as one might expect from someone who had had an affectionate husband, until his death in 1831, and a large family, is rich and

---

[84] See August Lange, *Wortschatz des deutschen Pietismus*, Tübingen, 1954, p. 311f.

[85] Schormann, *Bettine von Arnim*, p. 32.

[86] See Carol Diethe, 'Bettina von Arnim and "*Das Ewig-Kindliche*"' in *Women Writers of the Age of Goethe*, Occasional Papers in German Studies: 6, 1994, pp. 3–19, *passim*.

[87] Anna Brandes, 'Adele Schopenhauer in den geistigen Beziehungen zu ihrer Zeit', PhD Diss., Frankfurt am Main, 1930, p. 29.

exultant, which is not to say that Goethe had any sexually active part in the genesis of *Goethe's Briefwechsel mit einem Kinde* – beyond a kiss.[88]

With Bettina's intense individuality emerging on every page of *Goethes Briefwechsel mit einem Kinde*, her major work (though she published other important creative writings, most notably *Die Günderrode* [1840][89] and *Clemens Brentanos Frühlingskrantz* [1844]),[90] it is perhaps astonishing that Bettina should prove to be one of the most politically radical women writers of her age. Her sympathy always went out to the poor and suffering, and in 1832 she helped Schleiermacher in his work with victims of the Berlin cholera epidemic.[91] She also persuaded the King, Friedrich Wilhelm of Prussia, to allow the Grimm brothers to return from exile in Hannover to resume their posts at Berlin University, and in 1850 helped to bring about the release from jail of Gottfried Kinkel, husband of her good friend Johanna Kinkel. In 1843, the suffering of the poor in Berlin roused her to write a polemic, *Dies Buch gehört dem König*! This caused a sensation because of Bettina's outright attack on the state's supine refusal to deal with poverty, and immediately attracted censorship.[92] Placing her most radical words in the mouth of Goethe's mother, whose common sense she revered highly (and who also provided a shield of protection – the name of Goethe – to hide behind), Bettina challenged 'the belief that the ruled should exist in a state of dependence on the ruler',[93] arguing that there should be a level of collaboration between ruler and ruled, since this would protect the king from unscrupulous ministers. Bettina argues rhetorically:

[88] See Helmut Hirsch, *Bettina von Arnim*, Hamburg, 1987, pp. 41–55, for a succinct description of the relationship.
[89] Bettina von Arnim's *Die Günderrode*, first published in two volumes in Leipzig in 1840, treats the poet Karoline von Günderrode, who committed suicide in 1806 at the age of twenty-six.
[90] From the 1840s, Bettina collaborated with Varnhagen, who sympathised with her endeavours to arouse social consciences in Germany, but Feilchenfeldt in 'Die Anfänge des Kults um Rahel', p. 229, overestimates the importance Varnhagen had for her in ensuring that she had a place in posterity. However, this was true for Rahel, who would have sunk into obscurity but for Varnhagen.
[91] Konstanze Bäumer, 'Romantische "Gedankenerregungskunst" – Bettina von Arnim und Friedrich Ernst Daniel Schleiermacher' in *Bettina, Psyche, Mignon – Bettina von Arnim und Goethe*, Stuttgart, 1986, p. 91f.
[92] In 1844, Adolf Stahr was prevented from publishing his essay 'Bettina und ihr Königsbuch'. See Werner Vordtriede, ed., *Bettina von Arnims Armenbuch*, Frankfurt am Main, 1969, p. 7.
[93] Tim Bailey, 'Bettina von Arnim as an Apostle of Enlightenment' in *Women Writers of the Age of Goethe*, Occasional Papers in German Studies: 6, 1994, pp. 20–29, p. 21.

The state is a human being [*Mensch*] and its physical mission consists of helping people to develop their freedom … If humanity is a child, healthy potential lies in its seed. – The state must develop this seed, otherwise it is a bad mother [*Rabenmutter*] and just seeking to feed itself [*Rabenfutter*].[94]

The pun on ravens may be lost in translation, but not the rhetoric on the duty of the state as parent. The reference to the mother and child demonstrates that Bettina holds to the language of pietism, as she had done in 1835, though this time she tries – naively, perhaps – to set it in a political context whilst retaining a religious aura whereby, in Bailey's words, 'she successfully unites religious and political freedom'.[95] A surreptitious start had been made in this direction in *Die Günderrode*, which, Bäumer argues, 'despite its innocent appearance as a Romantic correspondence between two young women, contained a good deal of subversive criticism of society and church'.[96] Much of the polemic in *Dies Buch gehört dem König!* which so shocked Bettina's contemporaries, such as the argument for the abolition of the death penalty,[97] is years ahead of its time and, indeed, is still controversial.

In May 1844, Bettina was sent a list of the most destitute weavers in Silesia by Friedrich Wilhelm Schöffel, a factory owner who was tying to bring about an improvement in the weavers' conditions. This prompted her to publish an advertisement in the major German newspapers calling for information on poverty in Germany to be sent to her so that she could collate a report. More reports on the poverty of Silesian weavers soon reached her, in spite of police interception of her mail. Bettina now planned the publication of an *Armenbuch* to shame the authorities into doing something; however, in the event, the weavers' uprising of 9 June led to the arrest of Schöffel and scotched Bettina's plans to publish the book. According to Varnhagen von Ense, who was working closely with Bettina at this time, Alexander von Humboldt, who was beavering away at court on Bettina's behalf, advised her to have her report published abroad.[98] Vordtriede remarks that it is quite possible that Bettina may have had an inflammatory influence on the rebellion.[99]

[94] Bettina von Arnim, *Dies Buch gehört dem König!* in *Bettina von Arnim. Werke und Briefe*, 4 vols 1986–1995, ed. by Wolfgang Bunzel et al., Frankfurt am Main, III, 1995, p. 234.

[95] Bailey, 'Bettina von Arnim as an Apostle of the Enlightenment', p. 27.

[96] Bäumer, 'Margaret Fuller … and Bettina von Arnim', p. 51.

[97] Bunzel, *Bettina von Arnim*, III, p. 239.

[98] According to Varnhagen's diary entry for 24 June 1844. In *Tagebücher von K.A. Varnhagen von Ense*, 14 vols, II, Leipzig, 1861, p. 315.

[99] Vordtriede, *Bettina von Arnims Armenbuch*, p. 36.

Bettina, for her part, was furious that a desire to help the poor was twisted into incitement to riot.

As we have seen, Bettina was able to hold the respect of men who were actively engaged in liberal politics, such as Alexander von Humboldt. Bettina herself remained free to move on the margins of the political debate and was able to do so without any real fear of being arrested. She thus offers the first example of a woman writer who used her femininity strategically to her own advantage. However, she perhaps overestimated her seductive powers in her dealings with Fürst Pückler-Muskau, the writer, dilettante and *roué* to whom she attempted to draw closer in 1833, having first made his acquaintance through Rahel's salon. The correspondence begins in 1832, reaching a crescendo in the following late summer, when Bettina visited the Prince, apparently hoping for a love affair to bloom, since the tone of the letters had been nothing if not flirtatious. Pückler had to let her down as gently as possible, whereupon they corresponded on weightier matters centring on Schleiermacher's teaching. When Schleiermacher died in 1834, the bantering tone of the correspondence was no longer appropriate, and the letters petered out. Butler, whose sympathies are with the Prince in this non-affair rather than with Bettina, nevertheless grudgingly admits that she was not simply 'an artful old humbug of sixty' (actually, she was just fifty – *and so was Pückler!*):

> There was a real Bettina imprisoned inside the fake, whose qualities he [Pückler] recognised, and who appears sporadically in their correspondence, considerably modifying the general impression that truth and reality are to be found in Pückler's letters and mystical falsehood in hers.[100]

What Butler elides is the fact that Bettina routinely used flirtation as a way of gaining entry to the world of men; it was a means, not an end; the love affair did not need to be real, as was seen in the case of *Goethes Briefwechsel mit einem Kinde*. The point is that she managed to write about herself by this strategy, and moved woman's writing one step further towards the hitherto taboo realm of autobiography. Part of what she wanted to do was to express her own sexuality as a woman. Even in later life, she maintained a notion of the value of her own sexuality – something many of the women of her generation lost with the birth of their first child – and notwithstanding the misunderstanding with

---

[100] E. M. Butler, *The Tempestuous Prince: Hermann Pückler-Muskau*, London, New York and Toronto, 1929, p. 157.

Pückler, which she characteristically joked about as 'the battle of Muskau',[101] used her sexuality to her advantage in her dealings with men. In this way, she was quite unlike other Romantic women, such as Caroline de la Motte-Fouqué, who so often solves the problem of female sexuality by recourse to all manner of equivalents of the judicious sick headache. It is thus as a full-blooded woman that Bettina mounted the barricades, and others would follow. Bettina's brand of self-assuredness as a woman unnerved many women as well as men, yet she arguably did more for women's emancipation by her example than all the nineteenth-century tracts on female education put together.

---

[101] Pückler had divorced his wife Lucie when his fortunes were parlous, with the intention of finding a rich second wife. However, he could never actually bring himself to leave Lucie. She was therefore in the house when Bettina arrived, at Pückler's suggestion, and treated him as though they were engaged. Bettina was virtually shown the door. Her letter to Pückler written in 1834 mentions the 'battle of Muskau' without rancour. In Heinrich Conrad, ed., *Frauenbriefe von und an Hermann Fürsten Pückler-Muskau*, Munich and Leipzig, 1912, p. 199.

Luise Seidler, *Ottilie von Goethe*. Reproduced with kind permission of the *Stiftung Weimarer Klassik*.

2

WEIMAR CONNECTIONS

The cultural flowering of Weimar was already well under way by the time Goethe arrived there, at the young Duke Karl August's invitation, in 1775. The Duke's mother, Anna Amalia, was an art collector and had her own private collection, and the ducal palace in Weimar still houses a magnificent art collection. The death, in 1805, of Schiller, who had lived in nearby Jena, was a severe blow to Goethe, though the town had other luminaries, such as Wieland, and would have many more as the century progressed, amongst them Liszt and Nietzsche. Napoleon quartered himself briefly in the castle in 1806, but Weimar polite society was arguably more ruffled when Goethe married the humble Christiane Vulpius in the same year, probably to make his son August legitimate, though he was genuinely attached to Christiane. The marriage itself, which broke all the rules of etiquette, since Christiane was not even from the established bourgeoisie, was considered more offensive than the liaison. In fact, Goethe's mother in Frankfurt was one of the few women who was really kind to her; of course, Goethe himself was a patrician, and had come from below to enter the aristocratic circles he now frequented. A man could do this, a bourgeois woman might, but a commoner could not. We shall see that the tension between aristocracy and bourgeoisie continues to make itself felt in the writing discussed in this chapter. Adele Schopenhauer came from a background similar to that of Goethe, whilst Ottilie von Goethe descended from impoverished aristocracy. The chapter finally focuses on Annette von Droste-Hülshoff, who stemmed from ancient Westphalian nobility. Annette von Droste-Hülshoff, often

known affectionately as 'die Droste', never went to Weimar,
though in many respects – through her contact with Adele
Schopenhauer and Sibylle Mertens – Weimar came to her.

Johanna Schopenhauer, 1766–1838

Johanna Schopenhauer, a native of Danzig, was born into a
wealthy merchant family and received an education which was
'one equivalent to that of the society woman';[1] her burning regret
was that her desire to be trained as an artist was never fulfilled.
The refusal of her parents to encourage this artistic bent was her
first experience of rejection. Even after over sixty years, the
memory of the scorn with which this aspiration was greeted still
rankled; Goodman comments that the objection was founded on
the family's resistance to the thought of Johanna 'exercising a
trade'.[2] When in her late teens, Johanna Schopenhauer appears
to have had a sweetheart, although she is reticent about the
matter in her memoirs. At all events, soon after this, in 1784, she
was married, at the age of eighteen, to the respected and wealthy
Danzig merchant Heinrich Florian Schopenhauer, who was
nineteen years her senior. Like Marcus Herz, Schopenhauer tried
to educate his young wife to his views, especially to the scepticism
of Voltaire. He was more successful in bringing Johanna to his
point of view politically, converting her to outright republicanism
with regard to the French Revolution, so that they both rejoiced
over the fall of the Bastille, though with most other radicals they
revised their views when the Terror began. The widowed
Johanna was more of a neutral observer when Napoleon
occupied Weimar in 1806: in spite of the horrors of occupation,
she admired Napoleon, but by 1813 she had come to support the
struggle for German liberation and was disappointed that her
son Arthur (who was busy writing his dissertation) did not enlist
in readiness for the battle of Leipzig.[3]

---

[1] Kay Goodman, 'Johanna Schopenhauer (1766-1838), or Pride and
     Resignation', in *Out of Line/Ausgefallen: The Paradox of Marginality in the Writings
     of Nineteenth-Century German Women*, ed. by Ruth-Ellen Boetcher Joeres and
     Marianne Burkhard, Amsterdam, 1989, pp. 187–209, p. 188.

[2] Ibid., p. 188.

[3] According to H. H. Houben, ed., *Damals in Weimar. Erinnerungen und Briefe von
     und an Johanna Schopenhauer*, Berlin, 1929 [1924], p. 203: '[t]he intoxication of
     the national campaign for liberation had not gripped him [Arthur]; in this he
     followed the example of Goethe, who managed to stop his son from enlisting
     amongst the volunteers …'.

Three years after her marriage, Johanna Schopenhauer travelled with her husband to England, returning three months before Arthur was born in 1788; Adele was born in 1797. Johanna undertook a major journey through Europe with Arthur when he was fifteen, taking him to Holland, England, France, Switzerland, Austria, Silesia, and Poland. This journey inspired one of her first pieces of writing, *Erinnerungen von einer Reise in den Jahren 1803, 1804 und 1805*, which was then published under the title *Reise durch England und Schottland* and appeared in 1818. It is one of the first travelogues by a woman writer in the century: there would be many more. Johanna herself published her *Ausflug an den Niederrhein und nach Belgien in 1828* in 1831. Accounts of the journeys reappear in Johanna's posthumous memoirs *Jugendleben und Wanderbilder*, prepared for publication in 1839 by her daughter. In retrospect, Johanna remembers the joy she experienced when her husband told her they were going to travel to England:

> I was going to travel, travel! And to see a great many other towns and countries on the long way to Calais. I was dizzy with joy, I thought I was dreaming when my husband acquainted me with the fact that this unexpected pleasure was about to take place ...[4]

Johanna was not put off by the fact that one reason for the trip was for her husband to examine 'family life' in England with a view to moving there if the political situation in Danzig worsened. In the event, the partition of Poland in 1793, which drew Danzig into Prussia, made the Schopenhauers decide to leave Danzig to settle in Hamburg, and it was there that Johanna's husband died of a fall – though Johanna said it was suicide, which is likely to be the truth.

Johanna had found marriage to an irascible older man difficult, and had made many complaints to her children about her unhappiness. She experienced her sudden widowhood as an immense relief. She now travelled to Gotha and Weimar to see which she liked best, picked Weimar, possibly swayed because of the strong interest in art manifested in the town by luminaries such as Herzogin Anna Amalia and Carl Ludwig Fernow, and settled there in 1806. Having become a close friend of Fernow, she took him into her house in 1807 and nursed him there until his death in 1808. Johanna Schopenhauer's first publication in her own name was an essay 'Carl Ludwig Fernows Leben' (1810). Through Fernow and his friend, the painter Gerhard von

[4] Johanna Schopenhauer, *Jugend und Wanderbilder*, Tübingen, 1958 [1839], p. 178.

Kügelchen, she became an expert in the complex theory of art which characterised Weimar classicism around 1800. Fernow was a key figure in interpreting and disseminating this theory.[5] Johanna Schopenhauer was therefore a more central figure to Weimar classicism than her nervously charged fiction might suggest. Having become one of Anna Amalia's circle of friends, she was able to keep in touch with art criticism of the highest level, as is clear in her later work on Jan van Eyck, *Johann van Eyck und seine Nachfolger* (1822).

Now began the type of rebirth which was sometimes the welcome result of being widowed early: Johanna was still only forty, though that would have been classed as old by her contemporaries. This makes her achievement in establishing herself as writer and salon hostess all the more remarkable. It was enormously helped by Goethe's friendship, formed when Johanna was the first to invite Christiane von Goethe to her home – actually the day after Goethe had regularised their relationship by marrying her. Goethe visited her house regularly until 1814, the year in which Johanna quarrelled with her son, who by this time had become of interest to Goethe as a young man with promise. Arthur broke off contact with his mother because of her relationship with her lodger, Müller von Gerstenbergk, whom she had met in 1813. Though Johanna insisted that this relationship was not sexual, and indeed, Adele at one point thought her mother was trying to arrange a match for her with Gerstenbergk, Arthur felt that Johanna had insulted the memory of his father. Johanna, for her part, felt that she had been insulted. The quarrel was never resolved, and financial matters also made a rapprochement difficult. Arthur had insisted on having his inheritance paid to him in full, in advance, in 1814, an action which was highly propitious for him, since Johanna had invested in a Danzig bank which went bankrupt in 1819, leaving her in difficult circumstances. The quarrel even went beyond the grave: in her will, Johanna, who had scarcely anything to leave, expressly stated that Arthur was to have nothing. In spite of the financial shock of 1819, which would have far-reaching consequences for Adele as well as for Johanna, this was also the year in which Johanna's first novel *Gabriele* was published; it was followed by several other novels: *Die Tante* (1823), *Sidonia* (1827), *Richard Wood* (1837), many stories and other writings of non-fiction.

---

[5]   I am indebted to Harald Tausch for drawing this to my attention in his talk delivered to the *Stiftung Weimarer Klassik Stipendiarkolloquium*, Weimar, 11 March 1997, entitled 'Carl Ludwig Fernow und der Weimarer Klassizismus um 1800'.

Like Henriette Herz, Johanna Schopenhauer never actually complained about the social system in which young girls were married to much older men. In both cases, the husband was very pleased with his conquest, and this must have flattered the bride. Johanna was sent fresh flowers every morning of her five-week engagement, a common practice for Sundays; Heinrich Floris declared that 'every day was a Sunday' now that they were going to be married. What contaminated their relationship from the start was the fact that a few months earlier, Johanna had been in love and had had to give up all thought of marrying the man concerned. We know nothing of the details, but Dworetzki places her bet on a young artist.[6] What is certain is that Johanna did not love her husband, and her parents knew it. Like Henriette Herz, Johanna's memory of her wedding day, with snow still on the ground, is tinged with a bleak sadness.[7] It was worse for Johanna because she had had to renounce her first love. However, like Henriette, she never blamed her parents for encouraging her to make this marriage of convenience. Indeed, she makes it clear that she was not forced, a factor which becomes an important theme in her works.

In the novel *Sidonia*, there does at first sight appear to be a critique of marriages of convenience, and indeed of high society itself, which, Johanna Schopenhauer informs us in the authorial voice, is erroneously called 'good society' in German.[8] There is a marked contrast between the cheerful, sensible Sidonia and her decadent stepmother – who is scarcely older than Sidonia herself, having married Sidonia's father as his second wife when she was still, as she says, 'practically a child'.[9] The reason for the second marriage is gradually revealed. Sidonia's mother, when a young girl, had been in love with her childhood friend from the neighbouring estate, later destined to become the prominent and influential Graf Adelheim. Just why the parents on both sides oppose the match so bitterly is never revealed, but Sidonia's mother is married off to the much older Herr von Klarenbach at the age of fifteen, and proceeds to irritate him, from the wedding reception onwards, because she is not *au fait* with the manners of high society, and does not want to learn, either. She dislikes the artificiality of high society which her husband finds congenial,

---

[6] Gertrud Dworetzki, *Johanna Schopenhauer. Ein Charakterbild aus Goethes Zeiten*, Düsseldorf, 1987, p. 113.

[7] Johanna Schopenhauer, *Jugendleben und Wanderbilder*, p. 155f.

[8] Johanna Schopenhauer, *Sidonia* (i–iii), in *Sämtliche Schriften*, 24 vols, Frankfurt am Main, 1831, X–XII, i, p. 9.

[9] Johanna Schopenhauer, *Sidonia*, i, p. 12.

and is soon marginalised as 'gauche'. All her natural emotions are steadily crushed: for example, after the birth of her son (on her own sixteenth birthday), her desire to breast-feed him is refused and the baby is banished to a remote part of the house with the wet-nurse; the birth of Sidonia follows some years later. When Graf Adelheim meets Sidonia's mother again he naturally becomes a close friend, and wicked gossip results in Herr von Klarenbach divorcing her, though she has not been unfaithful. She is cast away, and moreover, forced to leave her children behind. Graf Adelheim offers to marry her but she refuses, feeling that, though still in her twenties, she is a burnt-out wreck who would hold Adelheim back in his career.

All of the sorry story recounted above is revealed to Sidonia when her dead mother's valedictory letter is forwarded to her by her aunt, Frau von Bornefeld. At that juncture, history is about to repeat itself in that Sidonia is being forced to marry an older man whom she detests, Herr von Binsenburg, though she has not been prised away from a lover. Her brother implicates himself in an intrigue to encourage the match. Sidonia, desperate, dresses up in man's clothing in order to escape, and after some far-fetched adventures involving students, throws herself on the mercy of an old friend, Seefeld, who turns out to be none other than Graf Adelheim, who now offers her his hand. The importance for the plot of Sidonia's marriage to her mother's former lover is completely omitted from Goodman's assessment of the novel.[10] The age gap, which *ipso facto* involves the man being old enough to be the father of his wife, a situation which Johanna Schopenhauer herself knew from experience, is glossed over. Adelheim feels rejuvenated at having a young wife, whereas his wife merely feels a calm satisfaction, since, she concludes, women are 'born moderators' who prevent the world from being burnt to cinders by the 'wild, bold men' who set the world on fire.[11]

The serene if short-lived marriage of Sidonia and Adelheim still leaves many unanswered questions about Sidonia's mother, whose wasted life is actually by far the most interesting detail of the whole plot of this three-volume marathon: for example, historically interesting information is sometimes provided unwittingly (such as the fact that a husband could prevent his wife from breast-feeding her own child, and had custody of the children after a divorce). The rest of the plot deals with Sidonia's

[10] Goodman in 'Johanna Schopenhauer …' just calls him 'a wealthier man', p. 204.
[11] Johanna Schopenhauer, *Sidonia*, i, p. 43f.

lonely wanderings in search of happiness after the death of Adelheim. In Bordeaux, the death of the painter Robert is blamed on her and Sidonia is ostracised. However, she has found a staunch ally in the aristocrat Belmont, who will now become her constant companion. They travel to Scotland together, tracing the steps of Ossian,[12] Macpherson's work not yet having been found to be a fake. No doubt Johanna also had her friend Goethe's early work, *Die Leiden des jungen Werthers* (*The Sufferings of Young Werther*) (1774), in mind at this juncture. She had already enthused over 'nature as Ossian painted it'[13] when she admired the rivers, rocks and primeval oaks of the region of Loch Tay on her journey to Scotland. However, the shared *frisson* of visiting Ossian's territory does not work the magic for Sidonia and Belmont as it did for Werther and Charlotte; Sidonia and Belmont believe that the primeval woods on the coast fringing Mull and Oban (Ossian's wooded 'Morven'[14]) have been destroyed by man's intervention, which serves to make their mood melancholy.

Belmont allows his relationship to Sidonia to be contaminated by a quarrel over a trivial matter provoked by ill-founded jealousy: history repeating itself again within the chronicle. As a result of this *contretemps*, Sidonia breaks with Belmont. Without his support, her life becomes aimless until she falls in love with a younger man, George Falkenberg. When Sidonia is about to give her hand to Falkenberg at the end of the novel, Belmont intervenes to say that she is being dishonest, since the relationship will not work. Without there being any proper explanation as to why it should not, the twenty-six-year-old Sidonia concedes that Belmont is right and breaks off with Falkenberg, only to become, like her mother before her, a burnt-out wreck. One has to assume that Johanna Schopenhauer intended her readers to feel sympathy for the fate of Sidonia and her mother, but it is hard to do so, since both are the authors of their own downfall when they reject offers from men they love and admire. It is their own lack of self-esteem which makes them old before their time.

Though Johanna Schopenhauer acquired a reputation for broad-mindedness when she invited Goethe's new wife into her home whilst the rest of Weimar high society sulked, she was by no means egalitarian, as Dworetzki has pointed out.[15] Only in one of her stories does she allow an aristocratic character, Egon von

---

[12] Johanna Schopenhauer, *Sidonia*, iii (XII), p. 88.

[13] Johanna Schopenhauer, *Reise durch England und Schottland* (i, ii) in *Sämmtliche Schriften*, XV, i, p. 295.

[14] Johanna Schopenhauer, *Sidonia*, iii, p. 87.

[15] Dworetzki, *Johanna Schopenhauer*, p. 97.

Hochberg in 'Herbstliebe' ('Autumn Love'), to say kind words
about the bourgeoisie – and the story takes place in the United
States, *locus* of egalitarianism. Otherwise Johanna, from a solid
bourgeois family herself, makes all her major characters members
of the nobility and, furthermore, places an embargo on their
marrying outside their class. Dworetzki argues that Johanna was
at pains to please the aristocracy with whom she was on such
cordial terms in Weimar; in addition, Johanna's heroines are
always the embodiment of perfection in terms of beauty, good
manners and intelligence, and thus necessarily shown off at their
best in an aristocratic milieu.[16]

The narrow-minded ethos of aristocratic society might well be
challenged in her plots, but marriage between the bourgeoisie
and the aristocracy is never allowed to take place. Though her
own crisis in love was possibly caused by the young man being of
a lower station than herself (as happened with Ottilie von
Goethe), Johanna leaves no room for regrets, merely making the
point that a marriage cannot flourish without the consent of the
parents, though the latter should not force a daughter to marry
against her wishes. As with Caroline de la Motte Fouqué, freedom
consists in choosing to do that which one does not want to do, a
recipe for frustration and dishonesty (if only towards oneself) in
the mind of the critic today, but in the early nineteenth century a
model for correct behaviour, notwithstanding the example
provided by certain individual Romantics. Dworetzki writes, '[i]n
Johanna's work the theme of conflict between feelings and
submission to the law of marrying in one's station is endless'.[17]

Johanna's warning to women not to have pretensions of
marrying above themselves into the aristocracy was somewhat ill-
timed: throughout the century, that type of liaison became ever
more frequent as the bourgeoisie gained wealth and the
impoverished aristocracy sought to acquire some of it through
'downward' marriages. Moreover, there is often an unpleasantly
complacent ring to some of her remarks, as in her description of
the ghetto Jews in Danzig, whom neither the poll tax they had to
pay nor the insults they had to bear could deter from creating 'a
disgusting clatter and screaming as they went about their
miserable business'; the 'daughters of Zion' are also spoken of
dismissively.[18] It should be added that this type of low-level anti-

---

[16] Ibid., p. 102.
[17] Ibid., p. 96.
[18] Johanna Schopenhauer, *Jugendleben und Wanderbilder*, p. 45f.

Semitism was so common at the time that it was probably unconscious on Johanna Schopenhauer's part.

In 1829 Johanna decided to move to the Rhineland, staying first in the Unkel property owned by Sibylle Mertens, Adele's friend, before moving to Bonn itself that winter. Johanna returned to Thuringia with Adele in 1837 and died in Jena, cared for by Adele, who spent their small remaining capital on care for her mother. The death of Johanna left Adele alone, since she had not seen Arthur since 1820 and would only see him again in 1848, just before her death. For a variety of reasons, partly because her star had waned with the collapse of her fortune and a simultaneous decline in visitors to her salon, and partly because her writing had come to seem dated to the younger generation, the late 1820s had seen a steep decline in Johanna Schopenhauer's popularity, and her daughter made it her first task to try to correct this trend after her mother's death, though as we shall see, Adele gradually conceived plans of her own in terms of creative fiction.

Adele Schopenhauer, 1797–1849

Adele Schopenhauer had inherited her mother's interest in art, and had also developed an unusual creative skill, that of cutting out exquisitely tiny silhouettes with scissors. She also had considerable acting skills. None of these talents was put to systematic use, though she apparently wrote the manuscript of a guide to Florence which has been lost. Though one can sympathise with Adele's exposed position, firstly as the daughter of an energetic and successful mother, and secondly as a single woman in an era when spinsterhood denoted failure as a woman, there is sometimes an unattractive tone of complaint in much of what she wrote. For example, her comment upon hearing that Arthur had made his housekeeper pregnant – 'I find it disgusting'[19] – gives a clue to the narrow-minded attitude she could adopt when convention was breached. Her many claims that she would be glad when her worthless life was over, reinforced by a tendency to be put out by trifles, such as not having the best lodging at an inn while travelling, detract somewhat from the high level of intellectual debate which her contemporaries praised in her. Houben states that recognition of

---

[19] Adele Schopenhauer, *Tagebücher der Adele Schopenhauer*, ed. by Kurt Wolff, 2 vols, Leipzig, 1909, I: p. 20.

her intellectual prowess was vital for her as compensation for her extreme ugliness, to which countless contemporaries testified.[20]

Adele's fear of remaining unmarried was all too justified: she herself constantly fell for men who did not return her affection – sometimes they did not even know about it. For example, it is highly questionable whether Ferdinand Heinke knew that she was madly in love with him in 1813, at the same time as was her friend Ottilie von Goethe (see below, p.62). Ottilie, her childhood friend, always remained close, and in later life Adele's loneliness was ameliorated by Sibylle Mertens-Schaafhausen, whom she met in Bonn in 1826. Sibylle was the daughter of the banker Schaafhausen and was also married to a banker: she therefore had considerable wealth, which enabled her to spend long periods in Italy. She was an amateur archaeologist and herself a minor poet. Sibylle introduced Adele to Annette von Droste-Hülshoff, and Adele introduced Sibylle to Ottilie. Thus, women's networks were formed and operated quite independently of men, though sometimes the men known to the women were drawn in, too: Annette's friend Levin Schücking became known to Adele, whose years with her mother in Bonn were enlivened by these contacts.

In 1909 the *Tagebücher der Adele Schopenhauer* were published; these are not systematic, but deal loosely with events prior to 1823, though in the 'Stammbuch' – a sort of scrapbook of favourite extracts from authors – there are other entries such as a quotation from Bettina (whose mind Adele admired, though otherwise she found Bettina eccentric[21]) and a poem by Ottilie.[22] These diaries are not to be confused with the quite separate *Tagebuch einer Einsamen*, edited by Houben and not published until 1921, a highly personal document intended originally for Ottilie von Goethe alone. Perhaps without Adele quite realising it, this developed into a psychological novel in the mode of Goethe's *Sufferings of Young Werther*, though as Houben points out, Adele is no Goethe.[23] Nevertheless, the intense egocentricity of both accounts is similar. The difference lies in Goethe's supreme mastery in suggesting, through Werther's account and from his perspective, the active return of affection on the part of Charlotte

[20] H. H. Houben and Hans Wahl, eds, *Adele Schopenhauer. Gedichte and Scheerenschnitte*, 2 vols, Leipzig, 1920, p. 10 (biographical commentary).

[21] Anna Brandes, 'Adele Schopenhauer in den geistigen Beziehungen zu ihrer Zeit', PhD Diss., Frankfurt am Main, 1930, p. 29.

[22] Adele Schopenhauer, *Tagebücher der Adele Schopenhauer*, II, pp. 108ff.

[23] H. H. Houben, foreword to Adele Schopenhauer's *Tagebuch einer Eisamen*, Leipzig, 1921, p. vi.

Kestner. Adele, however, has no male counterpart: we are in a neurotic world of unfulfilled desires. Adele's inner life between the years 1823 and 1826 is revealed in all its pain, whilst she seeks to document (or more accurately, persuade herself) that a variety of men, chief amongst them the young chemist Gottfried Osann, are in love with her. The entry for 4 January 1824 is typical:

> Fritz [sic] Osann came in the morning. He does everything I ask, writes to Arthur and gives me the news. How do I feel? Wonderful, absolutely wonderful! Before, I thought I would die of shame, face to face it went better than expected. I spoke unusually openly to an unusual man! I do not think he holds anything against me. When, after a while, we had both calmed down, he asked me to accompany him to see Schönberg's pictures. I accepted on condition Natalie came too. We had a very pleasant few hours whilst we were there – I thought of the future, which looked like paradise![24]

Tears of happiness flow, but on 30 March, the next entry, we are told that the whole framework of her happiness is wrecked (*zerbrochen*), not because Osann has deserted her (in real life, we should remember, the relationship never appears to have been anything other than warm friendship – if that), but because she is in love with someone else – Sterling. Charles Sterling was actually Ottilie's lover; she had met him in May 1823, when he came to visit Goethe on Byron's recommendation. Ottilie went to Berlin alone on 28 December, with Sterling in hot pursuit; predictably, her husband was furious. So much for the facts; Adele makes *herself* the recipient of Charles Sterling's love; in other words, through her literature she takes on the *persona* of her beautiful, aristocratic and sexually attractive friend and enjoys the affair to the full; she invents a scenario where she hopes Ottilie will not be jealous of her (!), and in which neither her reputation nor her relationship with Gottfried will suffer:

> At first I thought Sterling was cold, but when he came closer, he confessed his passion. I loved him more with every day! Six – no, seven weeks, from 1 January to 22 February, we lived together, cut off from the outside world ... At first, I thought his love would immediately cost me the peace of my soul or Ottilie's trust, a good part of her love, or my reputation – and Gottfried.[25]

The story told becomes very confused because certain facts - such as August's jealousy – do not transpose on to Adele: why should he be jealous of her? Adele has the answer ready: '... they all say

[24] Adele Schopenhauer, *Tagebuch einer Einsamen*, p. 84.
[25] Ibid., p. 86.

I am encouraging Ottilie's waywardness'.[26] After the steamy depiction of those 'six – no, seven weeks', Adele says rather lamely that Ottilie has gone off with Sterling for four days and she does not know if he loves her; she then comforts herself with the remark that she is so nationalistic that only a German could be of importance to her (Sterling was British). However, it is the shifting authorial first-person *persona* rather than the attempt to cover over any inadequacies with the German flag which is worrying, because the deluded effusions betray complete escapism on Adele's part; it is not good writing, and, if one is candid, it is not good to read, though the text has a fascination for readers because the autobiographical details cannot be overlooked. A novel it is not; as a diary, all that is accurate appears to be the friendship of Gottfried Osann, who seems to have been completely unaware that Adele pinned all her future happiness on him, and considered suicide when it was clear to her that his love was a lost cause.

As we have seen, Adele went to live with her mother in Jena in 1837, with the intention of making Jena her home. Marooned in Jena on her mother's death, and now even more fraught with financial difficulties, Adele first published her mother's memoirs before turning to her own work, encouraged to do so by Sibylle Mertens as well as Annette von Droste-Hülshoff, whom she visited in 1840 on her way back from a visit to Bonn. Adele had met a companion in Jena, Professor Gustav Schueler, with whom she planned to live and travel when he had sold the many collections and personal effects that took up sixteen rooms in his house. The sale of these articles was extremely slow, however, and by 1842, Adele was beginning to see that this plan was not going to work out, though for some time she continued to hope that it would. With Sibylle's constant encouragement, she brought out her *Haus-, Wald- und Feldmärchen* in 1844, the same year in which she delivered the manuscript of her novel, *Anna* (1845), to her publisher.

This lengthy novel begins with an autobiographical description of the young Anna's reaction to Napoleon's invasion of Weimar, an event which must have impressed the nine-year-old Adele when she moved to her new home in 1806. The novel places at the centre of the story a woman who is loved by several men, one of whom, Otto, dominates much of the narrative. His love for Anna is not returned, and he marries a young Swiss woman, Vrenely, who adores him and who has saved him from exposure

[26] Ibid., p. 87.

in the mountains. Otto is also loved by the dazzlingly beautiful Leontine, who is based on Ottilie von Goethe (to whom the novel is dedicated). Leontine is the niece of Kronberg, Anna's elderly first husband at the beginning of the novel. The game of musical chairs is sustained by suspense as to whether the widowed Anna will marry Gotthard, her sons' former tutor. She falls ill when she realises the strength of her attachment for Gotthard, and decides that she cannot marry him. However, after a lapse of five years, Anna is urged to marry Gotthard by her sons. The date of 1832 is provided at the end of the novel, so that clear parameters are set for the plot (such as it is). At the end of the novel, Anna (Adele) is happily married, leaving a peripatetic Leontine still whirling round Europe in search of happiness. The plot of the *Tagebuch einer Einsamen* is thus repeated on another level, though there is much less neurotic fantasy and indeed, quite a lot of action, most of it, however, trivialised to relate to Anna's emotional involvements. The influence of Goethe's *Die Wahlverwandschaften* (*Elective Affinities*) (1809) is apparent in the plot, where renunciation in affairs of the heart is continually demanded of the protagonists. Very occasionally there are attempts to introduce poetic images, such as a reference to the night peeping though the windows 'with a thousand black eyes'.[27] However, such images are rare.

Adele Schopenhauer's second novel, *Eine dänische Geschichte*, was published in 1848. It begins with comments on the feudal nature of society in Denmark which make it appear quite radical for the time, and the plot, too, is fundamentally radical since it hinges on whether a bourgeois painter, Thorald Cynerssen, will be able to marry the woman of noble birth with whom he is in love, Helene Gejer of Wallöe. The chief obstacle is the woman's brother, Christian, who opposes the match with a fanaticism which makes the reader pause to take a quizzical glance at Arthur Schopenhauer, though the situation has more in common with Johanna's friendship with Gerstenbergk. A sub-plot relates the story of Helene's aunt, who withered into obscurity, both mentally and physically, when her marriage to a young pastor was forbidden. The heroine's sojourn in a convent and ultimately successful appeal to the queen for permission to marry are made necessary because the lovers are too high-minded to elope. The novel strains against itself, with the high moral tone somewhat detracting from the radical premise that social standing should not prevent lovers from marrying. When they finally do marry, an irritatingly moralising tone creeps in which is, however, offset

---

[27] Adele Schopenhauer, *Anna*, 2 vols, Leipzig, 1945, II, p. 313.

at the very end by the birth of a healthy baby to prove beyond
doubt that the tired aristocracy can refresh its blood through
inter-marriage with the bourgeoisie – though of course, there is
no suggestion that the bourgeoisie should marry downwards.

The quality of writing in *Anna* and *Eine dänische Geschichte* does
not match that of the short stories, in which a wry humour can be
detected. Possibly, Sibylle overestimated her friend's literary
ability; she also wanted to provide Adele with something to
counteract her depression, though neither of them quite realised
that Adele was now ill with what would turn out to be a fatal
disease. Adele's low spirits were perhaps also partly a reaction to
her mother's literary acclaim. At all events, Adele's short stories
received early appreciation: Alexander von Ungern-Sternberg,
who had heard her vow, at a soirée held by Ottilie, that she would
never publish her work, wrote in 1844 to congratulate her on her
Haus-, Wald- und Feldmärchen: '[y]ou have shown how much the
world wins when one no longer needs to keep a promise.'[28]

The significant feature which characterises the *Haus-, Wald-
und Feldmärchen* is that they deal with the supernatural and are
self-consciously akin to Romantic tales; the first tale in the
collection, the *Waldmärchen*, begins with a stilted discussion of
what constitutes a tale, which even brings in a mention of the
German Romantic symbol *par excellence*, 'die blaue Blume' (blue
flower).[29] In the *Hausmärchen*, three elderly sisters, all spinsters,
take in the daughter of the woman their brother was unable to
marry because of his vocation as a Catholic priest. This young
woman, Marianne, appears to be connected to 'a higher world',[30]
as she is able to see the 'little people' who inhabit the house; like
the elves in the tale of 'The Elves and the Shoemaker', these
spirits do the work for Marianne so that the house is always
spotless. Worried about her inadvertent contact with the elfin
world, Marianne confesses all to her sweetheart, and is comforted
by this open-minded man whose religion is based on the
tolerance preached by Luther: '[w]e all believe in one God'.[31] The
magic elements are dealt with in a matter-of-fact tone which gives
these whimsical tales added force. They are well written and show

[28] Quoted in H. H. Houben, 'Neue Mitteilungen über Adele und Arthur
Schopenhauer. Aus dem Nachlass der Frau Sibylle Mertens-Schaafhausen', in
Sechzehntes Jahrbuch der Schopenhauer Gesellschaft, Heidelberg, 1929, pp. 79–184,
p. 133.
[29] Adele Schopenhauer, *Haus-, Wald- und Feldmärchen*, Leipzig, 1844, p. 4. A blue
flower is the central motif in Novalis' *Heinrich von Ofterdingen*, 1800.
[30] Ibid, p. 65.
[31] Ibid., p. 131.

a promise which unfortunately Adele Schopenhauer discovered in herself too late to develop.

By 1846, Adele had been told by doctors that her medical condition was incurable; she appears to have been suffering from cancer of the womb. Determined to use every moment she had left, and to spend her time in Italy if possible, she travelled to Rome, where Sibylle and Ottilie were also residing in grand style, and where she met Fanny Lewald. From Rome she went to Naples to study art in 1846 and, having revisited Jena, she went to Florence in 1847, where she fell desperately ill; in 1848, the Revolutions in Northern Italy prevented Sibylle (now widowed) from joining Adele as planned, and Adele was prevented from travelling home. Eventually, she managed to drag herself back to Germany, to die in Sibylle Mertens' house. Like Christiane von Goethe, she died in agony. Adele saw her brother Arthur before she died (not having seen him for nearly thirty years, though they had had a desultory correspondence since 1831). Unfortunately Arthur contested his sister's will, because in it she had bequeathed to Sibylle Mertens the lease of a property she co-owned with Arthur. The granting of the lease had been a convenient way of keeping up appearances: in reality, Sibylle was providing Adele with an income without wounding her pride.[32] The lease still had seven years to run when Adele died, so that Sibylle technically made a profit, which she was only too ready to hand over to Arthur. The delays in so doing, and mistakes – in 1850 she forgot to send Arthur the rent – made him suspicious and ultimately, Sibylle was the recipient of his ill-will, poor repayment for her devotion to Adele, for whom Arthur himself did nothing.

Ottilie von Goethe 1796–1872

Ottilie von Goethe, née Pogwisch, who is something of a writer *manquée*, as we shall see, is included in these pages because of her central place in anything to do with 'Weimar connections'. She was born in Danzig and brought up by relatives for several years, since her mother, who had married for love, was persuaded to leave her husband in 1802 because he could not support his family. Henriette von Pogwisch, having deposited her daughters with relatives, went to live with her mother in Weimar, and in 1809 her daughters were able to join her there. Henriette's mother was a lady-in-waiting at the ducal court in Weimar, and

---

[32] Houben, 'Neue Mitteilungen über Adele und Arthur Schopenhauer', p. 142.

was, incidentally, an eye-witness when Napoleon entered the castle to take up occupation in 1806.[33] Since the Duke was absent at that time, Duchess Luise asked Napoleon to stop his troops from marauding in the streets of Weimar. Taken aback, Napoleon agreed to do this, and kept his word.

Having arrived in Weimar as a girl of thirteen, Ottilie Pogwisch immediately became friendly with Adele Schopenhauer, who was just one year younger; it was not until 1811 that Ottilie and her sister were presented to Goethe at his house 'Am Frauenplan' in the centre of Weimar. This would later become Ottilie's marital home. Johanna Schopenhauer's salon was still at the height of its popularity when Ferdinand Heinke became a visitor to her house in November 1813. First-Lieutenant Heinke, a young lawyer[34] and now a volunteer in answer to the King of Prussia's appeal for men to enlist in March 1813, was quartered in Weimar and detailed to make ready for the arrival of his superior, an instruction which included gaining access to the best houses in Weimar, and this he promptly set about doing. The day after his arrival he called on Goethe, whose wife he had known in Halle in his student days (days which had been happier for Christiane Vulpius), and three days later he was presented at court. On his first visit to Johanna's house he was immediately struck by the beauty of Adele's friend, who was then just seventeen; Ottilie, for her part, swiftly fell in love. Two things stood in the way of a match: Heinke was engaged to the woman he later married, but far more drastic than this was his social status as bourgeois as against Ottilie's membership of the aristocracy. Though Ottilie's mother had married for love, there had not been a difference in social status, and in any case, the collapse of that marriage was enough to devalue love matches in the Pogwisch family. Heinke appears to have declared his affection to Ottilie that New Year's Eve, though both knew their love had no future; Ottilie still loved Heinke in 1833, when he wrote to offer his condolences on the death of Goethe the previous year.[35]

[33] Ruth Rahmeyer, *Ottilie von Goethe. Das Leben einer ungewöhnlichen Frau*, Stuttgart, 1988, p. 48.

[34] In his Introduction to the *Tagebücher der Adele Schopenhauer*, Kurt Wolff gives the wrong information that Heinke was a 'Lützow huntsman' (p. viii), and the mistake is repeated in Jenny von Gerstenbergk, *Ottilie von Goethe und ihre Söhne Walther und Wolf*, Stuttgart, 1901, p. 9 and in Houben and Wahl, *Adele Schopenhauer. Gedichte und Scherenschnitte*, I, p. 9. Rahmeyer in *Ottilie von Goethe* sets the record straight, p. 75ff.

[35] Rahmeyer, *Ottilie von Goethe*, p. 94.

August von Goethe already regarded Ottilie as his property and was wildly jealous of Heinke, even threatening a duel. For her part, Ottilie never loved August and tried unsuccessfully to extricate herself from the relationship. Writing to her mother at the end of July 1816, Ottilie commented that 'Herr von Goethe is not sufficiently my superior to be able to exercise a good influence over me'.[36] A marriage with Goethe's son was not quite the status symbol we might expect from the vantage point of today: even if his father was the Sage of Weimar, August was also the son of Christiane, never accepted by Weimar society and still whispered about as 'the housekeeper' ('*Mamsell*').[37] Nevertheless, Goethe's personal position was inviolable, and in addition, his affection for his daughter-in-law would remain unperturbed by her peccadillos. This gave her enormous protection, which she often needed. Not surprisingly, after her marriage, Ottilie was soon able to establish her own, glittering, salon.

At all events, the engagement between Ottilie and August von Goethe was announced in December 1816, and the marriage took place in June 1817. Ottilie's letter to Adele of 17 May 1817, shows how much courage she had to summon up in order to put a brave face on it:

> I am the same old hero sitting in the stirrups and keen to go forth in the name of God ... behold, fate smiles on me by giving me such strength, and I do not need to banish any thoughts from my soul; all those residual, haunting doubts, which will probably come back to see the light of day often enough, just make it [my soul] more holy, pious and strong.[38]

This was wishful thinking indeed. The marriage was doomed to be unhappy, though both parents loved their children. Their two sons, Walther (1819–1885) and Wolfgang (1820–1883), both of whom had pretensions to artistic creativity (Wolf as a writer and Walther as a musician), found it difficult to achieve independent recognition: they were blighted by the shadow cast by their grandfather.[39] August laboured under the same disadvantage; he himself collapsed and died in 1830, in Rome; ironically, he had

[36] Ulrich Janetzki, *Goethes Schwiegertochter. Ottilie von Goethe*, Frankfurt am Main, Berlin and Vienna, 1983, p. 25.
[37] Rahmeyer, *Ottile von Goethe*, p. 185.
[38] Quoted in Rahmeyer, *Ottilie von Goethe*, p. 43.
[39] In 1842, Wolfgang Goethe resided in Jena to be near to Adele Schopenhauer, as they were collaborating on the epic poem *Erlinde*, the tale of a pixie in the Ilm valley; Adele was at work on her own *Haus,- Wald- und Feldmärchen* at the same time.

gone to Italy for the good of his health. He had many ailments but was also, from around 1827, an alcoholic. By the time he left for Italy, Ottilie was implacably hostile to any amorous advances from him and even disliked any attempt on his part to be reconciled, since that would invalidate her own coldness towards him and place her in the wrong.[40] Ottilie and August also had a daughter, Alma, who was born in 1827 and who died, tragically, as a victim of the typhus epidemic in Vienna in 1844; Ottilie had summoned Alma to Vienna so that she could 'come out' in society. Insult was added to injury when rumours suggested that Ottilie, helped by her current lover, Romeo Seligmann, had poisoned Alma in order to get hold of her inheritance.

Ottilie von Goethe did not see herself as a writer, nor did she try to improve her precarious finances through trying to write for publication. Her output consisted merely of letters and sundry essays and poems, some of the latter being printed anonymously in the Weimar literary journal *Das Chaos*, of which she was founder and editor from 1829 until 1831. The publication was originally intended for her immediate circle of friends in Weimar, but the deaths of August in 1830 (which she found a relief), and of Goethe in 1832, saw it come to a halt. Goethe himself had been in favour of *Chaos*, and Adele Schopenhauer contributed two poems under the *soubriquet* 'Viator', and a short prose paragraph on 'Clouds'.[41] Ottilie's next literary attempts took place in 1837, when she was introduced to 'Young Germany' by Gustav Kühne. Here again, Ottilie found herself attracted to a much younger man: Kühne was twelve years her junior, and soon turned his attentions to a younger woman. The political situation in Germany was such as to wring a radical response from Bettina, but Ottilie's poems of the period are lukewarm as regards politics; in spite of Kühne's own radicalism, her interests remained literary. Having collaborated with her lover Charles des Voeux on a translation of Goethe's *Tasso* into English (with an introduction in English by Ottilie and an appendix of sundry poems), she now collaborated with Kühne, who in 1835 had begun publication of the *Zeitung für die elegante Welt*, a popular periodical in which some of Johanna Schopenhauer's hitherto unpublished writings appeared posthumously at Adele's instigation. Ottilie also wrote,

---

[40] Ottilie wrote to Adele Schopenhauer in May 1830 (quoted in Janetzki, *Goethes Schwiegertochter*, p. 90): '[e]verything which breaks the chain is welcome – as soon as he is quiet and friendly, I have less justification to change my lot, yet that is the only thing that would make me happy'.

[41] Ottilie von Goethe, *Chaos*, Bern, 1968 (facsimile of the original). Adele's contributions are on pages 48, 56 and 99.

in 1830, an essay for Anna Jameson on 'Rahel, Bettina and Steglitz'.[42] Ottilie felt drawn towards Anna Jameson, although she did not make the personal acquaintance of the Englishwoman until 1832. It is no coincidence that Ottilie, who herself flaunted convention, hailed the three women who were her topic for the essay as free spirits whose talents manifested genius. She writes:

> The Germans only really gained an appreciation of female genius through Rahel and Bettina. These two women actually brought about the intellectual emancipation of women ... if Rahel opened up the world of reflection for us and lit the Davy's lamp for the seam of our deepest thoughts and moods, Bettina released ... the wings of fantasy, which had been fettered until then.[43]

The question has to be asked: why did she not take up writing?[44] Why not, indeed? As with Henriette Herz and Rahel von Varnhagen, the latter of whom was her role model in many areas of her life, Ottilie seems to have preferred to collaborate with others rather than strike out on her own, though the publication *Chaos* is impressive evidence of her editorial capabilities. Her talent as a poet also had potential, as her poem 'Gebet' ('Prayer') of 1822 demonstrates:

> Father, you have everything,
> Give me love!
> Fame and gold, give them to others,
> Honours, too, give them to others,
> Let the path of others flow
> With the blessings you bestow
> Give me love!

The reason for the demise of *Chaos* is probably as much to do with Ottilie's unstable love life as with the cessation of Goethe's protection. Ottilie never managed to bring her life into focus and overcome the central disappointment of frustrated early love. As Ulrich Janetzki points out, 'two things play a central role in Ottilie's life: love, and the feeling that one has a right to it'.[45]

---

[42] Ottilie had met the Varnhagens when they visited Goethe in 1829 and she subsequently corresponded with Rahel; Bettina visited Weimar five times, but Ottilie does not seem to have known Caroline von Steglitz personally. Rahmeyer in *Ottilie von Goethe* states in a footnote on p. 377f that the latter committed suicide in 1834 so that the grief would spur her husband, Heinrich Steglitz, to greater literary creativity.

[43] Translated from an extract of Ottilie's essay in Rahmeyer, *Ottilie von Goethe*, p. 218f.

[44] Rahmeyer, *Ottilie von Goethe*, asks this on p. 218–9.

[45] Janetzki, *Goethes Schwiegertochter*, p. 179.

During and after her marriage, and well into her widowhood, Ottilie had several affairs which guaranteed that she would be the subject of gossip. Her attachment to the handsome Charles Sterling, who was eight years her junior and whom she met in 1823, has already been mentioned in connection with Adele Schopenhauer's fictionalised account (see above, n. 24); she met Charles des Voeux in 1826. The affair with Sterling was regenerated in 1832. Two months after Goethe's death, while Ottilie was waiting (in vain) for Sterling in Frankfurt am Main in 1833, she met the Englishman Captain Story. Anna Jameson tried to dissuade Ottilie from this love affair on the rebound,[46] but by early 1834, rumours were circulating that Ottilie had married Captain Story. Anna Jameson was right to be sceptical about these rumours, since Ottilie was still in love with Sterling, and became pregnant by him in early summer, 1834. By late September, Ottilie was forced to travel to Vienna to conceal the fact that she was pregnant, and there she met Romeo Seligmann for the first time. She gave birth to a baby girl in secret in February, 1835, but the baby died the following year. Seligmann now became Ottilie's lover. Seligmann was Jewish and considerably younger than Ottilie, two factors which would discourage her from contemplating marriage to him, though he accompanied her to Italy in 1845 and remained her friend.

Ottilie had met Sibylle Mertens as well as Anna Jameson in 1832; Sibylle Mertens would provide her with financial as well as moral support, whilst Anna Jameson would be her frequent travelling companion. Ottilie led a restless life, especially after the death of Alma. She had announced her intention to settle in Vienna when she left Weimar 'for ever' in 1842, however, like so many German aristocrats, she was drawn to Italy and made several extended trips there. Vienna was her base until the 1866 war between Austria and Prussia forced her to return to Weimar, where she died as a result of heart failure in 1872. Adele Schopenhauer remained loyally and indeed deeply affectionate until her own death in 1849, and gave Ottilie frequent advice in letters which sound ludicrously prim and proper and inappropriate for the circumstances. And yet it was the first concern of Sibylle Mertens, when she realised how ill Adele was in 1849, to send for Ottilie, who immediately rushed to her bedside. The networking of such women as Adele, Ottilie and Sibylle was

---

[46] Anna Jameson wrote on 16 October 1833, '[i]f that penchant (to le Capitaine) is happily past, let it be buried in *that* churchyard among the others ...'. She refused to believe rumours that Ottilie had married Story in a letter written 7 February 1834. In G. H. Needler, ed., *Letters of Anna Jameson to Ottilie von Goethe*, London, New York and Toronto, 1939, pp. 15 and 23.

common enough at the time; what makes this particular trio interesting is that it was made up of a faithful wife, Sibylle (though there was not much love lost between herself and her husband), a somewhat embittered spinster, Adele, and a society flirt, Ottilie, none of whom were actually judgemental towards each other.

In many ways, Ottilie felt that her behaviour was striking a blow for female emancipation. But again and again, her peccadillos brought her nothing but pain, including the embarrassment of an illegitimate child. August von Goethe had many faults of his own, but Ottilie herself seems to have blamed everything on the fact that she had not been able to marry Heinke. This deep rift in her psyche appears never to have healed. Many other women, as we have seen, had a similar tragedy to overcome, but Ottilie had the libido and energy to resist the simple renunciation expected of her. Furthermore, though Ottilie appeared to be a giddy society woman, and indeed acted giddily, she was the mainstay of the Goethe household after the death of Christiane in 1816, and remained, until Goethe died in 1832, the woman of the house. She also thereby maintained her position at the centre of Weimar society, in spite of continued gossip about her. Nobody was allowed to visit the ageing Goethe without Ottilie's knowledge and approval. With the death of Goethe in 1832, Ottilie was no longer protected from gossip, and in addition, she proved startlingly incapable of managing her finances, rather as Johanna Schopenhauer had been. Goethe's bequest to her had stipulated that this income would cease if she remarried; none of her lovers was sufficiently wealthy to be able to keep her. Thus, whether deliberately or not, Goethe made sure she did not remarry. Christina Ujma has recently suggested[47] that there was something of an eternal triangle in the Goethe household from the moment Ottilie entered Goethe's house, making August himself something of an outsider, and producing a situation calculated to disorientate Ottilie herself.

Annette von Droste-Hülshoff, 1797–1845

Annette von Droste-Hülshoff, who never went to Weimar herself, nevertheless had connections which link her to the network of friends discussed already in this chapter, though it is noteworthy

[47] Christina Ujma, 'Ottilie von Goethe zwischen Weimar, Wien und Rom', paper read at the Eighth Day School on Women Writers in the Age of Goethe, Lancaster University, 26 October 1996.

that her fame has eclipsed the short-lived writing careers of Ottilie von Goethe and Adele Schopenhauer. Earlier critics were content to accept her into the canon as a woman writer showing all the mildness of heart expected of the female writer, a view much influenced by Levin Schücking's biography, *Annette von Droste-Hülshoff: Ein Lebensbild* (1862), though there have been recent challenges to this perception.[48] Feminist interpretations have usually found instances in the poems themselves as a basis for an assessment of Droste-Hülshoff's portrayal of her position as a woman writer; Elke Frederiksen and Monika Shafi have also argued that the early prose pieces reveal that Droste-Hülshoff 'laments the limitation of the female role',[49] a role which placed certain specific expectations on the unmarried woman of high birth. Born into an ancient family of Catholic aristocrats who lived in the moated Hülshoff castle, Annette von Droste-Hülshoff led a sheltered life which both nurtured her talent (her father had an excellent library) and hindered her development (unlike her brothers, she did not attend school). In 1820, at the age of twenty-three, when many of the women discussed in this book had already been married for several years, Annette went to stay with her relatives at Bökendorff, and there became caught between two suitors, managing to alienate them both sufficiently for them to write her a joint letter of rejection. She was certainly not too immature to realise that this meant that she would have no further chance of marriage: it was a personal catastrophe.

In 1820, Annette had given her mother her first completed book of poetry, *Das geistliche Jahr*, which her pious mother locked away in a cupboard, probably because the poems verge on the supernatural at points, and also because they record Annette's struggle with her faith. This crisis is one of guilt rather than lack of belief; she appeals to God in a disconcertingly direct way:

> And see, I looked for thee with pain,
> Where could I find my God and King?
> Not in my heart, now dead again,
> Thine image vanished though my sin.
> Yet all around resounds my cry to thee,
> And, as in jest, it echoes back to me.

Therese von Droste-Hülshoff, used to the mediation of the priest in such matters, found the contents of the poems troubling; after a

---

[48] Various critical reactions to Droste-Hülshoff are detailed in Elke Frederiksen and Monika Shafi, 'Annette von Droste-Hülshoff (1797–1848): Konfliktstrukturen im Frühwerk' in *Out of Line/Ausgefallen*, pp. 115–136, p. 115ff.

[49] Frederiksen and Shafi, 'Annette von Droste-Hülshoff', p. 120.

week, Annette retrieved them from the cupboard where they had
been placed and nothing more was said about them; they were not
published until 1839. Given the fact that both Annette and her sister
Jenny were inordinately close to their mother, this silence was itself
significant and must have appeared as tantamount to a complete
denial of the value of the poems. Since Annette had blamed herself
for the events which had recently ended in such a complete fiasco,
a discussion of the emotional struggle which is so evident in these
poems would have been a kindness which Therese could have
performed. Sichelschmidt relates that Therese was 'stretched too
far'[50] in being asked to comment on something which was so outside
her remit as a devout Catholic, whilst Doris Maurer emphasises the
relationship between Annette and her mother as one of permanent
tutelage for Annette: 'Annette's problematic relationship towards
her mother is of particular significance for this life [which vacillates]
between renunciation and obedience.'[51] Though this was not an
unusual situation for the day, not all mothers had as puritanical a
standpoint as Therese, and not all daughters had the intellectual
and creative brilliance of Annette. For many years, her family
showed scant understanding of her sense of mission, and her
frustration at never being able to work at a concentrated pitch
without domestic interruption became the bane of her life.

It took Annette several years to recover from the fiasco at
Bökendorff; she was then plunged into grief on the death of her
father in 1826. Therese von Droste-Hülshoff now moved into the
Rüschhaus, not far from the castle, with her two daughters. This
became home to Annette for the rest of her life. Though Annette
obviously had made a monumental blunder when she destroyed
her marriage prospects, the men involved were by no means
innocent bystanders.[52] Her naivety can be better understood
when set alongside that of her sister Jenny, who bowed to her
mother's wishes and waited three years before she married the
man with whom she was in love, and who was, incidentally, an
ideal suitor in terms of wealth and standing. Therese Droste-
Hülshoff's resistance to the marriage was caused by the fact that
Joseph von Laßberg was at least twenty-five years older than Jenny
(there is no record of his actual age);[53] unfortunately, the good

---

50 Gustav Sichelschmidt, *Allein mit meinem Zauberwort. Annette von Droste-Hülshoff.*
    Eine Biographie, Düsseldorf, 1990. p. 81.
51 Doris Maurer, *Annette von Droste-Hülshoff. Ein Leben zwischen Auflehnung und*
    Gehorsam/Biographie, Bonn, 1982, p. 91.
52 Margaret Mare, *Annette von Droste-Hülshoff*, London, 1965, pp. 19–24.
53 Margaret Sloman, *Einsamkeit. Das Leben der Annette Droste-Hülshoff*, Bern, 1950,
    p. 171.

intentions of Jenny's mother meant that Jenny was thirty-nine
when she married and moved to Switzerland. From 1838, her
home was to be Schloß Meersburg on Lake Constance. Annette
visited her sister there several times, and it was in Switzerland that
some of her finest poems were written – even the ones which have
the Westfalian countryside as their setting. Because of the delay
imposed by Therese, Jenny was forty-one when her twin girls were
born; not surprisingly, it was a difficult birth. Once Annette had
regained her equilibrium after the death of her father and
marriage of her sister, she settled down to the tasks expected of a
maiden aunt, and in her spare time pursued writing in earnest. In
the course of time, her brother-in-law, a medieval scholar, became
a great help to her in the publication of her poetry.[54]

Annette von Droste-Hülshoff became a close friend of Adele
Schopenhauer, whom she knew through Sibylle Mertens, who had
been her friend since 1826. Adele and Annette had much in
common, though Annette was driven to write by inner necessity
rather than through the urging of a friend (the loyal Sibylle virtually
badgered Adele into becoming a writer). Though Annette's work
seems to belong stylistically to realism, she had a distinct 'penchant
for fantasy'[55] which takes her close to the mood of the short stories
written by Adele, especially the latter's *Haus-, Wald- und Feldmärchen*;
however, Annette had a certain capacity for extra-sensory
perception which gives her work a very distinct psychological
cutting edge, and places it on a quite different and higher level in
terms of artistry. For example, she once had a vision of herself
walking through the courtyard one evening when the servants were
having a celebration; she regarded this as a hallucination, since she
was standing by the open window at the time, but later on, one of
the servants mentioned that he had been worried to see her out at
night in case she should catch cold. Annette's poetry sometimes
contains allusions to second sight which are distinctly troubling
because one has the feeling that personal experience might lie
behind what is related. This applies to the following passage in the
masterly ballad 'Das Fräulein von Rodenschild':

> Do senses fail, my eyes deceive?
> What slipped along the stairs just then?
> Did I my mirrored form perceive?[56]

---

[54] Maurer, *Annette von Droste-Hülshoff*, p. 106.

[55] Gertrud Bauer Pickar, 'Annette von Droste-Hülshoff's "Reich der goldenen
Phantasie"' in *Gestaltet und Gestaltend*, pp. 109-123, p. 114.

[56] Annette von Droste-Hülshoff, 'Das Fräulein von Rodenschild', in *Sämtliche
Werke*, ed. by Clemens Heselhaus, Munich, 1966, p. 349–353, p. 350f.

Adele Schopenhauer was an important link for Annette, who ultimately found her much more congenial than she found Sibylle. There are similarities in their lifestyles: both failed to find a partner in life, both were ill for a good deal of the time; both lived with their mothers and in fact, Annette's mother outlived her. However, Annette never had Adele's hysterical tendency to place all her bets on the wrong man and then feel suicidal because he had not responded. The friendship with Adele Schopenhauer would provide Annette with her first effective critic. Through Adele, Annette heard about the Weimar circle at first hand. It was also Adele who inspired her to read English poets such as Byron (who was also Ida von Hahn-Hahn's favourite author), and it was Adele's advice she sought when seeking to get her first book of poetry into print in 1838. In the summer of 1840, Adele visited Annette in the Rüschhaus.

From 1834, Annette von Droste-Hülshoff was friendly with the blind Christoph Bernhard Schlüter, who lived in Münster. Schlüter had a literary circle in which he fostered religious poetry. Annette remained on the periphery of the circle, not necessarily through religious doubt – or should one say self-doubt of the kind she had struggled with in *Das geistliche Jahr*, with which she had come to terms – but through her desire to treat wider subjects, and also, it must be said, because she found the circle unbelievably small-minded. Sloman writes: ' ... basically, the literary chit-chat round the bubbling kettle got on Annette's nerves.'[57] One of the circle, Fräulein von Bornstedt, later distinguished herself though her *Schadenfreude* towards Annette by making sure that her relationship with Schücking received plenty of gossip, but in the main, the circle contained well-meaning and kindly people, amongst them someone whom Annette would come to view as her 'muse':[58] Elise Rüdiger, a minor poet whom Annette first met in 1837. Elise belonged to the same circle in Münster as Levin Schücking, a young poet of considerable talent whom Annette had first met in 1830, when he was seventeen and still at school. After Annette's infatuation with Schücking, discussed below, Elise was her confidante.

Schücking and Annette were to have a fertile collaboration in which Schücking was only too ready to acknowledge that Annette had superior talent. They drew the best out of each other, especially during the time they spent together at Meersburg in

---

[57] Sloman, *Einsamkeit*, p. 204.
[58] John Guthrie, *Annette von Droste-Hülshoff: A German Poet Between Romanticism and Realism*, Oxford, New York and Munich, 1989, p. 15.

1841/1842: Annette had persuaded her brother-in-law that he need a temporary librarian, and Schücking was duly appointed. Annette had to keep her plan to get Levin to Meersburg secret from her mother, who was still likely to open her letters and who, in general, still exercised the sort of control one expects in the parent of a young child. When Therese did learn, through a clumsily disingenuous letter from Annette, that Annette and Levin were together at Jenny's castle by some fortunate coincidence (actually through a concerted effort on the part of Annette and Jenny), she used her most ferocious weapon to make Annette feel guilty: silence. It is certainly true that Annette, starved of a man's attention, was now a new person; in short, she fell in love, though inevitably the much younger Schücking saw in her a mother-figure: Annette was forty-four, Schücking was sixteen years younger.

Peter Foulkes points out that the period at Meersburg was simply the culmination of an affection which had first begun in 1836, when the twenty-three year old Schücking was consigned to Annette's 'motherly care' on the death of his mother, Katharina Busch, Annette's former friend. Clearly, the 'intimate friendship with an undercurrent of strong erotic attraction' was 'doomed from the outset'.[59] To make matters worse, Schücking's attention was soon deflected towards a much younger woman, Louise Gall, herself a writer with whom he had begun to correspond; he was even thinking of proposing to her before they met.[60] As soon as they did meet, they embarked on a whirlwind romance and were subsequently very happily married. Though this (inevitable) rejection hurt Annette, causing an excess of grief when they parted, their time of collaboration at Meersburg saw the genesis of some of her best poems, as well as her one true masterpiece of prose, *Die Judenbuche*. Published in 1841, this is now numbered amongst the classics of German literature. Though in style it belongs to realism, the content is such as to rank it with the surrealism of the horror genre. The plot deals with the mystery of several violent deaths in the woods; the protagonist is Friedrich Mergel, and the first mysterious death is that of Friedrich's own father. At first this death appears to be from natural causes (alcohol abuse), but this does not explain why his ghost haunts the woods, nor is there an explanation for the murder of Brandis, the forester, though there is a motive for the murder of the Jew Aaron, as Friedrich owes him money for a watch. Aaron's people

[59] Peter Foulkes, Introduction to Annette von Droste-Hülshoff, *Die Judenbuche. Ein Sittengemälde aus dem Gebirgichten Westfalen*, Oxford, 1989, p. x.

[60] Sichelschmidt, *Allein mit meinem Zauberwort*, p.242.

appear in force to carve an inscription into the beech tree under which Aaron has been found dead: '[i]f you approach this spot, the same will be done to you as you did to me'.[61] Friedrich Mergel is supposed to have committed the crime and fled from the village with his cousin, Johannes Niemand. Friedrich's uncle has not acknowledged parentage of Johannes, who remains shrouded in mystery. Confusion over the identity of the characters and confusion over twists in the plot make it very hard to say what has really happened in the story, and to whom. Friedrich returns to his village after twenty-eight years, masquerading as Johannes, and declaring that he has 'escaped from Turkish slavery';[62] but when he himself is found hanged in the beech tree, a scar on his body reveals his true identity – though not to the satisfaction of the reader, who has not had any prior information about any wound. In addition, another Jew has already admitted to this crime. It is therefore not clear who killed Aaron nor indeed who killed Brandis. Friedrich Mergel? Johannes Niemand? And who or what killed Friedrich Mergel?

The story is one of the first crime novels: Annette herself called it a *Kriminalgeschichte*.[63] The skill with which the story line is handled reveals a talent for prose writing which Annette von Droste-Hülshoff either did not wish to develop or felt unable to pursue. The atmospheric details, with storms underlining the godless events taking place outside in the woods, interspersed with precise details of time and date and terse pieces of dialogue, have invited such comments from critics as Brigitte Schatzky's remark that 'Annette's *Wuthering Heights* was *Die Judenbuche*'.[64] An important element within the story is the role of the Westfalian landscape to which Annette always felt drawn; in this sense, she is like Eugenie Marlitt who, as will be shown in Chapter Four, was at her happiest when setting her tales in Thuringia and was herself, like Annette, a virtual recluse, and for similar reasons. The important difference is that Annette was an aristocrat, something which made her opportunities even more restricted if we consider that the bourgeois Eugenie was able to become an opera singer. For Annette, who was often short of money (partly because she gave rather too much of her small allowance away to the poor), the notion of actually earning money by that kind of public performance would be anathema. But – it cannot be said

[61] Annette von Droste-Hülshoff, *Die Judenbuche*, in *Sämtliche Werke*, p. 936.

[62] Ibid., p. 931.

[63] Foulkes, Introduction to Droste-Hülshoff, *Die Judenbuche*, p. xvii.

[64] Brigitte E. Schatzky, 'Annette von Droste-Hülshoff', in *German Men [!] of Letters*, I, London, 1965, pp. 81–98, p. 85.

often enough – writing was the one career open to women of all ranks, though the money to be earned was often the very least of their considerations.

Though Annette, like Adele, found solace in writing, like her friend she also found it impossible, given the life she was forced to lead, to avoid turning into the archetypal spinster. Even though she knew that Adele and Sibylle were close friends of Ottilie, she could not help spreading gossip about Ottilie in her letter to Elise Rüdiger of 31 July 1845. The gossip had to do with Alma von Goethe's death in Vienna in 1844: a tragic and unexpected death as already discussed, which gossip turned into an intrigue, with accusations against Ottilie herself and her lover, Seligmann.[65] Annette assumed that Ottilie was in allegiance with the Jew Seligmann, 'a really ghastly, inwardly mean fellow ...',[66] whilst Ottilie herself is described as no better than she ought to be. 'The general public [in Weimar] believe her capable of such a thing and would ... throw manure and stones at her if she dared to go back'.[67] The pious Annette is quite ready, it seems, to cast the first stone, although the verses prefixed to *Die Judenbuche* specifically warn against such *hubris* lest it should rebound on one's own head. Annette has no facts to go on (she wrongly states that Alma died in Paris, not Vienna) and is merely passing on malicious gossip with a good degree of *Schadenfreude* of her own, and more than a little anti-Semitism. Hence, although some networks amongst women flourished, there was no automatic fellowship of the type some feminists today might expect to encounter amongst female acquaintances. Annette brushed off Bettina's revolutionary zeal as 'nonsense', as she told Sophie von Haxthausen on 19 January 1846.[68] However, she was never publicly vindictive, as Fanny Lewald was towards Ida von Hahn-Hahn.

As we have seen, Annette had numerous tasks to perform in her capacity as maiden aunt: she was assumed to be free to help with any family problems, such as the illnesses of her nephews and nieces (her brother, ensconced in the family seat, had eleven children). Nevertheless, she pursued her calling as writer with single-minded devotion, and her name ranks with male writers of her generation, such as Heinrich Heine. This is no mean achievement. She did not welcome her unmarried state, but she came to realise the strength of her own personality. In her poem 'Am Turme' ('In the Tower')

---

[65] Rahmeyer, *Ottilie von Goethe*, p. 265f.

[66] Ibid., p. 265f.

[67] Karl Schulte-Kemminghausen, *Die Briefe der Annette von Droste-Hülshoff*, Jena, 1944, 2 vols, II, p. 415.

[68] In Schulte-Kemminghausen, *Die Briefe der Annette von Droste-Hülshoff*, II, p. 452; similarly to Wilhelm Junkmann, February 1846, II, p. 458f.

she bursts out with the one major expression of her frustration at having to conform to society's norms:

> Were I a hunter, open and free,
> A soldier, too, would be nice,
> A man! that's all I ask to be,
> Heaven would give me advice.
> Now I must sit all fine and sweet,
> Just like a well-behaved child,
> And let my hair down secretly,
> For the wind to ruffle it wild![69]

In spite of this rebellious example, Annette was fundamentally a conventional woman; the freedom she craved was simply the freedom to write uninterrupted. In other matters involving the position of woman in society, she upheld the conventions and bowed to necessity. It appears that she reconciled the conflicts with which she was confronted by splitting herself into two, whether consiously or otherwise, as Pat Howe has described:

> The sense of a divided self translates itself for Droste-Hülshoff, as it does for Marie von Ebner-Eschenbach, into ambiguity about where she belongs, into guilt, anxiety, constraint, a problematic view of herself in the context of her family, and a problematic experience as lyrical and fictitious self.[70]

As Annette aged, we find private utterances which contain an unpleasantly bitter and judgemental tone, especially in matters concerning Schücking, which belie the claim that Annette was reconciled to his marriage, even referring to him as her 'adoptive son'.[71] She had to struggle with her own resentment at the fact that Schücking had married a woman half her age.[72] Schücking offended her even more by drawing a portrait of her in his novel *Die Ritterbürtig* (1846), which went too close to the bone; she retaliated by making slighting remarks to others about both Schücking and Louise.[73] Schücking had no idea that he had

---

[69] The remarkable device used in this poem is the portrayal of the distinction between what Annette feels like doing in the wild wind, and what her position as woman allows her to do. The full poem 'Am Turme' is in *Sämtliche Werke*, p. 124f.

[70] Pat Howe, 'Breaking into Parnassus: Annette von Droste-Hülshoff and the problem of female identity', in *German Life and Letters*, 46, 1993, pp. 25–41, p. 29.

[71] Sichelschmidt, *Allein mit meinem Zauberwort*, p. 314.

[72] According to the Appendix in Schulte-Kemminghausen, *Die Briefe der Annette von Droste-Hülshoff*, II, p. 536, Annette wrote to the aunt of Helene von Dühring-Oetken, presumably in 1842, though no date is given: 'Schücking has consoled himself really fast and become engaged to a pretty and apparently very rich girl from the nobility! ... That's what you call fidelity in a man!'

[73] Sichelschmidt, *Allein mit meinem Zauberwort*, p. 318.

offended Annette, and worked tirelessly after her death to bring
out her unpublished works. He wrote her first competent
biography, as well as supervising the first edition of her collected
works in 1878. Whilst she was still alive, he published an essay on
her work in Gottfried Kinkel's annual *Vom Rhein*.[74] From the
vantage point of today, her jealousy towards Schücking seems
irrational, even ungrateful. From her viewpoint, this was the only
man who appeared to appreciate her, and he abandoned her. In
this sense she acted rather like Adele, another woman who had
desperately clung to the hope of finding a man; both women were
haunted by the knowledge that whatever else they had achieved,
society would judge them as old maids. This grotesque
Torschlußpanik (fear of the gate banging shut) is arguably as bad as
the despair encountered in marriages of convenience.

---

[74] Ibid., p. 317.

Malwida von Meysenbug. Reproduced with kind permission of the Richard-Wagner-Museum, Bayreuth.

3

The 1848ers

Towards Revolution

The 1840s were years in which the staple crops failed all over Europe. In many places of Germany, shortage of food was a relatively new experience. As Ritchie Robertson writes:

> Nothing on the Continent, admittedly, rivalled the Irish famine of 1846-1847, which killed a million people and drove another million to emigrate, but the potato blight also deprived the lower classes of northern France and Germany of their staple diet. Eastern Germany saw the first of several bad grain harvests in 1845. In 1847 there were bread riots in Berlin.[1]

However, economic factors alone did not account for the 1848 Revolution in Germany; even the uprising of the Silesian weavers in 1844 was quickly suppressed by troops and had, according to Bramsted, 'little direct political impact'.[2] Radical ideas were afoot, and the most radical demands were made in areas where the economic situation was less dire, namely Baden, Württemberg and Hesse, areas from which delegates were now sent to Heppenheim near Darmstadt with a list of demands. In broad terms, these included the demand for legal and educational reforms as well as for freedom of speech and assembly. The next revolutionary step consisted of a series of meetings in Frankfurt, which took place in St Paul's Church. These debates were often depressingly acrimonious and factional, as Fanny Lewald, who

---

[1] Ritchie Robertson, *Heine*, New York, 1988, p. 65.
[2] Ernest K. Bramsted, *Germany*, New Jersey, 1972, p. 127.

attended several, pointed out. She also feared that things were being rushed: '[t]hey want to proclaim a Republic immediately in Germany!', she noted in her account of these events.[3] The debates chiefly centred on the issue as to whether Germany would be 'great' (*Großdeutschland* – to include Austria) or 'small' (*Kleindeutschland* – dominated by Prussia). Simultaneously there were revolutions in Vienna against the Habsburg regime, resulting in the fall of Metternich and the re-establishment of stability through harsh police methods. This heavy-handedness weakened the case of the supporters of *Großdeutschland* in the Frankfurt assembly, which eventually voted in a constitution and sent a delegation to Friedrich Wilhelm IV of Prussia offering him the crown of the empire, which he promptly and unceremoniously refused because of its democratic origins.

The June days in Paris 1848, which demonstrated a retreat from the heady liberalism of February, affected the German radicals in that their demands came to seem ever more unrealistic in the new circumstances. At all events, the old powers returned, though in Prussia the king had at least been forced to grant a constitution with two houses of parliament. However, the National Assembly in Frankfurt had spectacularly failed to create a united Germany with liberal institutions. Amongst the 1848ers it was usually the case that the desire for liberal reform included a demand for a reform of statutes governing the Jews. Some radical women demanded reform for everyone, and did not necessarily see that the women's issue was a separate matter: this is the case with Johanna Kinkel, but others, like Fanny Lewald and Malwida von Meysenbug, thought that women's issues needed a separate campaign, though no such structure existed until Louise Otto-Peters laid the foundation for German feminism.

Fanny Lewald, 1811–1889

Fanny Markus was born in Königsberg into a Jewish family which no longer practised Jewish customs and was to all intents and purposes assimilated, especially when the family's two oldest boys were baptized. The Stein/Hardenberg reforms had stipulated that all Jewish documents had to be put into German, using regular

---

[3] Fanny Lewald, *Erinnerungen aus dem Jahre 1848*, 2 vols, Braunschweig, 1850, I, p. 124; Hanna Ballin Lewis' translation of this account (and others of the period) has now appeared under the title *A Year of Revolutions: Fanny Lewald's Recollections of 1848*, Oxford, 1997.

surnames, a regulation which occasioned a virtual stampede for Jews to register new names. Initially, the Markus family, which already had a recognised surname, found no necessity for change, though eventually the name of Lewald was adopted in 1831. In fact, Fanny did not even know she was Jewish until she was five, when a school-mate mentioned it, and she was promptly teased. From this early experience she became aware, not just of anti-Semitism, but of the type of Jewish self-hatred which was a significant factor with her mother. In due course, and unexpectedly, because Fanny's kindly if autocratic father did not usually explain his actions to his family, Fanny herself was baptized in 1830. For Fanny, the baptism represented a hypocritical entry into a world of edicts in which she did not believe, and her attitude to religion of any kind was henceforth one of scepticism. The problems surrounding the question of such a 'conversion of convenience' are dealt with fifteen years later in her second novel, *Jenny* (1842).[4]

Fanny's school closed down in 1824, when she was thirteen. Most girls went to school until the age of fourteen, but for Fanny, her school days were now over and she sorely missed the intellectual stimulus. As indicated in the Introduction to this volume, the Stein/Hardenberg reforms from 1807 onwards had had a wide impact on Prussian education, though this was irrelevant for Fanny Lewald, since girls could not attend grammar school or university; legally, they did not have to attend school at all.[5] Aristocratic families still engaged tutors for their daughters if they thought this was necessary, but Fanny's bourgeois parents certainly did not think it was necessary for her to have any further tuition beyond piano lessons, which she loathed. Fanny, as the oldest of the eight children who survived infancy, was now expected to help her mother run the large household, which was a minor hive of industry since all provisions were home produced. Fanny had a difficult relationship with her mother, whom she later believed to have been jealous of her wider aspirations; she was encouraged to read by her father, and he took her to visit relatives in Berlin in 1830. Here she saw Rahel, a distant relation, at the theatre but did not actually manage to meet her, something she regretted all her life. Fanny's uncle lived in the ghetto, which, though no longer closed off in order to confine Jews, as it had

---

[4]   Margarita Pazi, 'Fanny Lewald – Das Echo der Revolution von 1848 in ihren Schriften', in Walter Grab and Julian Schoeps, eds, *Juden im Vormärz und in der deutschen Revolution von 1848*, Stuttgart and Bonn, 1983, pp. 233–271, p. 237. See also n. 11.

[5]   See Brigitta van Rheinberg, *Fanny Lewald. Geschichte einer Emanzipation*, Frankfurt am Main and New York, 1990, p. 55f.

been in the eighteenth century, was still an unprepossessing area. Thus, Fanny Lewald was not particularly happy in Berlin. During this trip she also visited relatives in Breslau, where she fell in love with her cousin Heinrich Simon, but the affection was not returned, and it took Fanny several years to come to terms with the fact. In the event, Heinrich Simon fell in love with Ida Hahn-Hahn, who, though attracted to him, refused his offer of marriage in 1836. It was only much later, in 1844, that Fanny was able to talk to Heinrich about the passion she had had for him;[6] they were then close friends. In 1848, Heinrich Simon was a leading representative of the moderate left in the Frankfurt Parliament; when it was dissolved, he fled to Switzerland.

When they left Berlin after their stay in 1830, Fanny Lewald's father sent her to stay with another uncle in Breslau, and it was in this cultured milieu that she was at last able to develop her intellectual interests, or at least recognise that she had some. She was reluctant to return home to the stifling atmosphere of the family, where the expectation now placed on her was that she should find a husband. When, in 1834, Fanny Lewald turned down the much older suitor her father had selected for her, for no better reason than that she did not love him, her family were scandalised and treated her as an old maid, though she was still only twenty-three. Years of sterile and desultory household tasks now awaited Fanny. She herself called these years her *Leidensjahre*.[7] The situation was exacerbated by the fact that although Fanny loved her mother, she felt that she was never fully understood or appreciated by her.[8] Things were to change dramatically when, in response to her uncle's request for her to write a description of the festivities which marked the end of the visit of King Friedrich Wilhelm IV to Königsberg,[9] Fanny sent him an article which was then printed in its entirety in the journal which he edited, *Europa*. Encouraged by this and similar successes, Fanny turned to her first novel, *Clementine* (1841), which was followed in the next year by perhaps her best known work, *Jenny*, both initially published anonymously. From 1843 onwards, Fanny put her name to her publications, except for the spoof *Diogena* (1847), which will be

---

6   Ibid., p. 93.
7   Fanny Lewald in a letter to her uncle August Lewald in 1840; subsequently, in her autobiography *Meine Lebensgeschichte*, she gave the memoirs of her youth the title *Leidensjahre*, while the memoirs of her childhood had the title *Im Vaterhaus*. In Fanny Lewald, *Gesammelte Werke*, 10 vols, Berlin, 1871-1872; *Meine Lebensgeschichte* makes up vols I and II.
8   Lewald, *Meine Lebensgeschichte, i: Im Vaterhaus*, p. 180.
9   Lewald, *Meine Lebensgeschichte, ii: Leidensjahre*, p. 209.

discussed below. After the success of *Jenny*, Fanny went to Berlin, where, in the salon of Henriette Herz, she met Schleiermacher and the whole intellectual circle which clustered round Henriette, though of course, not Rahel, who had died in 1833.

In *Clementine*, Fanny dealt with the problems caused by a marriage of convenience and in *Jenny*, she described the kind of dilemma which could occur if a liberal Jew actually chose not to be baptised. The plot hinges upon the decision of Eduard Meier not to convert to Christianity in order to marry the woman he loves, Clara Horn, who has been his sister's inseparable childhood friend. Explaining his standpoint to Clara he declares:

> To the [Jewish community] I shall always remain Eduard Meier, who ... has always had everything in common with them, and they notice it if I do not show the same interest as they do in the doings of their uncle or great-uncle.[10]

Eduard feels that he cannot retreat from his trusted position within the ranks, and tells his father so; he wants to apply to the authorities for proper permission to marry a Christian, thus presenting a sort of 'test case' which he sees as being a first step towards true integration, and more dignified than baptism. His father points out that his decision, which is not actually based on religious conviction, since none of the family have practised their faith in any orthodox way and indeed criticise those who do, has further ramifications, since Eduard's sister Jenny is about to convert to Christianity in order to marry her fiancé, the theologian Reinhard. At the baptism, a profound change comes over Jenny: still barely seventeen, she realises she does not believe in the faith she is called upon to profess. She breaks off her engagement to Reinhard in a letter in which she confesses 'I do not believe that Jesus Christ is the Son of God'.[11]

Jenny now takes up the cause of freedom for Jews for which her brother is active, having been forced to forego his post as doctor: he turns down the offer of a post as municipal doctor in a clinic because he would have had to be baptised. He thus spurns both love and career for a faith in which he does not actually believe. Clara marries her cousin, an 'acceptable' husband, and becomes (in Jenny's eyes at least) a standard wife and mother, without vision or ideals. Renate Möhrmann points out that Lewald seeks to reveal that Clara's happiness is simply escapism.[12]

[10] Fanny Lewald, *Jenny* in *Gesammelte Werke*, IX, p. 99.
[11] Lewald, *Jenny*, p. 251.
[12] Renate Möhrmann, *Die andere Frau. Emanzipationsansätze deutscher Schriftstellerinnen im Vorfeld der Achtundvierziger-Revolution*, Stuttgart, 1977, p. 138.

In time, Jenny meets Graf Walter, a man who shares her own view of
the way the sexes stand in equality to one another. The image Walter
uses to explain his view is superimposed on the traditional view of
the relationship of man to woman. This had always figured the
female as ivy winding around the mighty oak, the male; Walter
wants to see the sexes on an equal footing. Jenny draws a sketch to
illustrate his idea: two trees with interlocking branches; underneath
she writes 'growing freely from the same soil, high into the sky'.[13]
These ideals, so dear to Jenny and Eduard, will bring tragedy in
their wake, since Walter, when taunted for marrying a
'Judenmädchen',[14] fights a duel in which he is fatally wounded;
Jenny dies of the shock. As Möhrmann points out, the ending does
not invalidate the ideal of happiness for which Jenny has been
striving, it simply shows how wrong society is to seek to crush those
ideals and to try to perpetuate outmoded concepts of what
constitutes happiness.[15] Eduard's final defiance, that he will continue
in the struggle 'for the emancipation of our people',[16] reminds the
reader of the main purpose of the novel: which is to demonstrate the
entrenched nature of German prejudice towards the Jews.

In *Clementine* and *Jenny*, then, Fanny Lewald had set out the two
themes which would recur constantly in her work; another major
theme which would become dominant is that of the authoritarian
father; this theme is uppermost in her last novel, *Die Familie Darner*
(1887). This novel is set in Königsberg in the years 1806/1807 and
raises the question of the hostility of Christians towards nascent
Jewish emancipation.[17] Fanny Lewald also deliberately set out to
write from what we would now call a feminist political position; the
politics in question were the liberal politics of 1848, which merged
seamlessly with Jewish aspirations, and these were close to her
heart. Her style is uncluttered and she intensely disliked the
verbose and sentimental style of Ida Hahn-Hahn, her rival as a
writer as well as her rival for the love of her cousin Heinrich Simon.
In 1846, Fanny wrote a biting satire on Ida Hahn-Hahn, *Diogena
(Pseudonym). Roman von Iduna H… H…* (1847). In this, as well as
parodying the title of the collection of high-minded contributions
entitled *Iduna. Schriften deutscher Frauen* which appeared in 1820,[18]

---

[13] Lewald, *Jenny*, p. 271f.
[14] Ibid., p. 328.
[15] Möhrmann, *Die andere Frau*, p. 138.
[16] Lewald, *Jenny*, p. 332.
[17] Pazi, 'Fanny Lewald', p. 245.
[18] Helene von Chezy, ed., *Iduna. Schriften deutscher Frauen*, 2 vols, Chemnitz, 1820.
The nationalistic moral high ground for German women is claimed in the
contributions.

she also 'parodied her [Hahn-Hahn's] neurotic aristocratic heroines'[19] and criticised them for their selfish heartlessness to the point where she felt sorry for the men they tormented. According to Marieluise Steinhauer, Fanny Lewald took the novels of George Sand as her model on the question of love, finding that her heroines 'loved honestly and were destroyed by their love in all honesty, if that could not be avoided'.[20] Fanny had taken particular exception to Ida Hahn-Hahn's novel *Sibylle* (1846), which she had read in Berlin on her return from Italy in 1846. She had seen some merit in Hahn-Hahn's earlier novels *Ilda Schönholm* (1838) and *Der Rechte* ('Mr Right') (1839), where there are occasional challenges to conventions which restrict women,[21] but she drew the line at *Gräfin Faustine* (1841). Though Lewald did not attempt to emulate Hahn-Hahn's sentence structure in *Diogena*, she mimicked the pretentious use of foreign words: for example, the incomparably lovely Diogena is described as a 'veritabler Tresor'.[22] Since *Diogena* was initially published anonymously to considerable acclaim, people were subsequently astonished to learn that the author was a woman.[23]

Diogena, though in its own right extremely funny, is only fully understood as a reply to Hahn-Hahn. Ida Hahn-Hahn's tendency to place her protagonists within an impressive genealogy is topped by Diogena, who, the daughter of Sibylle and niece of Faustine, traces her ancestry back to the ancient Greeks, to Diogenes.[24] More immediately, Sibylle's second husband, Astrau, who was repulsed in Hahn-Hahn's novel, as are all the other men who are bewitched by her attractions, is claimed to have fathered Diogena in a rare moment of peace between the married couple. Within two months of her marriage to her cousin Bonaventura, the son of Faustine and Mario, Diogena has affairs with the Vicomte Servillier, Lord Ermanby and Graf Gallenberg before being deserted by her husband. She now seeks happiness through religion, retiring to a cell which she makes into a laboratory.[25] Her dabblings in electro-magnetism show an awareness of the

[19] Van Rheinberg, *Fanny Lewald*, p. 126.

[20] Marieluise Steinhauer, 'Fanny Lewald, die deutsche George Sand. Ein Kapitel aus der Geschichte des Frauenromans im 19. Jahrhundert', PhD Diss., Berlin, 1937, p. 56.

[21] Ibid., p. 56.

[22] Fanny Lewald, *Diogena (Pseudonym). Roman von Gräfin Iduna H ...H...*, Leipzig, 1847, p. 88.

[23] Steinhauer, *Fanny Lewald, die deutsche George Sand*, p. 62f.

[24] Lewald, *Diogena*, p. 5.

[25] Ibid., p. 106.

scientific discoveries being made at that time, though this being a spoof, Diogena's perception of science has more to do with Mesmer than Faraday, not to mention the effect Diogena has on her father confessor, who flees from her, this 'serpent ... serpent in seductive form'.[26] Of course, the retreat into seclusion satirises Faustine's decision to leave her family in order to live in a convent as well as anticipating Ida Hahn-Hahn's actual retreat into a cloistered life, as discussed in the next chapter, and indeed, the pain caused by this spoof could have been a contributing factor. Like Sibylle, Diogena travels the world in order to quell her longing for love: within two pages she traverses Italy, France, Russia, Britain, Turkey and Greece, before deciding to travel to the Orient (again, a direct allusion to Hahn-Hahn's *Orientalische Briefe*). At last she ends up with a tribe of Indians in Delaware and throws herself at the brutish but manly Indian chief Coeur-de Lion, who *rejects* her because she is past her physical prime, and sends her back to her own people; at which point there is only China left for her to go to. In China, she goes mad, occasionally screaming that 'she never found "Mr Right"'[27] (another allusion to Hahn-Hahn). The faithful Gallenberg is still with her, no doubt an allusion to Hahn-Hahn's companion Bystram. As indicated, the novel is very witty, but almost recklessly destructive towards Hahn-Hahn.

In 1845, Fanny travelled to Italy, and it was in Rome that she first came in contact with the female intelligentsia of Weimar, in other words, Ottilie von Goethe and Adele Schopenhauer, who had decamped to Rome and were busy having a very good time indeed, often in the palatial apartment of Sibylle Mertens. She also met Adolf Stahr, a married man with five children with whom she was to fall deeply in love. The beginning of the friendship is described in great detail in Fanny Lewald's *Römisches Tagebuch 1845/46*, written as a Christmas present to give to her husband in 1865, and never published during her lifetime. It was finally published in 1927, though extracts had appeared in *Westermanns Monatshefte* in 1897. What Fanny Lewald did publish was her *Italienisches Bilderbuch* (1847). Konstanze Bäumer has given a very thorough critique of the place this travelogue has amongst its rivals; Lewald herself knew that it was almost an anachronism to write yet another book on a journey to Italy. She therefore focused on her position as a woman travelling on her own (with a female companion) at her own expense. This made the book

[26] Ibid., p. 103.
[27] Ibid., p. 179.

interesting to women readers and it therefore had publicity value for the novels, which were now her principal source of income. Though the wonders of Italy are duly visited, Lewald takes pleasure in describing more personal matters such as her lodgings, details not to be found in travelogues written by men. As Bäumer stresses, Lewald also takes the opportunity to criticise other women's narrow perspectives.[28] The mere fact that it was possible to roam around unchaperoned impressed many German women who visited Italy. In 1869, Stahr and Lewald published their joint work, *Ein Winter in Rom*.

Fanny's first impression of Stahr's relationship with his wife was that he was happy; however, when he read aloud a letter he had received from her, Fanny was shocked that it contained nothing but small-talk and domestic detail:

> It contained nothing, absolutely nothing but chitchat about the housekeeping which any normal wife does every day, and which I had done for years, in the main in a very narrow-minded and difficult atmosphere, and which is really only to be seen as an unavoidable means to an end.[29]

Fanny thought that the intellectual Stahr was demeaned by receiving such a letter. It is true that she herself had had more experience of running the household for her mother than she wished to remember; she had shown the greatest determination in refusing a marriage of convenience and in eventually earning sufficient to live by her pen. What she did not sympathise with was the way Marie Stahr had allowed herself to become set into a domestic routine. On Marie Stahr's behalf we can say several things: she had married her early sweetheart for love, which was unusual enough for the time; she had encouraged Stahr to go to Italy to try to cure his throat condition, and she had kept in affectionate touch with him whilst he was away. She was the type of wife whom the Germans held up as an example. On a less positive note, the birth of five children had no doubt prevented her from developing her intellectual interests, and there probably was a sense in which Stahr had 'outgrown' her intellectually. It is still very hard for a feminist to speak warmly of Fanny Lewald's

[28] Konstanze Bäumer, 'Reisen als Moment der Erinnerung: Fanny Lewalds (1811-1889) "Lehr- und Wanderjahre"', in Ruth-Ellen Boetcher Joeres and Marianne Burkhard, eds, *Out of Line/Ausgefallen: The Paradox of Marginality in the Writings of Nineteenth-Century German Women*, Amsterdam, 1989, pp. 137–157, p. 152.

[29] Fanny Lewald, *Römisches Tagebuch 1845/46*, ed. by Heinrich Spiero, Leipzig, 1927, p. 71f.

love affair with Stahr without at the same time mentioning that this was at the cost of Marie Stahr's happiness.

Marta Weber has been the only critic so far to defend the hapless Marie Stahr, though Konstanze Bäumer has dropped heavy hints about the overweening nature of Lewald's personality, which was not easily brooked;[30] the problem is that Weber's tone is sanctimonious, and even anti-Semitic, when she accuses Fanny of bringing her 'whole sophistry and Jewish rhetoric' to bear in her letters to Stahr. Weber asserts that without her persuasion to the contrary, Stahr would have 'returned to his duty'.[31] For ten years, the future of the relationship between Fanny Lewald and Adolf Stahr rested in the balance, until his wife, no match for the determined Fanny, finally agreed to a divorce, and they were married in 1855. By that time, Fanny was too old to have children (though she forged a close relationship with Stahr's eldest son, Alwin). Fanny had at one point thought that she could live with the Stahrs in a harmonious relationship, and in late December 1847, after the publication of *Diogena* (which Fanny had been inspired to write at Stahr's suggestion), she took herself off to Oldenburg, home of the Stahr family, where Marie, with what reluctance one can only guess, had found a flat for Fanny. Here, Fanny worked on her novel *Prince Louis Ferdinand* (1849), which deals with the friendship between Pauline Wiesel (Rahel von Varnhagen's close friend) and the Prince, using the original (though expurgated) letters which Varnhagen had purchased from Pauline. The novel is dedicated to Varnhagen and reads like a 'who's who' of Rahel's salon at its height, where princes feel at their ease, though the salon itself, it is stressed, was a simple attic room.[32]

Fanny travelled extensively during the decade 1845–1855, uncertain, for most of this time, whether Stahr would leave Marie or not; she even suggested that they could live on her money, so that he could leave Marie even without her consent, but he could not bring himself to take the step of leaving his family until 1852, and even then, three more years would elapse before the divorce came through. This period of instability for Fanny Lewald was also the period of her most overt political activity. After leaving Oldenburg in 1848, Fanny heard about the fall of Louis Philippe and rushed to Paris to be at the centre of events; here she mixed with Heinrich Heine and Georg Herwegh. She then travelled to Frankfurt, where she attended the meetings in St Paul's Church

---

[30] Bäumer, 'Reisen als Moment der Erinnerung', p. 148.
[31] Marta Weber, *Fanny Lewald*, PhD Diss., Zurich, 1921, p. 35.
[32] Fanny Lewald, *Prinz Louis Ferdinand*, Breslau, 1849, 2 vols, I, p. 67f.

and became ever more disillusioned with the unrealistic expectations of the liberal delegates, coming to the conclusion that the Germans were not yet ready for a Republic. Like her old friend Johann Jacoby, she thought that the interests of Jews would be served by a joint effort towards liberalising the whole of society, including women. Some of these ideas are treated in Fanny Lewald's novelle *Auf roter Erde* (1850). Boetcher Joeres has argued that the actual revolutionary activity takes place at a suitable distance in *Auf roter Erde*,[33] but there is plenty of discussion amongst the characters about the dangers of supporting constitutional demands. Consternation reigns amongst the democrats in the story when the King of Prussia refuses to be Kaiser 'of a Germany which does not yet exist'.[34] Actually, the events of 1848 are convenient but not crucial to the plot, since it hinges on Marie's lower status: nobody expects Geheimrath Werder to allow his son Anton to marry a 'Bauerntochter' (country girl).[35] The sub-plot, the reconciliation of old Margarethe, herself wronged by Anton's grandfather, has nothing to do with politics, though the ending does – Anton and Marie flee from Germany as political emigrés, as Lewald's acquaintance Johanna Kinkel was forced to do, in their case to Mississippi.

Fanny Lewald's apparently revolutionary, but in fact reformatory zeal very soon became beset with doubts about the left-wing radicals, and these doubts would continue to grow for two decades. By 1859, her friendship towards Jacoby had begun to cool, possibly because she had struck up an enduring friendship with the enlightened Duke Karl Alexander of Weimar, whom she had met in 1848 and visited again with Stahr in 1851. She had met Johanna Kinkel in Bonn in the spring of 1850, before Johanna left for exile in England; Fanny, too, undertook a journey to Britain that year; the literary result, her travelogue *England und Schottland* (1851), coincided with a further cooling of her political enthusiasm, possibly through her conversations with the gradualist Kinkels, as witnessed in her letters to Johanna Kinkel during the years from 1850 to 1854. The letters to Johanna show that Fanny is beginning

[33] Ruth-Ellen Boetcher Joeres, '1848 From a Distance: German Women Writers on the Revolution' in *Modern Language Notes*, 97, 1982, pp. 590–614, p. 596. Boetcher Joeres deals with the following texts: Louise Aston, *Revolution und Contrerevolution* (1849), Fanny Lewald, *Auf rother Erde* (1850), Claire von Glümner, *Fata Morgana* (1851), Louise Otto, *Drei verhängnißvolle Jahre* (1867); Gottfried Kinkel, *Die Heimatlosen* (1849), Adolf Streckfuß, *Die Demokraten* (1850) and Melchior Meyr, *Vier Deutsche* (1861).

[34] Fanny Lewald, *Auf roter Erde* in *Gesammelte Werke*, XIII, p. 98f.

[35] Lewald, *Auf roter Erde*, p. 104.

to think that Gottfried Kinkel's political aims might be too optimistic, and, coupled with this, is her enthusiasm for Karl Alexander's relaxed relationship with his people:

> So long as power remains in the hands of the princes, I think it is the duty of well-meaning persons like us to take the light to a place where it can shine for centuries.[36]

Pazi argues that although Fanny saw republicanism as ultimately the most suitable form of government for Germany, she was pessimistic about how it could be achieved, and this pessimism communicated itself to Stahr until he, too, shared that opinion. But Fanny had not yet parted company with Jacoby, and shared his rejection of the necessity of the war between France and Prussia in 1866. Gradually, she came to regard Bismarck and his reforms as necessary, so that in 1870 there took place in Fanny Lewald the 'final transformation from the enthusiastic supporter of democracy to the unchallenging adherent of Bismarck's politics'.[37]

As has been shown, Fanny Lewald was nothing if not pragmatic in her political stance, and the same is true of her stance on female emancipation. She had met and admired Bettina when the latter was in Berlin in the winter of 1847/1848, just four years after the fiasco with the *Armenbuch*. Some readers will be alarmed to find Steinhauer describing Bettina as 'an old woman' (at just turned fifty), and others will be delighted to hear that Bettina had dyed her hair purple,[38] and was thus no disappointment to those used to her eccentricity. At all events, she could still inspire her friends. Like Bettina, Fanny did not just fight exclusively for women, but for the unfortunate or downtrodden of either sex. However, since women tended to be more disadvantaged than men once they were destitute – especially if they had the care of children – Fanny Lewald's comments on the amelioration of the lot of women must now be examined. She was strenuously in favour of women being allowed to work and thus achieve independence if necessary – in this, she completely agreed with Louise Otto-Peters;[39] she was in favour of state help for the setting up of such institutions as refuge shelters for women in towns, and was a member of the committee which set up one such shelter in January 1869. She was in favour of education for women, in particular poor women and women in

---

[36] Letter from Fanny Lewald to Johanna Kinkel, 1851, cited in Pazi, 'Fanny Lewald', p. 249.

[37] Pazi, 'Fanny Lewald', p. 259f.

[38] Steinhauer, 'Fanny Lewald, die deutsche George Sand', p. 19.

[39] Van Rheinberg, *Fanny Lewald*, p. 192.

service, and helped to set up educational societies for servant girls, remarking that a spin-off from such groups was that prospective employees could be vetted – another example of 'the scrupulously practical' Fanny Lewald (in Ulrike Helmer's words[40]). She berated wealthy women for their vanity and love of show, which set such a bad example to their servants, and said it was in their own interest to change:

> ... if we want to produce a healthy atmosphere for ourselves and our children in our family life, an atmosphere which means that our servants leave our homes as industrious girls to take their place as well-behaved women in the world of work, then above all *we ourselves and our daughters must behave well*.[41]

Fanny Lewald also supported the communal kitchen which was pioneered by Lina Morgenstern in Berlin in 1866,[42] but remained in general terms a bourgeois feminist who supported marriage and family life. To that end, she was an implacable opponent of the 'double standard' which so often resulted in the exploitation of poor women by rich men. She and Louise Otto-Peters disliked the way the radical feminists, amongst them the writer Louise Aston, challenged men by opening a ladies' club in Berlin, provocatively called 'Die Emancipierten'; conservatively minded women found it just as shocking as did men. In this club, such George Sand-like infringements of decorum took place as the wearing of men's clothes and the smoking of cigars. In general, Fanny Lewald's ultimate desire was for people – not just women – to be happy, and for that they had to be educated. In view of the lack of opportunities for female education at the time, her aspiration thus involved a polarisation whereby she campaigned for issues of specific concern to women. Her pressure for women's education was a life-long interest.[43] She did not go so far as asking for women to have the vote; this aspiration had not the remotest practicality at the time. Fanny Lewald's main achievements as a feminist, which mark her out from later bourgeois feminists who would be chiefly concerned with gaining recognition of woman as a *Persönlichkeit*, consisted in the support she gave to women of the lower orders.

[40] Fanny Lewald, *Politische Schriften für und wider die Frauen*, ed. by Ulrike Helmer, Frankfurt am Main, 1989 [1863], p. 12 (Introduction).

[41] Lewald, Fifth 'Osterbrief' in *Politische Schriften für und wider die Frauen*, p. 50.

[42] In 1866, just before the poor of Berlin were hit by the outbreak of war with France and a cholera epidemic, Lina Morgenstern swung into action with her 'Volksküche', which provided nourishing food at cost price. By June 1869, there were ten such kitchens functioning in Berlin. See Fanny Lewald's eighth letter in *Politische Schriften für und wider die Frauen*, pp. 154–60.

[43] Van Rheinberg, *Fanny Lewald*, p. 197.

Johanna Kinkel, 1810–1858

Johanna Kinkel grew up a Catholic in Bonn as the daughter of the *Maitre d'études* at the French *Lycée*;[44] a musically gifted girl, she was taught music by the same man who had taught the young Beethoven, Franz Ries, though it must be said that her parents were more than challenged at having a daughter of such intelligence, and unrelenting in their attempt to discourage her musical propensity.[45] However, at the age of nineteen she ran the local music lovers' society and from the age of twenty began to compose her own pieces, including songs and cantatas; at the same time she wrote articles on music, including, according to Ruth-Ellen Boetcher Joeres, 'a still useful treatise on giving piano lessons and an exceptional study of Friedrich Chopin',[46] and began to give private music lessons, principally on the piano. Still only twenty-one, she married Johann Mathieux, but left him after six months. He apparently abused her by quarrelling with her non-stop, though Helmer notes that Bonn gossip blamed the breakdown of the marriage on Johanna's 'masculine education' and 'lack of femininity'.[47] Since Johanna's first husband was looked upon as religious, people tended to take his side, and she stopped going to church, though according to Schulte, she had in any case lost her faith at the age of sixteen.[48] Johanna now went to Berlin to study music, living for a while in Bettina's house and teaching her two daughters music. In 1836, she completed her music studies and was now able to support herself as a qualified teacher of music. This step was taken against the wishes of her parents, and was unusually independent for the day.[49] Having returned to Bonn in 1836 to seek a permanent position, Johanna met Gottfried Kinkel in 1839, and they married in 1843 after the

---

[44] For this and the following biographical details I am indebted to the *Nachwort* by Ulrike Helmer, to be found in Johanna Kinkel, *Hans Ibeles in London. Ein Roman aus dem Flüchtlingsleben*, Frankfurt am Main, 1991 [1860], pp. 384–401.

[45] J. F. Schulte, *Johanna Kinkel nach ihren Briefen und Erinnnerungs-Blättern*, Münster, 1908 [to mark the fiftieth anniversary of Johanna Kinkel's death], p. 7.

[46] Ruth-Ellen Boetcher Joeres, 'The Triumph of Woman: Johanna Kinkel's *Hans Ibeles in London 1860*', in *Euphorion*, 70, 1976, pp. 187–197, p. 187.

[47] Helmer, editorial *Nachwort*, in *Hans Ibeles in London*, p. 395.

[48] Schulte, *Johanna Kinkel*, p. 7.

[49] In her short story *Musikalische Orthodoxie* (in Gottfried and Johanna Kinkel, *Erzählungen*, Stuttgart, 1883), Johanna Kinkel describes some of the problems a gifted female pianist might encounter in trying to make her way in the world. It is rather wishful thinking at the end to find the heroine, Ida, happily married, with two lovely children, performing with her husband to loud acclaim.

death of Johanna's first husband and her conversion to Protestantism. Within the next six years they had four children.

Gottfried Kinkel, whose intended career as theology professor at Bonn University had been abruptly foreshortened by his relationship with the Catholic Johanna, her conversion notwithstanding, re-established himself as a highly successful lecturer on art history.[50] He was, like Johanna, a gifted musician and writer, and soon became involved in radical politics; as Malwida von Meysenbug points out, from being the darling of the aristocratic circles he now became the hero of the revolutionary farmers, artisans and workers,[51] and was elected leader of the Bonn democrats. As such he was delegated to go to Berlin, where he was arrested in 1849 for his active role in the 1848 uprisings in the Pfalz and Baden. He was at first condemned to death, only for this to be commuted at the last minute to life imprisonment. Apparently with the help of Bettina, whose daughter laid a petition on behalf of Kinkel at the feet of the King, Friedrich Wilhelm IV, a royal blind eye was turned when Kinkel was sprung from Spandau jail in 1850 by one of his pupils, Carl Schurz.[52] Johanna and Gottfried Kinkel were now able to emigrate to London, and the experiences of their arrival there, and the years following, are mirrored in Johanna's witty and well-written novel – the only one she wrote – *Hans Ibeles in London. Ein Roman aus dem Flüchtlingsleben* (*Hans Ibeles in London. A Novel of Emigré Life*), published posthumously in 1860. There are some passages, especially at the beginning, which, in the affectionate portrayal of the neighbours' prejudice towards the new German arrivals, curtains a-twitching, are highly reminiscent of Elizabeth Gaskell's *Cranford* (1851).

Johanna fully shared the revolutionary fervour of her husband, but their ideals centred on bourgeois aims and thus differed from the Communism of Marx. Indeed, Marx loathed both Kinkels because of what he viewed as their watered-down socialism, and labelled Gottfried a 'churchy-aesthetic-liberal parasite'.[53]

---

[50] Malwida von Meysenbug, *Der Lebensabend einer Idealistin* (1898) included in the two-volume *Memoiren einer Idealistin*, Stuttgart, Berlin and Leipzig, 1929 [1876], II, p. 382. The roman numerals denote the volume for this edition, not the division of the memoirs into three parts, though for the sake of accuracy, Part 1 and 2 are found in vol. I, and Part 3 and the *Lebensabend einer Idealistin* are found in vol. II.

[51] Meysenbug, *Der Lebensabend einer Idealistin*, II, p. 383.

[52] Arthur Helps and Elizabeth Jane Howard, *Bettina: A Portrait*, London, 1957, p. 194f.

[53] Christine Lattek, 'Im englischen Exil 1852-59. Der Rückzug der Demokratin ins Privatleben,' in *Malwida von Meysenbug. Ein Portrait*, ed. by Gunther Tietz, Frankfurt am Main, Berlin and Vienna, 1985, pp. 71–110, p. 86.

However, Alexander Herzen liked Gottfried Kinkel's conciliatory approach and relished his visits to the Kinkels, who held virtual open house to the German emigrés in these years. Kinkel's brand of socialism, which Johanna fully shared, is characterised by Malwida von Meysenbug as follows:

> His whole nature protests against the arid systems of uniform, bureaucratic Communism, and the destructive levelling down which wipes out the age-old natural right to individuality ... His social ideal is a free organism, the laws of which are aimed at the independence of the individual, the full development of all work skills and each individual form of manual work.[54]

As indicated, Johanna Kinkel shared her husband's political stance, and collaborated with him in all matters. Indeed, as Ruth-Ellen Boetcher Joeres points out with justified exasperation, it has become received wisdom for historians of literature to comment that Johanna was superior in talent to her husband, whose only generally agreed work of merit remains the epic poem *Otto der Schütz* (1843).[55] Both Gottfried and Johanna wrote short stories of considerable interest, but the crowning achievement in their partnership remains Johanna's novel, which, as well as providing insights into the life of exiles living in London[56] – which can be checked for accuracy by a parallel reading of Malwida von Meysenbug's memoirs – also contains clues as to her own life with Kinkel, though, as discussed below, the novel is not a direct *roman à clef*. However, it is easy to assume that Dorothea Ibeles' experiences of London life in exile are a fictional rendering of many of Johanna Kinkel's own experiences, in spite of the fact that the character of Hans Ibeles is thinly drawn in comparison with the other characters, whereas Gottfried was very much the central point of Johanna Kinkel's life.

Though many other details in the novel are different from real life – the Ibeles have seven children, the Kinkels had a mere four – what we can glean from the novel is an insight into the depth of depression to which Johanna must have sunk when, in 1858, ostensibly suffering from a heart attack, she opened a second-floor window and fell to her death. The type of drudgery which the heroine Dorothea shoulders in giving endless piano lessons to

---

[54] Meysenbug, *Der Lebensabend einer Idealistin*, II, p. 383.
[55] Boetcher-Joeres, 'The Triumph of Woman', p. 187f.
[56] See Helen Chambers, 'Johanna Kinkel's novel *Hans Ibeles in London*: a German View of England' in *Exilanten und andere Deutsche in Fontanes Londone. Festschrift für Charlotte Jolles zum 85. Geburtstag*, ed. by Peter Alter and Rudolf Muhs, Stuttgart and London, 1996, pp. 159–173 *passim*.

dull pupils in order to help the ailing family finances will strike a chord with anyone who has ever given private tuition. As a gifted pianist herself, Johanna became artistically frustrated as well as snowed under by the grinding routine of tuition, housekeeping and the demands not just of her family, but of their many friends and acquaintances. Hans Ibeles' roving eye is dealt with firmly in the novel, where Dorothea manages to divert Hans' interest away first from the fascinating (and selfish) Countess Blafoska, who is discovered to be a spy, and then from the *femme fatale* Livia, alias Lora O'Nalley, who turns out to be the murderer of her own husband. Dorothea's spirits are kept up by the friendship of the young emigrée Meta Braun, based directly on Malwida von Meysenbug, portrayed in the novel as a governess with a powerful intellect and proto-feminist leanings. In spite of Johanna's decision to give the novel a happy ending, warning signals are sent out at the very beginning through the description of the reaction of the 'locals' in Dessau to the marriage of the sensible Dorothea to the handsome young musician, Hans Ibeles, which ends with the following comments:

> The town philistines could not understand how such a reasonable woman could have fallen in love with a young Adonis, and believed that if she had waited a little, a more suitable partner might have become available, for example, the widowed mayor and the retired Major could both be viewed as suitors. And the young women of the town complained tearfully about the terrible fate of the young man who had been landed with a wife who was not just ugly, but also, *horribile dictu*, a few years his senior.[57]

We should note the above humorous comment on philistines who regard a musician as frivolous; this is a recurrent theme in Johanna Kinkel's short stories. A musician is often seen as little better than an acrobat or juggler, as in the story *Der Musikant* (published posthumously in 1883[58]), where a father's prejudice towards his daughter's lover, a musician, is criticised. However, Johanna, in referring to Ibeles as a 'young Adonis', is making a statement which can be seen as a thinly disguised comment on Gottfried Kinkel's handsome features compared to her own ugliness. Though Boetcher Joeres remarks that critics have 'irrelevantly' commented on Johanna's lack of beauty,[59] she immediately provides a footnote which shows that Johanna herself did not find her lack of beauty irrelevant at all; in fact, quite the

---

[57] Kinkel, *Hans Ibeles in London*, p. 22.
[58] Johanna Kinkel, *Der Musikant*, in Gottfried and Johanna Kinkel, *Erzählungen*.
[59] Boetcher-Joeres, 'The Triumph of Woman', p. 192.

reverse. Malwida von Meysenbug commented that the first time she saw the Kinkels – she actually went to their house in London uninvited (like all the rest!), having corresponded with Johanna from Germany – she was struck at how unhandsome Johanna was:

> Johanna Kinkel had nothing about her outward appearance that one would usually call beautiful or attractive; her features were strong, almost masculine, she was very tall, but over her whole presence reigned her wonderful deep eyes, which gave proof of a spiritual world of sensitivity whilst in her full, low-pitched voice rang a wealth of feeling ...[60]

Malwida adds, tellingly enough, that Gottfried Kinkel, who was five years younger than Johanna, 'was in the full bloom of his manly beauty', and it is easy to sympathise with Johanna when, under stress, she felt at a physical disadvantage. Within a society in which, as pointed out in the Introduction to this volume, beauty in a woman mattered very much indeed, it is my contention that Johanna came to feel that the years of drudgery in London had taken their toll on her, making her seem, and more importantly feel, even older than she was in relation to Gottfried. She had already been depressed about this during Gottfried Kinkel's imprisonment, which had made him a glamorous hero for many radicals, whilst Johanna tore out her hair trying to manage the family finances and keep up political pressure for her husband. Fanny Lewald reports a conversation she had with Johanna in 1850, in which the latter said she was considering asking for a divorce:

> 'What has put that into your head?' I cried.
> 'My mirror!' she answered, so calmly that it was rather frightening at that moment. 'You know I'm five years older than Kinkel, I have always been ugly. It has always hurt me and the worry [about Kinkel in jail] has aged me years in months – and in spite of all this trouble Kinkel is so handsome! So handsome!'[61]

Clearly, Johanna Kinkel's preoccupation with her lack of beauty amounted to an inferiority complex.

From the descriptions of life in exile which Johanna sent to Fanny, in which she complained that she was being buried alive along with her talents, and described the money problems the family had, exacerbated by the endless flow of emigrés through the house, it can be seen that she was perhaps not always the cheerful and resourceful wife and mother that her heroine

---

[60] Meysenbug, *Memoiren einer Idealistin*, II, p. 265f.
[61] Fanny Lewald, *Zwölf Bilder nach dem Leben*, Berlin, 1888, pp. 1–32, p.6.

Dorothea is in *Hans Ibeles in London*. There are passages in the novel which remind us of the crushing workload which took its toll on Johanna, such as the description of a walk on Hampstead Heath which would bring tears to Dorothea's eyes because it made the rest of the world seem, by comparison a 'joyless workhouse'.[62] Furthermore, Johanna's own reaction to the fellow emigrée Baroness Brüningk's dealings with Gottfried (which was to bar her from the house) indicates that even if those dealings did not amount to flirtation, liberties appear to have been taken: the Baroness tended to abuse the Kinkels' hospitality, like everyone else. Eventually, the Baroness presided over her own 'emigré centre' in St John's Wood. There was thereafter a coolness between the two houses which belies the energetic handling of the parallel affair of Hans and Madame Blafoska in the novel. Malwida clearly took the side of the Kinkels, though she continued to visit Baroness Brüningk on occasion and, just before the latter's death at the end of January 1853, conveyed parting greetings from the baroness to Gottfried Kinkel, 'a friend whom she had loved very much and who had been separated from her by a misunderstanding.'[63] It is possible that Johanna might have thought there had been more than a 'misunderstanding' if she barred her house to her former friend. However, Camille Pitoullet has painstakingly shown that the novel is 'essentially fictive and imaginary'.[64] Pitoullet's chief concern is to refute Geiger's premise that Johanna Kinkel's novel was a 'satire on Kinkel', motivated by revenge.[65] Pitoullet quotes a lengthy letter from Carl Schurz, who became a frequent visitor at the Kinkel home in London, to corroborate his thesis:

> The atmosphere in the Kinkel household seemed to me to be a cheerful and happy one up to the time of Kinkel's trip to America [1851]... He took upon himself this fantastic undertaking out of a feeling of duty for the party. ... During most of the time Kinkel was absent, I was at Frau Kinkel's house at her request and I could observe how this second separation from her husband clouded the mood of this formerly so cheerful woman.[66]

---

[62] Kinkel, *Hans Ibeles in London*, p. 101.

[63] Meysenbug, *Memoiren einer Idealistin*, I, p. 356.

[64] Camille Pitoullet, 'Sur un prétendu roman à clef de Johanna Kinkel' in *Revue Germanique*, 3, 4, July/August 1907, 261–402, p. 380.

[65] Ludwig Geiger, 'Vergessene satyrische Romane des 19. Jahrhunderts', in *Zeitschrift für Bücherfreunde*, 2, 1903/1904, p. 367.

[66] Letter from Carl Schurz to Camille Pitoullet, 1 December 1905. Quoted in Pitoullet, 'Sur un prétendu roman à clef de Johanna Kinkel', p. 405.

Both Schurz and Pitoullet are at pains to minimise the tensions between the Kinkels, and to blame external factors for trouble between the two of them. Schurz ends his letter by saying:

It could be that a woman like Johanna Kinkel might be inclined to jealousy. As far as I know, no individual ever gave cause for suspicion. The tendency towards jealousy was probably directed at everything which in any way came between her and her husband.[67]

Such jealousy, which Johanna confessed to Fanny Lewald was a character fault but which we can view, within the context, as understandable, was made much worse by Johanna's overwork and resultant depression, all within a situation where she felt insecure by definition: as an emigrée and as a woman. Coupled with this, she had lost her father and had been forbidden by the doctor to work because of her heart problems. This placed an even greater strain on Gottfried Kinkel, whose teaching duties kept him away from home for hours on end. It is noteworthy that Johanna had felt liberated in the summer of 1858, having finished her novel, and had told Malwida von Meysenbug that she had not been so happy since the time she was a bride.[68] Her happiness thus depended on her husband to an inordinate degree in the months prior to her death. Nobody seems to have realised the 'deep depression'[69] into which Johanna Kinkel had sunk, not even her friend Malwida, as we can see from an incident between Johanna and Malwida a few days before Johanna died. Apparently Malwida had asked to bring a lady to visit Johanna, which drew from Johanna a comment which was insulting to Malwida. Though Malwida talks round the issue without being precise, it is possible to read between the lines and we can presume that Johanna had perhaps said that her husband would have someone new to flirt with. Malwida, the aristocrat with tender nerves and without the stresses of caring for a husband and family as well as ill-health, all of which were obviously bearing down on Johanna, took the high ground and was put out by the supposed insult that she would be capable of being party to such a thing. Though both women appeared to make things up at the time – with Johanna unfortunately asking Malwida to say nothing to her husband – Malwida nursed her grudge, and refused to answer Johanna's letter of apology; the next thing she heard was that Johanna was ill with bronchitis, and, just when she had decided to visit her, she

---

[67] Schurz, in Pitoullet, 'Sur un prétendu roman à clef de Johanna Kinkel', p. 407.

[68] Meysenbug, *Memoiren einer Idealistin*, II, p. 119.

[69] Schulte, *Johanna Kinkel*, p. 113.

received the news from Kinkel that Johanna was dead. Perhaps it was partly to rationalise a feeling that she, too, had let Johanna down that led Malwida to agree so vehemently with Kinkel that Johanna could not possibly have committed suicide,[70] even though many of their exile friends appear to have held him morally responsible for Johanna's death.[71] That death robbed Germany of a writer of great promise, and German feminism of a true early radical.

Malwida von Meysenbug, 1816–1903

Malwida Rivalier was born in Kassel to a father of French Huguenot stock, Philippe Rivalier, the eleventh of twelve children (ten of whom survived childhood), in the same year in which the last of the line of the von Meysenbug family died. The Duke of Kassel, to whom Malwida's father was chief advisor, subsequently gave Rivalier the title of 'von Meysenbug' in 1825 for services rendered; thus, Malwida was not from an ancient family of nobility, though there were times in her life, especially when she mixed with the Wagners, when she behaved as though she was. Her most important work was her *Memoiren einer Idealistin*, published in 1876, a work which was to inspire a generation of young women with feminist zeal, though the tone and indeed content of the memoirs is frequently over-sentimental and vague. In that sense she was a true follower of Bettina, whose work, along with the letters of Rahel, she took as her example. Significantly enough, Malwida, like Bettina, only achieved celebrity in later life: she was sixty when her memoirs were published. What was important to her predominantly female readers was that here was a woman who dared to earn her own living and who dared to appear at protest meetings, a woman who would have been arrested by the police if she had not emigrated to England: a woman who could claim to be noble, if only just. This was the acceptable face of German feminism.

The fortunes of the Duke of Kassel fluctuated through his own subservience to his mistress, to the great annoyance of the people of Kassel, and there came the moment when the Duke abdicated, leaving the duchy to his son. This was also the point at which the family fortunes of the newly ennobled von Meysenbugs faltered; the older children now being adults, the family was scattered in different directions and Frau von Meysenbug took Malwida and

[70] Meysenbug, *Memoiren einer Idealistin*, II, p. 123.
[71] Lattek, 'Im englischen Exil', p. 86.

her younger sister to Detmold. The family idyll which had taken up
the first hundred pages of the *Memoiren* had come to an abrupt end.
Malwida had been brought up a Protestant and was confirmed,
though her journey towards scepticism had already begun before
she took her first communion; however, she attended the sermons
of Georg Althaus, and was impressed when his son stood in for him
one Sunday. Theodor Althaus would eventually engage in radical
politics to the point of turning his back on the church, but at this
point – 1844 – he had just returned from Bonn, where he had
studied theology under Gottfried Kinkel. Though six years younger
than Malwida, who was now twenty-eight, the relationship became
serious and for Malwida, crucial; this was '*the* great love in Malwida's
life'.[72] Though Malwida preferred to skirt over the issue later,
Althaus ended their relationship in 1847 because he loved another
woman, something which shocked Malwida to the core.[73] Tietz
surmises that as they were never unchaperoned, the relationship
never had a chance to develop, though he also hints at Malwida's
frigidity,[74] but on the positive side, the lack of privacy meant that
they had long political discussions focused on the matter of equal
rights.[75] What Malwida now did was transfer her concern about
equality to the matter of rights for women; she maintained that a
woman had a right to a proper education and to training for paid
work so that she could provide for herself if necessary. These were
ideals which Malwida maintained throughout her life, and which
were, as we have seen in Chapter One, well in advance of her time.

In 1848, Malwida was in the right place, Frankfurt, at the right
time; she had come to visit her father, who was ill, and was
spellbound as events unfolded. On 31 March, she watched the
procession of delegates entering St Paul's Church, two by two and
in great solemnity for the declaration of the constitution, after
which the cannons thundered to the applause of the watching
crowd. Malwida had managed to gain a vantage point from the
house of complete strangers.[76] Still full of revolutionary zeal, she
began to study for teacher training in Hamburg; at which point
Althaus, who had been in prison and was now *persona non grata* in
society, came back into her life briefly, a sick and broken man; he
soon fell seriously ill and died in 1852. Before he died, Malwida

---

[72] Gunther Tietz, 'Das Paradis der Jugend. Malwidas Jahre in Kassel und
Detmold' in *Malwida von Meysenbug. Ein Portrait*, pp. 19–42, p. 41.

[73] Meysenbug, *Memoiren einer Idealistin*, I, p. 255. Even after a quarter of a century,
Malwida remembers the grief as 'one of the decisive moments of my life'.

[74] Tietz, 'Das Paradies der Jugend', p. 36.

[75] Ibid., p. 40.

[76] Meysenbug, *Memoiren einer Idealistin*, I, p. 145f.

had been able to render him little services which she hoped would convince him that 'when a woman is greatly in love, mother love is included; it does not demand, but gives, helps, comforts and reconciles'.[77] Thus Malwida rationalised what was actually a rejection into an ethereal and heroic friendship; Theodor was enshrined in her heart as a 'beautiful individual'.[78] We also realise that she had already formed her conception of love as motherly, a stance which would become one of her defining characteristics, as Elisabeth Förster-Nietzsche would later point out.[79] Of course, the *Memoiren* were written two decades after the events with Althaus had taken place, which in itself provides us with a fascinating insight into the way the cutting edge of Malwida's idealism began to become blunted by effusive sentimentality such as that which was common currency among her friends, Cosima Wagner and the much younger Elisabeth Förster-Nietzsche.

The Hamburg teacher-training establishment attended by Malwida, which was incidentally run by the nephew of Friedrich Fröbel, had to close down, partly for financial reasons but partly, it has been suggested, because the young ladies were becoming too radical. But at least the seed had been sown, as Malwida pointed out:

> The thought of bringing about woman's full freedom for intellectual development, economic independence and all civil rights was in the process of becoming reality; this thought could never again die out.[80]

Althaus had inspired Malwida with democratic ideals which she then widened to apply to women; however, according to Lattek, Malwida's political sentiments would become ever more elitist as time went on (hardly surprising in view of her close contact with Wagner and Nietzsche):

> She increasingly came to see the inequalities amongst people as a necessary expression of the different strength and intelligence of the individual, and even viewed nature as organised along aristocratic principles. More and more she rejected all the 'mad attempts at levelling down', and saw no solution in the democrats' 'new craze', the *Volk*.[81]

For the time being, however, Malwida remained a radical. She now went to Berlin, where she wrote articles for a democratic

---

[77] Ibid., I, p. 223.
[78] Ibid., I, p. 235: '[d]ie schöne Individualität'.
[79] Elisabeth Förster-Nietzsche, *Friedrich Nietzsche und die Frauen seiner Zeit*, Munich, 1935, p. 82.
[80] Meysenbug, *Memoiren einer Idealistin*, I, p. 237.
[81] Lattek, 'Im englischen Exil', p. 101.

publication, ultimately to find herself in trouble when the police raided her house. Her connection with Althaus made her a prime suspect, and she was forced to flee to London, her first port of call being the house of Gottfried and Johanna Kinkel, whose political ideas she whole-heartedly endorsed.

In London, Malwida gave private German lessons, which were in demand in view of the fact that Queen Victoria had married a German consort, Albert, and became even more so when Queen Victoria's daughter, Princess Victoria, married Friedrich Wilhelm IV of Prussia in January 1858. Malwida had been completely against taking a post as a governess, but after she became friendly with Alexander Herzen, she moved in as governess – and family friend – from 1853 to 1856. It was in this capacity that Johanna Kinkel knew Malwida when she devised the character of Meta Braun in *Hans Ibeles in London*, though Johanna used the occasion to give a biting critique of the abuses to which governesses were exposed.[82] These abuses certainly had nothing to do with Malwida's experiences with Alexander Herzen, who appreciated her as a 'completely free and mature person', though, as one has come to expect, such descriptions often spare nothing with regard to physical features, and Herzen, no exception to this rule, added that she was 'outwardly ugly'.[83] Herzen was a Russian emigré whose house was, like the Kinkels', a virtual thoroughfare for Russian 1848ers passing through London. Herzen's wife had died in 1852, and Malwida rapidly became a substitute mother to Herzen's youngest daughter, Olga. This was the defining relationship in Malwida's life.

Malwida had made important contacts in London, some of them famous, such as Mazzini, who remained a life-long friend, and some of them rich, such as Madame Salis Schwabe, who was often glad to have Malwida's company when travelling. Madame Schwabe had a house in Manchester and property in Wales; on her invitation, Malwida was able to see the major art exhibition in Manchester in 1857, staying with Madame Schwabe in Manchester and afterwards travelling with her to Wales, where they made the fleeting acquaintance of Mrs Gaskell. Malwida wrote to Johanna Kinkel from Manchester, complaining that Madame Schwabe's house was continually full of guests, so that she had no peace; Johanna replied that it could not be worse than

[82] Kinkel, *Hans Ibeles in London*, Chapter 11: 'Die deutsche Gouvernante (Manuskript)', pp. 143–159.
[83] Lattek, 'Im englischen Exil', p. 95.

what she was experiencing in London, with emigrés still abusing her hospitality with depressing regularity:

> The way we have been plagued by people in the last few days is beyond belief; one simply cannot have any pleasure from life in London without having three locks fitted to the front door.[84]

In 1858/1859, Malwida spent the first of many winters in Paris, where she encountered Richard Wagner and his first wife. She was immediately convinced of Wagner's genius, and when she returned to London in 1860, once again to the hospitality of Madame Schwabe, who had rented a house there, she asked Madame Schwabe to send Wagner a sum of money, for which he wrote a note of thanks dated 20 May 1860; a few weeks later, another petition from Wagner resulted in more cash from Madame Schwabe via Malwida.[85] From this time on, Malwida remained on terms of intimate friendship with Wagner. She also became party to Wagner's appreciation of the philosophy of Schopenhauer, not as a treatise on pessimism but as a theory which gave prominence to art as man's highest calling. She would later share with Nietzsche a high estimation of art.

In response to a request from Herzen in 1860, Malwida collected Olga from him for a visit to London. Olga was so ecstatic to be with Malwida again that Herzen handed her over to Malwida's care in the following year, 1861. Malwida construed this as a stroke of fate which had placed her in the position of educator and mother, and resolved to devote the rest of her life to the task.[86] That winter, Malwida travelled to Paris with Olga. Here she was able to witness the success of Wagner's *Tannhäuser*, before proceeding to Italy in 1862, with Olga and Olga's older sister, Natalie Herzen. Malwida now lived a somewhat nomadic life with Olga (and often with Natalie, too), visiting the major cities in Italy and storing up experiences for later collections of essays, such as *Stimmungsbilder* (1879). This contains essays with titles such as 'Die Frau in der Gesellschaft' ('Woman in Society') and 'Das Bedürfnis einer Philosophie' ('The Need for a Philosophy'); perhaps one title sums up all the rest: 'Toleranz'. Malwida was a keen literary critic, making shrewd assessments (Ibsen, for example, is branded 'a vivisectionist of human nature[87]). She also wrote stories and two novels, *Phädra* (1885) and *Himmlische und Irdische Liebe* (1905). Her creative work

---

[84] Letter from Johanna Kinkel to Malwida von Meysenbug, cited in Meysenbug, *Memoiren einer Idealistin*, II, p. 89.

[85] Gaby Vinant, *Malwida de Meysenbug 1816–1903. Sa vie et ses amis*, Paris, 1932, p. 180.

[86] Meysenbug, *Memoiren einer Idealistin*, Ii, p. 184.

[87] Meysenbug, *Der Lebensabend einer Idealistin*, II, p. 466.

has received far less acclaim than her other writing, especially her memoirs, which have a place in the feminist canon in Germany.

Wherever she was in Europe, Malwida always kept in touch with her many friends, and left behind a voluminous correspondence. She maintained close touch with Wagner and Cosima, whom Wagner married in 1868 (after the birth of Siegfried that June). As part of the Wagners' 'inner circle', Malwida was present at the laying of the foundation stone for Bayreuth in May 1872, and it was on this occasion that she met Nietzsche. Werner Ross has suggested that when Olga married, Malwida found it hard to face up to this 'catastrophe',[88] and was keen to gain a son. Nietzsche seemed a prime candidate, though her real 'substitute son' would be Romain Rolland, fifty years her junior, with whom she was friendly for the last ten years of her life.[89] For several years, Malwida made Bayreuth her base until she moved to Rome in 1877. Here, she would hold house-parties where young people would join her for intellectual or cultural discussions. She had one winter-long house-party in the winter of 1876, hosting Nietzsche, Paul Reé and Alfred Brenner. Nietzsche had hoped that his stay with Malwida would be relaxing, but actually he was bored, especially when the other two men departed, leaving him alone with Malwida.[90]

Though Malwida's memoirs had just been published in that year, it is probably fair to guess that Nietzsche did not want to discuss them with her. The radical politics inherent in the term 'Idealist' of the title would be sufficient to put him off, since he was opposed to democracy on principle, believing that it had a weakening effect on culture. It is a mystery how Nietzsche and Malwida could have been close, since one of the people Malwida most admired was Madame de Staël, about whom she wrote, as well as other prominent women in cultural history, in her collection of essays *Individualitäten* (1901). Yet Nietzsche in *Jenseits von Gut und Böse* (*Beyond Good and Evil*) (1886) singled out Madame de Staël for scorn as 'one of the three *comical* women as such',[91] the reason being that she was a woman writer, for Nietzsche, a contradiction in terms. How could Malwida, now

---

[88] Werner Ross, 'Das konnte nicht gut gehen! Impromtu über Malwidas Freundschaft mit dem jungen Nietzsche', in Meysenbug, *Malwida von Meysenbug. Ein Portrait*, pp. 127–46, p. 133.

[89] Ibid., p. 134.

[90] Carol Diethe, *Nietzsche's Women: Beyond the Whip*, Berlin and New York, 1996, p. 79f.

[91] Friedrich Nietzsche, *Beyond Good and Evil*, VII: 223, in *Basic Writings of Nietzsche*, trs by Walter Kaufmann, New York, 1966, p. 354; the other two 'comical' women are Madame Roland and 'Monsieur' George Sand.

going to press herself, brook such comments? And how could Nietzsche remain on good terms with Malwida when she insisted on making a cult of her friendship with Wagner, whose whole outlook he now rejected? In 1878, Malwida enthused over *Parsifal*, a work which aroused Nietzsche's contempt, writing to Rée, '... yes, dear friend, I cannot help it, that is religion!'[92] Since she was actually an atheist, her comment is to be construed as an expression of what she understood as humanism:

> What makes us human cannot be discovered in a chemist's laboratory. If it is a product of the historically developed human spirit (*Geist*), our prospects are limitless, because we are capable, nay, obliged to idolise ourselves.[93]

Nevertheless, Nietzsche and Malwida remained close friends, with Malwida always on the lookout for a wife for him. It was at another of her house-parties, in Rome 1882, where both Reé and Nietzsche were present, that Nietzsche was introduced to Lou Salomé.

Clearly, Malwida's admiration for Wagner verged on hero worship, and indeed, that was a stipulation for his friendship, the realisation of which caused Nietzsche to withdraw from the whole Wagner circle in 1876. It is typical of Malwida that when Nietzsche wrote her insulting letters in 1889, just prior to his mental collapse, she was more upset about his animosity to Wagner than any insults towards herself. Years later, she recorded her hurt feelings vividly in *Individualitäten*.[94] Tietz has argued that at first, Malwida needed to look up to people in this manner, though as time went by, she accepted homage from those who looked up to her.[95] The point is that there never seemed to be a meeting between equals. Nevertheless, as already indicated, Malwida is an important figure for feminism in Germany. Her writing inspired young women to take up the cause, and although she became less radical, she never lost her enthusiasm for the campaign for proper education for women. Her influence on the Russian Lou Salomé, the Austrian Resa von Schirnhofer and the Swiss Meta von Salis-Marschlins, all of whom would have important things to say on the woman question in the decade prior to the turn of the century (though in Salomé's case the message would be a conservative one, as discussed in Chapter Six), indicates how international her reputation was, though as she aged, her influence was restricted to a small circle of protégés.

---

[92] Meysenbug, *Der Lebensabend einer Idealistin*, II, p. 317.
[93] Ibid., p. 317.
[94] Malwida von Meysenbug, *Individualitäten*, Berlin and Leipzig, 1901, p. 37.
[95] Tietz, 'Das Paradies der Jugend', p. 30.

Ida Hahn-Hahn. Lithograph from *Europa*, 1842 (shelfmark PP 4793C), signed by Hahn-Hahn with the words 'Only someone who fights, struggles and strives – lives'. Reproduced with kind permission of the British Library.

4

POPULAR LITERATURE

This chapter will deal with three writers who were immensely popular in their day, but of whom only Marie von Ebner-Eschenbach has retained a place within the literary canon. The most neglected writer, Eugenie Marlitt, was the one who was most read and Ida Hahn-Hahn was the most prolific. All three criticised aspects of contemporary society in their writing. Ida Hahn-Hahn became so disgusted with the prevailing morality that she turned her back on the world for a life of contemplation, converting to Catholicism in the process; Catholicism, with its certainties and patriarchal system, offered a safe haven for such women. The Protestant Eugenie Marlitt and the Catholic Marie von Ebner-Eschenbach maintained a prolonged attack on religious bigotry, a fact which makes their novels interesting documents from the perspective of the History of Ideas, especially as the official Prussian stance of tolerance towards Catholics was not always upheld.[1] Indeed, though the Catholic political party, the Zentrum, gained seventeen votes in the Reichstag elections of 1871, Bismarck conducted a campaign against it during the 1870's in his

---

[1] According to John E. Groh, *Nineteenth Century German Protestantism: The Church as Social Model*, Washington, 1982, p. 195, anti-Catholic measures came into force almost by accident in the Rhineland, which had been controlled by Prussia since 1815. There, Catholics were in the majority by 80 percent, but were forced to obey the Prussian command that children of 'mixed marriages' were to be brought up in their father's religion. As most of these marriages consisted of Catholic women married to Protestant men who had moved into the area on official business, the law blatantly discriminated against women. Further trouble in Cologne in 1844 ultimately led to a hardening of Catholic resolve to form a political presence within the state.

Kulturkampf, albeit for political rather than theological reasons (he needed the support of the liberals). Furthermore, as we see in the life of Marie von Ebner-Eschenbach, some who regarded themselves as German were cast off as a result of the war between Prussia and Austria in 1866, and felt their very identity threatened through these political upheavals.

Gräfin Ida von Hahn-Hahn, 1805–1880

Ida von Hahn-Hahn held a predominant position amongst female writers of popular fiction, especially during the years from 1838 until 1850; the novels of the thirty years after her conversion to Catholicism focus single-mindedly on social Catholicism, and appealed to a narrower clientele. The conversion itself made her into something of a joke figure – unfairly, to be sure – and somehow devalued the earlier work. This was a woman who had a bizarrely cavalier attitude towards her writing, as we shall see. All attempts to label her as having anything to do with Romanticism, Young Germany or Realism – or as poised between all three[2] – do not really mean very much. Gräfin Ida von Hahn-Hahn was born into an aristocratic family and spent the early years of her life at her father's newly inherited castle in Replin, Mecklenburg-Schwerin. The family fortunes began to be troubled when Ida's father developed a passion for the theatre, and had his own theatre built at enormous expense. It was very much appreciated by those who visited it, who included Achim von Arnim in 1806.[3] Unfortunately, Duke Carl von Hahn was no businessman, and his attempts to make a profit by hiring the best actors never worked out: he was outrageously extravagant, and within four years of inheriting his property he was in grave debt. His wife began to sell her jewels. In the end, unable to cope with her husband's obsession, she had no choice but to divorce him, and he became a travelling hanger-on in whatever theatre would employ him as prompter, dying in poverty in 1858.

Naturally, the sense of belonging to impoverished nobility haunted Ida's youth and indeed pushed her into a hasty marriage to her cousin at the age of twenty-one, largely in order to secure sufficient money to keep her mother and sister from the breadline. The man Ida had married was almost as obsessive as her father: this time the passion was for racing horses. His

---

[2] Erna Ines Schmid-Jürgens, *Ida Gräfin Hahn-Hahn*, Berlin, 1933, p. 121.
[3] Katrien van Munster, *Die junge Ida Gräfin Hahn-Hahn*, Graz, 1929, p. 14.

expensive horses and luxurious stables with marble stalls became legendary. Duke Friedrich Hahn-Basedow disliked the fact that his wife showed no interest in horses and took pleasure in tormenting her by such pranks as sitting her on an untrained horse. However, it was he, not she, who asked for a divorce. Ida von Hahn-Hahn was pregnant when she and her husband went for a cure at Wiesbaden in 1828; here, they met Gräfin Schlippenbach, who would become the Duke's second wife. At the same time, Ida met the man who would be her companion until he died in 1849, Baron Adolf von Bystram. Though the story of Ida von Hahn-Hahn's life so far sounds like a comic mixture of the plots of Goethe's *Wilhelm Meister's Apprenticeship* (1796) and *Elective Affinities* (1809), farce became tragedy when Ida's husband trapped her into agreeing to the divorce by planting forged incriminating evidence in her luggage. She subsequently gave birth to a daughter, Tony, who was both physically and mentally severely handicapped. Ida tried to look after Tony herself, but eventually handed her over to private foster parents who cared for her until she died at the age of twenty-four. One of Ida's recurrent themes in her writing is the potentially desperate situation of a woman trapped in an unhappy marriage of convenience such as hers had been.

Bystram had been widowed after only one year of marriage, and had promised his Polish wife on her death-bed that he would never remarry. Nobody has been able to assess whether the friendship he now enjoyed with Ida von Hahn-Hahn was platonic or not. Since they lived together, travelled together and were ostensibly 'a couple', there was naturally much gossip at the time about the liaison. I would like to suggest that it probably was platonic, if only because of Ida von Hahn-Hahn's strict moral stance in her novels even before her conversion to Catholicism in 1850. Also, she seems to have had no further children after Tony. There is, too, the fact that she was very attracted to Heinrich Simon, Fanny Lewald's cousin, who proposed marriage to her in 1836. Perhaps she rejected him because he was both bourgeois and Jewish, sufficient reasons to make any aristocrat pause at the time. After her conversion, Ida von Hahn-Hahn would become fanatic in her religious proselytising, and this involved her in anti-Semitic postures.[4] Perhaps she just rejected Simon because she feared another marriage. At all events, Simon took 'no' for an answer and Ida went back to her familiar lifestyle with von Bystram.

---

[4] Ida von Hahn-Hahn, *Maria Regina*, Regensburg, 1861, p. 131: '[t]he Jews take their revenge for the tyranny [against them] by trying to alter and destroy conditions which are based on a principle to which they are opposed.'

Ida von Hahn-Hahn's first collection of poems appeared in 1835; Bystram had actively encouraged her to write and he now supported her switch to prose. She embarked upon a series of journeys which would prove to be fertile breeding ground for both her travelogues and her plots. In 1835/1836 she went to Italy, in 1837 to Vienna, and on to Italy and Sicily in 1838/1839. In 1838, her first novel, *Ilda Schönhelm*, appeared and in 1839, *Der Rechte* (*Mr. Right*), followed by *Jenseits der Berge* ('On The Other Side of the Mountains') (1840), and her best-known work *Gräfin Faustine* (*The Countess Faustine*) (1840); *Ulrich* also appeared in 1841. *The Countess Faustine*, which appeared in English translation as early as 1845, had been dedicated to Bystram, who had stood by Ida in 1840 when an eye operation to cure a squint went badly wrong, leaving her blind in her left eye. She travelled to Nice that winter, then through southern France to Spain, the fruit of this journey appearing in due course as the travelogues *Reisebriefe* and *Erinnerungen aus und an Frankreich* (1842). Having travelled to Denmark and Sweden in 1842, the travelogue of the journey, *Reiseversuch im Norden*, appeared in 1843 together with the novel *Sigismund Forster*. During an ambitious trip to Egypt and Greece, Ida actually bumped into Grillparzer, who was staying in the same hotel. Predictably, the travelogue *Orientalische Briefe* appeared in 1844, together with the novel *Cecil*. The following year, weary of travel (which was making Bystram ill), Ida von Hahn-Hahn settled in Dresden. In 1846, *Clelia Conti* and *Sibylle* appeared. After her conversion to Catholicism in 1850, she moved to Mainz and lived in a convent there for the rest of her life.

The above list of works and punishing travel schedule suggest that Ida wrote quickly, and indeed, she prided herself on the ease with which things came to her. She was not a writer who planned ahead, but one who thought with her pen; she tended to write as things occurred to her, and as she felt at the time. This is partly why it is so hard to say whether or not she was influenced by any particular writer, though for sheer originality in both life and work (not to mention the religious dimension), she has been compared to Bettina von Arnim. She did not bother to alter what she had already written; her manuscripts had hardly any corrections. Schmid-Jürgens criticises this aspect of her writing, commenting that she did not really bring the concept of 'work' to her writing: '[i]n the strong self-confidence that everything she writes is good lies her major error'.[5] The result is that there are often inconsistencies in her characterisation and even story line.

---

[5] Schmid-Jürgens, *Ida Gräfin Hahn-Hahn*, p. 88.

However, perhaps we can say, in her defence, that it was entirely up to her what she did with her time: she did not seek fame or glory, and only attended the odd soirée to keep in touch with what was going on. Her diffuse method of composition could be seen as a typical example of a woman writing *as a woman*, a point made by Gerlinde Geiger, who mentions Irigaray and Cixous in this context.[6] However, in my view, Ida von Hahn-Hahn – blissfully unaware of any theoretical correctness[7] – was not using 'woman-speak' so much as descending to the occasional lapse in style.

Ida von Hahn-Hahn's tendency to waffle provided a measure of justification for the many attacks on her creative ability. The two novels *Sibylle* and *The Countess Faustine* caused such offence to Fanny Lewald that she wrote her enormously successful spoof on Ida's writing, *Diogena (Pseudonym). Roman von Iduna H… H…* in 1847, as already discussed in Chapter Three. In the first novel, Sibylle grows up adoring her older brother, though he treats her condescendingly, as the reader is informed: '… actually, I was Heinrich's doll.'[8] Sibylle's family are carried off in swift succession – father, brother and sister in one page – and she is left in the company of her now much-enfeebled mother and various servants, with her collection of books by Scott and Byron. The music teacher, Fidelis Sedlaczech, teaches her to appreciate music and art. Having been brought up a strict Catholic, he cannot respond, years later, to Sibylle's amorous approaches even though he is in love with her throughout the novel. Her first husband, her cousin Paul, to whom she is betrothed at the age of fourteen and whom she marries the following year, had at first been engaged to her older sister, now deceased. Paul is devoted to his bride, but the more he shows affection, the more Sibylle realises that she does not love him. 'I was in love with the idea of love – not with Paul'.[9] They have a daughter whom they name Benvenuta, though she is actually not welcome; Sibylle had wanted a boy. Sibylle falls in love with her husband's friend, Otbert Astrau, and marries him after the death of Paul. Astrau is a cold and shallow man. Always longing for love but never finding it, Sibylle lives separated from Astrau and journeys with the teenager Benvenuta to Italy, where a young man falls in love, not

---

6   Gerlinde Geiger, *Die befreite Psyche. Emanzipationsansätze im Frühwerk Ida Hahn-Hahns (1838–1848)*, Frankfurt am Main, Bern and New York, 1986, p. 36.
7   Toril Moi used the phrase 'theoretical correctness' to highlight the current orthodoxy in feminist academic discourse in a talk delivered to the Radical Philosophy conference *Torn Halves*, London, 9 November 1996.
8   Ida von Hahn-Hahn, *Sibylle. Eine Selbstbiographie*, 2 vols, Berlin, 1846, I, p. 22.
9   Hahn-Hahn, *Sibylle*, I, p. 71.

with Benvenuta, as both women assume, but with Sibylle. In a rather grotesque scene, Sibylle begs Wilderich to marry her daughter, who dies as a result of her disappointment (on her mother's birthday, All Souls' Day, which has a general curse upon it). The many deaths, the slavish devotion of men to Sibylle – except for those in whom she is interested – place the novel in a sentimental category, even allowing for the misunderstanding of health issues (Sibylle blames herself, at the end of the novel, for failing to listen to her heart, which is now taking its revenge in the form of heart disease). On the other hand, there is nothing as unbelievable in the novel as Ida von Hahn-Hahn's own real-life experiences. In addition, Sibylle's marriage when she is only fifteen to virtually the only young man she has ever seen (apart from Fidelis) makes its own comment about the contemporary marriage arrangements in high society, as well as on the remoteness of Ida von Hahn-Hahn's native Mecklenburg, where the novel is set.

In *The Countess Faustine*, the heroine's name alone is sufficient to alert us to the fact that she will be engaged upon a quest. Although she appears to be independent, and is a proficient painter, many men find themselves tongue-tied by her, though women like her.[10] She proves to be a life-line for Cunigunde von Stein, who is terrified at the prospect of marrying a man she does not love. Faustine's friend and future husband, Mario Mengen, finds a post for Cunigunde as companion to his sister, at Faustine's instigation. By making Cunigunde's fiancé a model of rectitude, Ida von Hahn-Hahn is able to show, very shrewdly, that some women just cannot face marriage, however upright the man. She is even more clever in setting off Cunigunde's chosen path of celibacy against that of Adele, Faustine's sister, who is completely domesticated and never happier than when making butter. The feminist issues lie in the contrast between the choices made by Cunigunde and Adele rather than Adele and Faustine, though as the latter are sisters, one can be excused for drawing analogies between the domesticated Adele and her restless sister in the same way that analogies can be drawn between the twin sisters in *Zwei Frauen* (1845) and *Zwei Schwestern* (1863).[11] Faustine, for all her spontaneity and strength of purpose, does not find what she requires. Having divorced her husband before the novel begins,

---

[10] Ida von Hahn-Hahn, *The Countess Faustine*, 2 vols, I, London, 1845, pp. 39ff.

[11] See Patricia Herminghouse, 'Seeing Double: Ida Hahn-Hahn (1805–1890) and her challenge to Feminist Criticism' in Ruth-Ellen Boetcher Joeres and Marianne Burkhard, *Out of Line/Ausgefallen: The Paradox of Marginality in the Writings of Nineteenth-Century German Women*, Amsterdam, 1980, pp. 255–78. (The novels in question are discussed on pp. 268–275.)

she has a relationship with Andlau, who unwisely absents himself, so that when Faustine is besieged by Mario Mengen, she finally overcomes her profound reluctance towards remarriage. As Möhrmann points out, Ida von Hahn-Hahn has tried to portray 'the other woman', the one who is 'not just a projection of male desires'.[12] She hopes for everything from Mario, only to find that his views are typically conventional. Even their son Bonaventura cannot make amends for her disappointment, and she begs Mario to let her live in a convent – one belonging to the most austere order of the *vive sepolte*: '… now let me go, my beloved Mario, and, like the anchorites of old, commune with God alone.'[13] Within six months of taking the veil, she is dead.

Helen Chambers has argued that this novel has realist credentials as well as innovatory aspects, such as Mario Mengen's acceptance of responsibility towards his son, when the child could be left in the care of servants.[14] Chambers is right to say that Faustine, though exceptionally gifted, is beset, not by extraordinary problems, but by 'ordinary problems of the relation of the self to the other'.[15] Perhaps she should add that this is quite enough to make a woman go off the rails – one only needs to compare the fate of the artistic Olly in Böhlau's *Rangierbahnhof* (discussed in Chapter Five) to see how impossible women authors found it to portray a woman who could combine family duties with creative endeavour. Furthermore, Mengen's 'new man' image is only visible at the very end of the novel: his patriarchal attitudes, on the other hand, have been well established and rehearsed. A final point one might make is that neither Benvenuta in *Sibylle* nor Bonaventura in *The Countess Faustine* come alive at all. It could be that Ida von Hahn-Hahn herself had conflicting emotions about her handicapped daughter which these portrayals of children are masking. Her contact with Tony was through visits rather than through every-day family life, which with Ida von Hahn-Hahn never really existed, since she was constantly engaged on travels in her life prior to 1851, and never stirred from the convent in Mainz from 1851 until 1880. The label of 'realism' must thus be regarded with some suspicion. A final point regarding both *Sibylle* and *The Countess Faustine* is that they provide internal evidence that Ida

---

[12] Renate Möhrmann, *Die andere Frau. Emanzipationsansätze deutscher Schriftstellerinnen im Vorfeld der Achtziger Revolution*, Stuttgart, 1977, p. 106.

[13] Hahn-Hahn, *The Countess Faustine*, II, p. 334.

[14] Helen Chambers, 'Ein schwer definirbares Ragout: Ida Hahn-Hahn's *Gräfin Faustine*', in *Perspectives on German Realist Writing: Eight Essays*, ed. by Mark G. Ward, pp. 82–94. p. 94.

[15] Chambers, 'Ein schwer definirbares Ragout', p. 87.

von Hahn-Hahn was already considering moving over to the Catholic Church. Sibylle's conversations with Fidelis on the spirituality of Catholicism and Faustine's withdrawal into the convent build a bridge towards Ida von Hahn-Hahn's own decision to convert to Catholicism and withdraw from the world.

For Fanny Lewald, one of the objectionable features about Ida von Hahn-Hahn's novels was their aristocratic choice of character and milieu (though Lewald herself would become pompously sure of her position),[16] and it is clear that she had no compunction at all in publicly humiliating Ida von Hahn-Hahn.[17] This lack of solidarity towards another woman writer, moreover one who had suffered so much, is another instance of the lack of any automatic solidarity amongst women during the century. Though Fanny Lewald became a highly active proto-feminist, and Ida von Hahn-Hahn founded a convent in Mainz affiliated to an order she had come across in Ireland which was dedicated to helping fallen women (a cause Fanny supported in Berlin), there was no central network, no way of knowing who was doing what and, it seems, not much sisterly warmth. Fanny Lewald was just one of a number of critics who made vicious attacks on Ida von Hahn-Hahn during her lifetime, though it must be added that the critics were usually men. Heinrich Heine used a typical brand of sexist joke (of the type which would become familiar to readers of *Simplicissimus* later in the century) when he penned the following comment:

> Oh, women! ... When they write, they have one eye on the paper and the other on a man, and this is true for all women writers with the exception of Gräfin Hahn-Hahn, who only has one eye.[18]

Part of Fanny Lewald's success with *Diogena* was that she had chosen an appropriate moment to attack aristocrats: 1848 would

---

[16] Konstanze Bäumer, 'Reisen als Moment der Erinnerung: Fanny Lewalds (1811–1889) "Lehr und Wanderjahre"', in Boetcher Joeres and Burkhard, eds, *Out of Line/Ausgefallen*, pp. 137–157, p. 154f.

[17] Van Munster in *Die junge Ida Gräfin Hahn-Hahn* writes (p. 188): '*Diogena* ought to be valued higher than Ida Hahn's average output and it would be easy to applaud this fine example of Fanny Lewald's literary talent, if only the work did not speak with a tone of the most personal, touchy and small-minded revenge.' Van Munster assumes that Fanny Lewald was still slighted because Heinrich Simon had rejected her love in favour of Ida, and there may be something in this theory, although by this time Fanny was in love with Stahr, whom she had met in Rome in 1845. Since the original idea for the satire came from him, the chief motive is more likely to be that Fanny wished to impress Stahr.

[18] Heinrich Heine, 'Geständnisse' in *Sämtliche Schriften in Zwölf Bänden*, ed. by Klaus Briegleb, Munich and Vienna, 1976, XI, p. 453.

soon bring with it the (unsatisfied) demands for democracy which would repel Ida and make her despair of her native land. Though one could be forgiven for asking why on earth men like her father and husband had any claim to be the élite of the land, Ida von Hahn-Hahn never challenged the status quo in society, and bitterly disapproved of any criticism of the aristocracy. The post-revolutionary state of the country, coupled with the fact that Bystram had died in 1849, led her to turn her back on the first forty-five years of her life as being full of useless pomp and show. She refused to allow her publishers to bring out a collected edition of her works because she could now only agree with ten percent of what she had written.

Ida von Hahn-Hahn had plenty of admirers as well as detractors, amongst them Fürst Pückler-Muskau, though one has to doubt how much of his praise was genuine. Suspicions had been raised that Pückler might have been the author of *Diogena*, though these were swiftly laid to rest by Varnhagen von Ense.[19] Nevertheless, Ida von Hahn-Hahn had been referred to as a 'female Pückler-Muskau',[20] not something he would automatically welcome even if he meant his fulsome praise of her work when he began a correspondence with her in September, 1844. Pückler had corresponded flirtatiously with Bettina until the latter had taken him at his word and visited him. Now nearly a decade older and wiser (he was fifty-nine in 1844), Pückler, who had already met Ida and had read her first two novels (without liking them), wrote to her to congratulate her on *Sigismund Forster*, which had appeared in 1843 and which he liked very much. There followed the obligatory yet insincere invitation to visit Muskau (1 October, 1844). By 2 March, Ida had seen through him: 'You, dear Fürst, always up in the air, easy, broad-minded [*umfassend*], versatile, *vague*: me with my feet on the ground, awkward, one-sided, serious, something I struggle to overcome [*das harrassiert mich zu überwinden*].'[21] What actually caused the rupture in their correspondence was Pückler-Muskau's attempt to get the thirty-year-old writer to visit him alone when they happened to be staying in the same hotel in Dresden. He wrote to her on 31 March 1845:

[19] Unpublished letter from Varnhagen von Ense to Ida von Hahn-Hahn, handwritten manuscript in the Preußische Staatsbibliothek, cited in Van Munster, *Ida Gräfin Hahn-Hahn*, p. 188f.
[20] Van Munster, *Die junge Ida Gräfin Hahn-Hahn*, p. 176; also on p. 88, n. 2, Van Munster mentions that Ida was pleased about the comparison.
[21] In Hermann Conrad, ed. *Frauenbriefe von und an Hermann Fürsten Pückler-Muskau*, Munich and Leipzig, 1912, p. 261.

If you want to see me alone, receive me alone (because your *cavaliere servente* bothers me, and if you have shown him my letters I do not want anything more to do with you), so, alone, in the evening, with lamp turned low or lying on your sofa with half-closed eyes, preferably in the dark, because I am *very* abashed towards you, more shy than a badly brought-up child.[22]

Ida von Hahn-Hahn, no doubt offended by the slighting reference to Bystram and the whole tenor of this *billet-doux*, merely sent Pückler her visiting card in reply, and retaliated by using his characteristic traits for Astrau in *Sibylle*, published the following year.

We should note in passing the flippant treatment meted out to Ida von Hahn-Hahn by Pückler's partisan biographer, E. M. Butler, who now comments on the end of this friendship:

He [Pückler] may sometimes have intruded on her thoughts during her noisy and theatrical devotions in the convent she founded at Mayence [Mainz], for she became a Roman Catholic in 1850 and free-lance nun a few years later, who was by no means immured from the world.[23]

Clearly, Ida Hahn-Hahn has never lacked detractors and is never likely to; Butler's comments are a gratuitous slur on Ida von Hahn-Hahn, since she has provided no evidence at all that Ida thought lustfully about Pückler or any other man, for that matter, whilst in her retreat; however, one must add that Butler is not alone in taking the sort of view which automatically marginalises Ida von Hahn-Hahn and her writing.[24] Geiger has pointed out that a more recent critic of Ida von Hahn-Hahn, Gerd Oberembt, in an impressively thorough analysis of her work from the standpoint of the sociology of literature, has consistently dealt with the writing from a male point of view, so that she emerges as little more than a *Trivialautorin*.[25] Oberembt laboriously tries to pigeon-hole her work with scant regard to other factors. He therefore dismisses her casual attitude towards the art of writing with the criticism that it is 'a surrogate for life', a quotation from *The Countess Faustine* that is brought in as a damnation of the author herself.[26]

[22] Ibid., p. 302.
[23] E. M. Butler, *The Tempestuous Prince: Hermann Pückler-Muskau*, London, New York and Toronto, 1929, p. 163.
[24] Herminghouse gives an overview of the critics in 'Seeing Double', pp. 255–59.
[25] Geiger, *Die befreite Psyche*, p. 30.
[26] Gerd Oberembt, *Ida Gräfin Hahn-Hahn. Weltschmerz und Ultramontanismus*, Bonn, 1980, p. 19.

As discussed in the Introduction, the social conditions which made it possible for women's writing to be spoken of in this way need to be scrutinised before sweeping statements are made. Oberembt sees Ida von Hahn-Hahn as the archetypal aristocrat who fears the coming 'of machinery, democracy, the mass' and wishes to stop progress.[27] Though there is much truth in this comment on the reactionary nature of Ida von Hahn-Hahn's views, she remains of interest as a woman writer who wrote about women's problems, however narrowly defined. In her fictional work, the central problem is nearly always pivotal on love which is not fulfilled; indeed, there is scarcely a happy marriage in her novels. One should view this not as idle *Weltschmerz*, but as an accurate assessment of many women's experiences, including her own. Ida von Hahn-Hahn's refusal to say anything positive about the nascent campaign for women's rights lay in her certitude that women needed to be under the control of men, but treated with respect. Like Lou Andreas-Salomé later in the century, she thought it would be 'laughable' if women tried to ape men at the work-place, since 'it is a man's world'.[28] Hence, the move to Catholicism represented less of a disruption than one might think, though there was a change of emphasis: examples abound of women as patient martyrs, such as the nun Maria Regina.[29] The demand for woman's right to autonomy, however, such as is seen in problematic form in *The Countess Faustine*, is elided after her conversion to Catholicism, the impossibility of divorce within the Catholic Church being glossed over in a manner which scarcely does justice to Ida von Hahn-Hahn's own earlier beliefs in the freedom of the individual; nor is the general tenor of reverence for the Pope convincing for anyone not already a believer.[30]

Paul Haffner, one of the few critics to praise Ida von Hahn-Hahn's later work, claimed that she had wished she had been born a Catholic: for her, it represented authority and above all permanence and stability in a world of decaying values and transient moral positions.[31] Ida von Hahn-Hahn was accepted

[27] Ibid., p. 18.

[28] Hahn-Hahn, *Sibylle*, II, p. 223: '[t]he world is made for men, so they can fight, compete ... This can be ruinous for a woman and will always make her suffer.'

[29] Eda Sagarra, 'Gegen den Zeit-und Revolutionsgeist. Ida Gräfin Hahn-Hahn und die christliche Tendenzliteratur im Deutschland des 19. Jahrhunderts' in *Deutsche Literatur von Frauen*, II, pp. 105–119, p. 118.

[30] See, for example, Ida von Hahn-Hahn, *Der briete Weg und die enge Straße. Ein Familiengeschichte*, 2 vols, Mainz 1877, I, p. 9.

[31] Paul Haffner, ed., 'Gräfin Ida Hahn-Hahn. Eine psychologische Studie', in *Frankfurter zeitgemäße Broschüren*, I, Frankfurt am Main, 1880, pp. 133–166, p. 149.

into the Catholic faith in Berlin by Wilhelm von Ketteler in 1850
and followed him to Mainz when he was promoted to the position
of Bishop that same year.[32] On Church advice, she burnt her
boats by publicly repudiating her earlier works in a newspaper
announcement in April 1851; the Church also encouraged her to
take up her pen in the Catholic cause.[33] She immediately
published the highly controversial tract *Von Babylon nach Jerusalem*
(1851), in which she made propaganda for the Papist
ultramontanism which was sweeping through Europe after the
1848 revolution, and which can be seen in its turn as a reaction
to the liberal tendency of German Catholicism. Though the
tract was construed as confessional in nature, Eda Sagarra has
pointed out that it revealed nothing of Ida von Hahn-Hahn's
personal reasons for her conversion (which she never divulged),
its 'aggressively bigotted tone'[34] merely constituting a panygyric
for Catholicism.

For Ida von Hahn-Hahn, the next thirty years would be taken
up with making keen propaganda for the Catholic Church
through novels and tracts which, written with her customary
speed, were well received within the ranks of the believers: *Maria
Regina* (1860), *Doralice* (1861), *Zwei Schwestern* (1862), *Peregrin*
(1864), *Eudoxia die Kaiserin* (1866), *Die Erbin von Kronenstein* (1868),
Die Geschichte eines armen Fräuleins (1869), *Die Glöcknerstochter*
(1871), *Die Erzählung des Hofrats* (1872), *Vergib uns unsere Schuld*
(1874), *Nirwana* (1875), *Eine reiche Frau* (1877), *Der breite Weg und
die enge Straße* (1877) and *Wahl und Führung* (1878). These
'Tendenzromane'[35] were all written while Ida von Hahn-Hahn
inhabited a small room in the convent of the Sisters of the Good
Shepherd, living in poverty like those who had actually taken the
veil. In 1853 she had written a pamphlet entitled *Ein Büchlein zum
guten Hirt* to describe the Order, which was dedicated to the
'betterment of repenting sinners',[36] in other words, fallen women.
Ida von Hahn-Hahn tended to view these women from the *male*
perspective of her mentor, Bishop Ketteler, as women who had

---

[32] According to Herminghouse, 'Seeing Double', p. 263 n. 10, Ketteler had been
a republican at the Frankfurt National Assembly of 1848 but left it because the
plan for German unification excluded Austria. He became known for his social
Catholicism.

[33] Herminghouse, 'Seeing Double', p. 265.

[34] Sagarra, 'Gegen den Zeit- und Revolutionsgeist', p. 113.

[35] Ibid., p. 118.

[36] Ida von Hahn-Hahn, letter to Cardinal Diepenbrock, 14 April 1851, in
Briefwechsel des Kardinal Diepenbrock mit Gräfin Ida Hahn-Hahn, ed. by Dr Alfons
Nowack, Munich 1931, p. 62.

infringed the patriarchal code rather than as victims of that code, and Schmid-Jürgens comments drily that 'basically, the novels all work on the same principle – believers are good, non-believers are bad; the former are rewarded, the latter punished'.[37] Patricia Herminghouse, in a detailed examination of the difference in treatment of the twin sisters in the novels *Zwei Frauen* and *Zwei Schwestern*, comments:

> ... the moral, political and social decomposition of Germany is deplored ... [e]ven though events in the outside world loom larger than they did in the earlier novel, one looks in vain for any overt sign of concern for the particular situation of women at any level of the world which Hahn-Hahn portrays – a surprising omission, given what she must have glimpsed through the mission of the Sisters of the Good Shepherd.[38]

Though from today's perspective, such an omission can be viewed as virtual heresy in terms of women's emancipation, Ida von Hahn-Hahn wrote *for* women, albeit acccording to her own lights. As Sagarra has shown, her works were seen as valuable reading matter for pious young ladies and matrons and were even read in Protestant circles, in spite of their 'fanatic Catholicism'.[39] Ida von Hahn-Hahn remained resolutely true to her conversion and busied herself with good works in the town; the loss of a large section of her former readership does not appear to have troubled her serenity in the least. When she died, her funeral was suitably low-key, her coffin being carried by six nuns to its burial place.[40]

Eugenie Marlitt, 1825–1887

Friedericke Christiane Henriette Eugenie John, who adopted the pseudonym Eugenie Marlitt when she began to write in 1863, was born in the small Thuringian town of Arnstadt in 1825 to parents who became much impoverished through the business incompetence of the father, who was only saved from ruin by his brother. It would become Eugenie's driving ambition to re-establish the fortunes of the family. Eugenie's mother was from a rich family and was gifted musically; when Eugenie, who had

---

[37] Schmid-Jürgens, *Ida Gräfin Hahn-Hahn*, p. 114.
[38] Herminghouse, 'Seeing Double', p. 275f.
[39] Sagarra, 'Gegen den Zeit- und Revolutionsgeist', p. 118.
[40] Haffner, 'Gräfin Ida Hahn-Hahn', p. 133. The funeral took place on 14 January, 1880, in Mainz.

distinguished herself at school, showed musical promise – she had an excellent voice – her mother approached the ruling family at Sonderhausen for help. The Fürstin Mathilde von Schwarzburg-Sonderhausen took the sixteen-year-old Eugenie under her wing, and for three years she was trained by the best teachers the court could provide. In 1844, Fürstin Mathilde gave Eugenie the choice of either being trained to teach or trained to perform. Probably because she thought she could amass more money by performing, she chose to become an opera singer, and was sent to Vienna for three years. This was a period she later looked back on as her 'golden age'.[41] It was also the period in which she stored up experiences which she would later use as plots, since when she actually did take up writing, she lived as a virtual recluse. In 1848, Vienna was a turbulent place and Eugenie, though herself keenly interested in the demands of the democrats, left Vienna temporarily; on her return, she finished her training and tried in vain to gain employment in Vienna. Once again she was rescued by the Sonderhausen family and, having been made *Kammersängerin* (the equivalent of having a Royal charter) by the Fürst von Sonderhausen, she gave performances at Linz, Lemburg and Graz as well as at court in Sonderhausen. The terrible truth now had to be faced that she could not conquer her stage fright; it plagued her performances and could have been a psychosomatic cause of the deafness which now set in.[42]

Eugenie Marlitt left no diary and hardly ever wrote a letter. The events of her life are therefore difficult to document with certainty. However, it was probably the Sonderhausen family who paid for her to have (unsuccessful) medical treatment for her deafness in Munich. While there, she stayed with the 'Young German' writer Bodenstedt, who encouraged her to consider taking up writing, though it would be a further eleven years before she did. In 1852, Fürst Sonderhausen divorced his wife Mathilde, and Eugenie Marlitt went to live with her as her companion; for most of the time they lived in Munich. More plots for novels were stored away for future use. Potthast has hinted that Eugenie refused a suitor at this time because she felt she had to provide financial assistance to her family.[43] At all events, Fürstin Mathilde was ill and in straitened circumstances and Eugenie, who was not well either, eventually had to leave her and

[41] Berta Potthast, 'Eugenie Marlitt. Ein Beitrag zur Geschichte des deutschen Frauenromans',PhD Diss., Bielefeld, 1926, p. 8.
[42] Cornelia Brauer, ed., *E. Marlitt. Maienblütenhauch. Die Gedichte*, Rudolstadt and Jena, 1994, p. 54f. (Nachwort).
[43] Potthast, *Eugenie Marlitt*, p. 9.

go back to Arnstadt. At the age of thirty-eight, ill, deaf, single and penniless, she crawled back home, having failed to achieve every single goal she had set herself. 'Home' was now the home of her favourite brother, Alfred, a teacher at Arnstadt grammar school, who also had his widowed father under the same roof. In desperation, Eugenie Marlitt sent her first two literary efforts to Ernst Keil, the editor of the magazine *Die Gartenlaube*, a publication which published the 'Young German' writers; it welcomed work from liberals and *Freidenker*. Louise Otto-Peters worked for the magazine for a while, and it published the work of Levin Schücking and Rudolf Gottschall. Keil, who had actually spent a year in prison in 1852 for his revolutionary activities, would become a close personal friend to Eugenie, one of the very few who could visit her at home without being turned away.

Eugenie Marlitt's very first story, *Schulmeister Marie*, was rejected as being too similar in style to Auerbach, but her first novel, which she had begun in Munich and which her brother persuaded her to finish, *Die Zwölf Apostel*, was accepted and printed under the name of 'E. Marlitt'. The publishers assumed they were dealing with a male author and asked him (!) to send more scripts; Eugenie now sent them *Goldelse* with the request that it be published as a book, as *Die Gartenlaube* tended to print only shorter stories. Instead, in 1866 it was printed in its full length in the magazine, to extraordinary acclaim from the readers of *Die Gartenlaube* and from reviewers. In swift succession more novels followed, all greeted with the same near-ecstatic reception from readers: suddenly, Friedericke John, alias Eugenie Marlitt, was rich, and, hiding behind her *nom de plume*, a world celebrity. For the next few years, Eugenie Marlitt produced virtually a novel a year; all were published in *Die Gartenlaube*, to whom she remained faithful for every one of her works. These now included the short story *Blaubart* (1866), *Das Geheimnis der alten Mamsell*[44] (1867), *Reichsgräfin Gisela* (1869) and *Das Heidenprinzeßchen* (1871). As a 'loyalty bonus', Eugenie was allowed to keep the entire proceeds from the hugely successful *Reichsgräfin Gisela*, and with it she had a house built – an impressive villa, 'Marlittsheim', with views of the Thuringian forest she loved so much. When, in 1871, she and her family finally moved in (Alfred, his wife and children and her father), Eugenie was in a wheel-chair, crippled with gout; she hardly ever left the house and was in constant pain. Not surprisingly, her

---

[44] The word *Mamsell* often meant housekeeper, but this would not fit the context here as the woman in question is of good birth. See also n. 58 below.

output slowed down: *Die Zweite Frau* appeared in 1874, followed
by *Im Haus des Kommerzienrats* (1876), *Im Schillinghof* (1879),
Amtmanns Magd (1881) and finally *Die Frau mit den Karfunkelsteinen*
(*The Woman with the Sparkling Gems*) (1885).

During the late 1860s and the 1870s, the reviewers tended to be
as favourable towards Eugenie Marlitt as the rest of her
readership, and it is no surprise to find Fürst Pückler trophy-
hunting. After the final 'adieu' from Ida von Hahn-Hahn,[45]
Pückler's laddish existence had continued unabated; he had
reluctantly sold Muskau, and now lived at Branitz near Kottbus.
His amorous affairs, whether semi-serious or 'lighter dallyings',[46]
are well-documented by Butler; suffice it to say that at eighty-two
(he was to die three years later, in 1871), Pückler managed to enter
into correspondence with Eugenie Marlitt; his first letter, actually
addressed to 'Eugenie John', begins: '[b]eautiful unknown dearest
authoress' and is dated 9 February 1868; Pückler signed himself
'The Author of the *Letters of a Dead Man*' (*Briefe eines Verstorbenen*
had first appeared in 1830), with a postscript asking for an answer
to be directed to his intimate friend, Fürst Pückler-Muskau.[47] For
once, Eugenie replied to one of the many letters of admiration she
received; she responded to Pückler's joke by addressing the letter
'[t]o the author of the *Letters of a Dead Man*' and thanked him for
his interest in her work. But she ignored his strong hint that he
would like to visit her, and was adamant in remaining *incognito*.
She could just about be persuaded to reveal her address: at the
head of her letter of 4 March 1868, she put 'Arnstadt, Thüringen',
and said she had scarcely been able to force her pen to write it. She
told Pückler that if he wanted to know her opinion about things,
he should read *Goldelse*, since her views expressed in that novel
were incontrovertible.[48] She also responded to his curiosity by
informing him at the end of the same letter that her family called
her 'Eugenie'. Her joy at the birth of Alfred's son, reported in her
letter of 5 May 1868, shows that Butler did get one important
thing right when she wrote that Eugenie Marlitt was 'very happy
in her modest domestic circle'.[49] Pückler was indifferent to such
domestic details. Eugenie John was resisting his charm offensive,
and was therefore a challenge. By July, Pückler was pressing for a
meeting, but Eugenie had other things on her mind – the baby

---

[45] Letter from Ida von Hahn-Hahn 24 March, 1845: '[o]h, what a child you are...
Adieu, dear Pückler!'. In *Fraueuenbriefe*, ed. Conrad, p. 297.
[46] Butler, *The Tempestuous Prince*, p. 166.
[47] In *Frauenbriefe*, ed. Conrad, p. 307.
[48] Ibid., p. 316.
[49] Butler, *The Tempestuous Prince*, p. 172f.

had died.[50] She now had to catch up with her work, which her own bad health and the birth (and death) of her nephew had interrupted – though *Die Gartenlaube* never actually insisted on deadlines. By the end of the year, the correspondence had fizzled out.

The correspondence with Pückler provides us with a very rare insight into the world of Eugenie Marlitt in the first person. It is astonishing that she should state so openly that her views are expressed in her writing. Unlike Ida von Hahn-Hahn, who wrote as the mood took her, Eugenie carefully planned her novels and wrote them in complete secrecy: Alfred and his wife never knew what she was writing until she had finished, and was ready to read extracts aloud to them. The fact that they called her 'Eugenie', and that she named her dream-house 'Marlittsheim', demonstrates the extent to which she identified with her fiction. As we have seen, Ida von Hahn-Hahn has been accused of using literature as a 'surrogate for life'; Eugenie Marlitt, too, seems to have fled into literature as a safe haven from a life which had many disappointments. Her secrecy with her work is also an indication of how important it was to her. Keil having died in 1878, Eugenie was left somewhat exposed to bad reviews in the early 1880s, though her books continued to sell well; we can therefore understand how devastated she was in 1885, when there was a veritable attack on her work from several quarters, and subsequent defence from her admirers. The instigator of the attack was Hermann Friedrichs, the editor of the *Magazin für Literatur des In- und Auslandes*, who had stated that Eugenie's work contained a subterranean sensuality which could be harmful to young people.[51] Nothing could be calculated to hurt the shy and high-minded Eugenie more deeply; in addition, she had badly injured herself in an accident in her wheelchair in 1883, and never properly recovered. Like Ida Hahn-Hahn, she did not reply to her critics, but continued to work on her last novel (*Das Eulenhaus*, which she left unfinished) and fell ill in 1886, dying the following year. Now practically forgotten, she was much loved by her readers and her death was marked by numerous tributes from all over the world.

Since Eugenie Marlitt herself indicated that her values were to be gleaned from *Goldelse*, it is worth considering this novel from that perspective. There is much in the novel that reminds the reader of the type of Romantic setting familiar from the work of

[50] Pückler-Muskau, *Frauenbriefe*, p. 347f.
[51] Potthast, *Eugenie Marlitt*, p. 20.

Caroline de la Motte Fouqué: an aristocratic home is the setting
for most of the action, though when aristocratic behaviour is
described it is full of hypocrisy of the type deplored by Ida von
Hahn-Hahn. Eugenie Marlitt branches away from both these
writers, however, since her bourgeois heroine marries the
aristocratic Herr von Walde at the end of the novel, a
dénouement quite unthinkable in the work of de la Motte
Fouqué, and a happy ending out of key with the renunciatory
longing to be found in Ida von Hahn-Hahn's works. However,
the emancipatory import is lessened by the fact that Frau Ferber
is found to have an aristocratic title at the end of the novel,
though the family decide not to use it, the name Ferber having
stood them in good stead hitherto. The story is a rags-to-riches
romance with gothic interludes: the heroine, Elisabeth Ferber, is
locked in the tower of a disused convent by her uncle's ward,
Bertha, who believes 'Goldelse' to be her rival for the affections of
Hollfeld. Hollfeld turns out to be a seducer and charlatan who
has made Bertha pregnant and is determined to conquer
Goldelse. Herr von Walde has so little confidence in his own
ability to attract the fresh young Goldelse that he gives his
permission for the marriage between Hollfeld and Goldelse,
which prompts Goldelse to resist the match in a melodramatic
scene. There are many misunderstandings to be cleared up, but
the ending is unashamedly happy. Since the above synopsis might
wrongly give the impression that the novel has little depth, I shall
now focus on three other women characters.

Herr von Walde has a disabled sister, Helene, who is madly in
love with the worthless Hollfeld; von Walde's mother, Helene's
sister-in-law, Baroness Lessen, has moved into the castle in the
absence of Herr von Walde and has effectively taken it over,
sacking servants who do not share her pietism, which Marlitt
portrays as a veil for total philistinism. Goldelse, representing the
authorial view, declares herself to be a good Lutheran and is not
intimidated by the revivalist rhetoric which seeks to forcibly
produce converts and which her mother, Frau Ferber, has
denounced as 'a very bad method of awakening the spirit of
Christianity in the people'.[52] Goldelse is, however, intimidated by
Baroness Lessen's many manoeuvres to make her conscious of
her inferior position as employee (she plays piano duets with
Helene). Baroness Lessen has a spoiled daughter, Bella, who
torments her puppy and is in general as objectionable as can be
imagined, though Marlitt has the good sense to lay the fault at the

[52] Eugenie Marlitt, *Goldelse*, Leipzig, 1866, p. 58.

door of the mother. When Baroness Lessen is sent packing at the end of the novel, Herr von Walde provides a small annuity for the 'proper' education of Bella; Marlitt thus manages to slip in her own argument in favour of women's education, which is that it is a matter of values rather than knowledge. Helene's weakness is both physical and emotional; she is entirely enslaved by her attachment to Hollfeld, and dies an early death, providing another instance of the typical escape into mortal sickness of the frustrated or hysterical nineteenth-century heroine.

If the aristocratic women all behave with weakness and hypocrisy in contrast to Goldelse and her worthy mother, the portrayal of the peasant girl, Bertha, is particularly interesting. This naive girl has promised Hollfeld not to breath a word of their relationship to anyone, and has pretended to be completely dumb, though she is forced to relinquish this masquerade when her pregnancy can no longer be concealed. Eugenie Marlitt, unlike nearly every other novelist of her time, refuses to condemn Bertha and marries her off to a working man who emigrates with her to America – an astonishingly merciful fate. Most fallen women in nineteenth-century literature are considered too polluted to be allowed to live: even Mrs Gaskell felt that the eponymous Ruth had to die, as did Esther in *Mary Barton* (1848). Bertha, whose characteristics have been portrayed as sinister if not outright evil, is shown to be a victim and set back on her feet. In this portrayal at least, Marlitt shows herself to be remarkably ahead of her time.

In assessing the actual achievement of Eugenie Marlitt's novels, the comments from her contemporary, Friedrich Kreyßig, are indicative of how an author can be condemned by faint praise. Kreyßig writes:

> When she speaks of the major issues of the time (her preferred topic and directly tendentious when it comes to questions of religion) she speaks as a genuine woman, using the language of feeling rather than that of thought.[53]

Frau Ferber's comment (n. 52, above) indicates that Marlitt did indeed condemn the heartlessness of the neo-pietists. Her criticism of hypocrisy in religion, which Kreyßig finds tendentious (and which is itself tendentious), was ignored by Butler when she commented on 'the sentiment which drips from these books'.[54] Yet Pückler, whom Butler admires, also allows plenty of his own

---

[53] Friedrich Kreyßig, *Vorlesungen über den deutschen Roman der Gegenwart*, Berlin, 1871, p. 294f.

[54] Butler, *The Tempestuous Prince*, p. 173.

sentiment to emerge in his writing – in fact, his letters can
occasionally sound maudlin – reminding us that sentimental
phrases were often regarded as *polite* at the time. Furthermore,
though Eugenie was labelled sentimental because that was a
woman's sphere, Pückler felt perfectly able to discuss his old friend
Schopenhauer with her (letter of 25 February 1868), playing on
the notion of immortality which had been mooted in his initial
letter to Eugenie and which was virtually his signature tune, for all
his banter (a rift in his nature which, as Butler points out, the
perspicacious Bettina had spotted[55]). Eugenie replied in kind,
dismissing Schopenhauer's life-denying philosophy roundly; true,
she argues for the existence of the soul, but she also demonstrates
that she has grasped the essence of Schopenhauer's pessimism,
belying the notion that women cannot argue rationally.[56] Indeed,
her female characters are sometimes coolly logical (for example,
Felicitas in *Das Geheimnis der alten Mamsell*), leaving the emotional
struggle to men. Any sentimentality of style which Eugenie Marlitt
employed was, then, quite deliberate; it is pitched at achieving a
'pot-boiler' with a keen view towards captivating the reader's
interest: one must not under-estimate the very strong financial
motivation Eugenie Marlitt had. She therefore had to please her
readers by giving them what they wanted; if she had indulged in
too-radical political statements or even too-rational philosophical
excursions, her sales would have suffered. There is no denying the
uniform nature of the themes, which centre on clashes between
the aristocracy (often decadent and nearly always conservative in
politics and hypocritically evangelical in religion) and the
bourgeoisie (liberal in politics and *Freidenker*), with the latter
usually coming off best unless they are too cocksure.[57]

A favourite plot involves people of the opposite sex, who dislike
each other at first, falling in love by the end of the novel. This
happens in *Das Geheimnis der alten Mamsell*, where the old lady
herself, another mad woman in the attic,[58] Tante Cordula Hellwig,
is the fairy godmother to Cinderella/Felicitas, a *Spielerskind* (child
of entertainers), who turns out to have aristocratic blood in her
veins after all. As usual, Marlitt savagely attacks showy religious
piety, which acts as a cover for vanity and avarice, all gathered

---

[55] Ibid., p. 298.
[56] In *Frauenbriefe*, ed. Conrad, p. 317 (letter dated 4 March 1868).
[57] Potthast, *Eugenie Marlitt*, p. 32.
[58] Cordula Hellwig is consigned to the attic rooms of the Hellwig house and
   treated as an outcast when by rights, she should have been allowed to marry
   the legal owner, now long dead, who turns out to have been a distant relative
   of Felicitas. This is the 'secret' of the title.

together in the person of Frau Hellwig, who, like a typical philistine, thanks God that her family are not entertainers.[59] Frau Hellwig's son Johannes has to experience a steep learning curve when forced to acknowledge the hollowness of his mother's faith and actions, and the sincerity of Felicias' beliefs and actions. He is delivered from his quandary as to how to marry a women so far beneath him in social terms when Felicitas is acknowledged to be a member of a noble family, though the story of her mother, cast out from her family because she chose to marry a Polish entertainer, is a fascinating sub-plot which shadows the similarly iniquitous treatment meted out to Tante Cordula by her family. Eugenie Marlitt reinforces the message that neo-pietism can do nothing but harm through her comments on Felicitas' education. Frau Hellwig cuts Felicitas off from formal learning because of her lowly station, but Tante Cordula educates the young girl in secret, so that her intellect ultimately puts Frau Hellwig, her so-called benefactress, to shame. The plea for a child-centred education is made through the reference to Defoe's *Robinson Crusoe*, the only book Rousseau considered fit for the young Emile to read; the servant Heinrich spirits this away from Johannes' brother, Nathanael, for Felicitas to read.[60] Nathanael dies in a duel, leaving debts for his pious mother. *Das Geheimnis der alten Mamsell* ends with a familiar device in Marlitt's fiction: the plot is engineered so that that the male and female protagonists marry, having overcome seemingly insuperable hurdles. In *Die zweite Frau* (the most overtly religious of the novels), the couple are actually married: having married for convenience, and having quarrelled until a parting seems inevitable, they find they are actually deeply in love. Although this plot might seem dated today, and there were plenty of critics ready to jeer, it must have seemed like a fairy-tale ending, pure escapism for the thousands of women trapped in similarly loveless matches.

Eugenie Marlitt, the middle-class woman in a world where things were changing fast, supported the new liberal ideals but had benefited too much from the generosity of the aristocracy to simply turn her back on it as a class. By the same token, she had seen the aristocracy, with all their foibles, at close quarters for too long to simply portray them in idealised terms. If Fanny Lewald's own early radicalism was seen to cool, Eugenie Marlitt's political stance represented a shrewd sitting on the fence, though she welcomed Bismarck and the new Reich, founded in 1871. The

---

[59] Eugenie Marlitt, *Das Geheimnis der alten Mamsell*, 2 vols, Leipzig, 1867, I, p. 75.
[60] Ibid., p. 90.

same guarded tone is maintained in Eugenie's comments on women's rights. Single, she still puts forward the idea of marriage as woman's goal, but comments bitterly on the misery caused by arranged marriages. She did not agree with feminist calls for equality or the vote, and like Ida von Hahn-Hahn, thought that women ought to take second place to men. Her female characters are the helpmeets of their busy husbands, whom they soothe with their magnificent singing voices or other talent: Johannes Hellwig relishes the thought of giving his wife the frequent command, 'Fee – a song!'. Eugenie Marlitt's ideal woman appears to be the *Hausfrau* who is sufficiently interested in current affairs that she can converse with her husband on an intelligent level. However, she did support the idea that women should be allowed to work and be properly paid. In many of these aspects she is annoyingly conservative to the reader of today, but would appear mainstream or even rather radical to her contemporaries. Levin Schücking was no doubt right to highlight her capacity to understand female psychology; she had grasped (probably unconsciously) that women had internalised certain attitudes which might well go against their own interests, but which they, like everyone else, believed to be basic for upholding the morals of society. Perhaps more importantly, Schücking added that Eugenie Marlitt could always tell a good tale.[61] We should note the close identification she made with her work: it gave her back her self-esteem as well as her lost voice.

Marie von Ebner-Eschenbach, 1830–1916

With the Catholic Marie von Ebner-Eschenbach we return to the same social level as Ida von Hahn-Hahn as a point of departure, but encounter an aristocrat with the liberal concerns hinted at in Eugenie Marlitt's work. With Marie von Ebner-Eschenbach, however, social critique is incorporated fearlessly into the text. She shared Eugenie Marlitt's scrupulous attitude towards her writing, which had been encouraged by her stepmother, Gräfin Xaverine Kolowrat, who was her father's fourth wife. His first wife had died after two years of marriage, leaving him rich; his second, the bourgeois Marie Vockel, had borne him two daughters, the younger of whom, Marie, cost her her life. He then married a Baroness, Eugenie Bartenstein, who proved to be an excellent stepmother. She bore three more children, the last of

---

[61] Cited in Potthast, *Eugenie Marlitt*, p. 13.

whom died, and she herself died a few weeks after the birth. Xaverine therefore inherited four stepchildren and had three of her own, only to die of puerperal fever after the birth of her youngest child. Graf Dubsky had loved each of his wives, and each had been kind to his motherless children. One really does not need a theory – beyond a recognition of the Grim Reaper in action – to work out part of the reason why women of childbearing age were marginalised during the nineteenth century, and I would argue that the quite different birth control methods and neo-natal health care of today have made women's lives so dramatically different that it is a false equation to continue to speak in terms of biological determination, as though it meant the same thing in the last century as it does in the writing of some feminists today. Women have choices today scarcely dreamed of by the women under discussion.

After the death of Eugenie Bartenstein, Graf Dubsky's sister, Helene, moved into the family home at Zdislawitz, then part of the Austro-Hungarian empire, and was frequently visited by her son Moritz, who was fifteen years older than his niece Marie. Nevertheless, in spite of a warning from Xaverine about how unwise it was, in view of in-breeding, for such close relatives to marry,[62] Marie very early made the decision that 'Uncle Moritz' was the only man she could possibly marry. In the event, and to their great regret, they remained childless. They were engaged in 1845 when she was fifteen, and married in 1848; as Moritz was an officer in the Imperial (Austrian) army, their wedding had to be brought forward in case Moritz was summoned for duty in the war Austria was fighting in northern Italy (the same war which made it impossible for the sick Adele Schopenhauer to return home from Italy). In the event, they were first stationed in Vienna, before being posted to the remote Klosterbruck. Moritz was sympathetic to his wife's first attempts at writing and was an invaluable guide and even teacher to her, in the same way that Marcus Herz had been towards his young bride, but in Marie's case, she herself had chosen her much older husband, and had married purely for love. Marie was lucky that both her stepmother and her husband encouraged her aspirations as a writer. Indeed, Xavarine even sent her stepdaughter's early poems to Grillparzer for his comment. Grillparzer replied favourably, but it would be another two decades before he and Marie von Ebner-Eschenbach actually met. He then became a close personal friend to her until his death.

---

[62] Marianne Wintersteiner, *Ein kleines Lied, wie fängt's nur an … Das Leben der Marie von Ebner-Eschenbach*, Heilbronn, 1890, p. 90f.

More so than any other writer mentioned, apart from Bettina, Marie von Ebner-Eschenbach was politically aware if not politically active. She and her husband lived through the rumbling trouble of the question of Prussia's co-operation with Austria, which was settled when Austrian troops were defeated by the Prussian armies at Königgrätz on 3 July 1866. This was a severe setback for the Prussian liberals who had still hoped that a *Großdeutschland* policy would prevail. Bismarck was careful to exercise leniency towards the defeated Austrians, fearing their revenge as a powerful Austro-Hungarian Eastern power, but he was severe towards their former allies in Northern Germany.[63] Of course, Austria was now excluded from the North German Federation, which accepted the rule of the king of Prussia (Schleswig-Holstein had been regained from Denmark in 1866). However, it was not until after the successful war against France in 1870 that the Second Reich was formed in the following year. In the midst of this turmoil, which had ended with a victory for the aristocratic Junkers and the conservatives in Prussia and the trouncing of the Austro-Hungarian empire, Marie von Ebner Eschenbach's family were engaged in military conflict at crucial moments. Marie's husband Moritz was called to serve in the Adriatic and her brother-in-law, Graf August Kinsky, was wounded in Bohemia, on Austria's northern front, shortly before the battle of Königgrätz. Marie and Moritz were of the same mind over this conflict: they thought the Emperor Franz Josef, who was now forced to abdicate, had led Austria into a meaningless conflict which had burdened the country with a reparation debt of twenty million Thalers. Moritz was particularly disaffected with the army, and in 1870, he wrote a pamphlet which exposed the conditions within the military. This caused offence amongst his superiors and forced him into early retirement. The von Ebner-Eschenbachs were not the only aristocrats who desired to see social change. Many Austrian liberals from all sections of society still felt German; Eduard Devrient wrote to Marie on the subject in 1866, just after the Peace Treaty had been signed in Prague:

> In particular, we Austrians must prove, through our works, that we belong to Germany ... We are who we are through the German spirit [*Geist*], through German culture and in spite of any attempt they might make to get us to forget it.[64]

---

[63] Ernest K. Bramsted, *Germany*, New Jersey, 1972, p. 148.
[64] Wintersteiner, *Ein kleines Lied*, p. 239.

The above explains the noticeable insistence on the part of Marie von Ebner-Eschenbach that she is a German writer.

Marie von Ebner-Eschenbach was still only eighteen when she witnessed the revolutionary events in Vienna as a young bride. With bourgeois blood from her mother's side, she was fascinated by the struggle of the bourgeoisie to shake off the injustices imposed by the aristocracy, but she was interested in all echelons in society, including the lower orders. Her works cover a wide range, and indeed, she began as a dramatist. Unfortunately, her early plays were not well received, partly because of a certain inevitable immaturity and partly because she had strayed into an acknowledged male domain where women practitioners were unwelcome; women writers were more likely to be tolerated in poetry or prose. As Edith Toegel informs us, Marie von Ebner-Eschenbach's family, including her 'otherwise immensely supportive husband', were uncomfortable with her high-profile failures: '... the family censoriousness grew as her dramas became a public embarrassment to their well-known name'.[65] Reluctantly, Marie von Ebner-Eschenbach turned away from drama, but not before she had written a dozen plays, her first (if we believe her denial that *Aus Franzensbad* [1858] was a serious work), *Maria Stuart in Schottland* (1860), clearly inspired by Schiller. She wrote numerous short stories which appeared either singly or in various collections, the first in 1875 (*Erzählungen*), and several novels, including two acknowledged masterpieces, *Das Gemeindekind* (1877) and *Unsühnbar* (1890); she also wrote a good deal of mediocre work, some of which has not been preserved, since she was quite capable of destroying a whole manuscript if she thought it let her down. The list of her publications is extensive, and includes letters, reviews and a somewhat fictionalised autobiography. Ferrel Rose has pointed out that the animal stories, such as *Krambambuli* (1883) and *Der Fink* (1897) are worthy of note and have been unjustly neglected.[66] Marie von Ebner-Eschenbach was thus a prolific and confident writer, corresponding with the foremost men of letters of the day, such as Paul Heyse, who greatly admired her work, singling out the novella *Die Freiherrin von Gemperlein* (1883) as a treasure.[67]

In spite of the liberal views adopted by the von Ebner-Eschenbachs, they were not radicals, and Marie can be viewed as

[65] Edith Toegel, 'The "Leidensjahre" of Marie von Ebner-Eschenbach: Her Dramatic Works' in *German Life and Letters*, 46, 2, 1993, pp. 107–119, p. 117.

[66] Ferrel V. Rose, *The Guises of Modesty: Marie von Ebner-Eschenbach's Female Artists*, Columbia SC, 1994, p.10.

[67] Anton Bettelheim, *Marie von Ebner-Eschenbach*, Berlin, 1900, p. 127f.

conservative in her portrayal of the domestic role of women. However, in her own life, rather than through her female characters, she had a very positive effect on early feminists. As Helga Harriman has pointed out, it was of prime importance that she was awarded an honorary doctorate in 1900 – 'the first ever awarded to a woman by the University of Vienna'.[68] Although Moritz encouraged his wife's fictional output, its sheer scale indicates that there must have been times when she had to choose between family duties and creative work. Rose suggests that some of Marie von Ebner-Eschenbach's headaches could have been caused by the frustration of being thus thwarted (Annette von Droste-Hülshoff's migraines may have been of the same ilk).[69] Toegel blames much of the tangible frustrations in Marie von Ebner-Eschenbach's works on the early embargo placed on her career as dramatist:

> The recurring themes of alienation, frustration and resignation in her later prose works which we admire today reveal a persistent inner struggle which had an impact on her psyche as a woman and as a writer. It is very likely that her misadventure in the drama intensified the broad range of feelings of exclusion and disillusionment that recur throughout the later works, especially in the women characters and their relations with men.[70]

Part of the trouble was that, as we have seen, women writers tended to identify very closely with their writing, but they also accepted the domestic role of woman as the correct one. Therefore, any sentiment experienced that went against this assumption was construed as, quite simply, wrong. This was bound to cause an inner conflict, but they often failed to recognise it as such, and even if they did, they still did not think that the campaign for women's rights had anything to offer them. Thus, when the first *Frauenverband* was formed by Louise Otto-Peters in 1866, neither Marie von Ebner-Eschenbach nor Eugenie Marlitt made any attempt to join. Nevertheless, Marie von Ebner-Eschenbach's solidarity with other writers was tangible, and she did join the Verein für Schriftstellerinnen und Künstlerinnen in Vienna. Through this, she helped other writers such as the poet Betty Paoli. Furthermore, Marie von Ebner-Eschenbach's very conservatism was something that attracted mainstream 'moderate' feminists, who sought to re-evaluate the woman's position in the

---

[68] Helga Harriman, 'Marie von Ebner-Eschenbach in Feminist Perspective' in *Modern Austrian Literature*, 18, 1, 1985, pp. 39-37, p. 29.
[69] Rose, *The Guises of Modesty*, p. 5f.
[70] Toegel, 'The "Leidensjahre" of Marie von Ebner-Eschenbach', p. 110.

home and therefore applauded her resolute refusal to write in a 'mannish' way. This was the stance taken by the feminist Marie von Bunsen in 1893.[71] Marie von Ebner-Eschenbach was, in Toegel's phrase, 'foremost a humanist'.[72]

In the light of the sheer wealth of Marie von Ebner-Eschenbach's literary output, one is tempted to make a comparison with Dickens; indeed, there are elements in the realist novel, *Das Gemindekind*, such as very convincing dialogue and character-isation, which are equal to what Dickens produced. In terms of characterisation, too – one thinks of *Oliver Twist* (1838) – *Das Gemeindekind* is convincing. Pavel and Milada are at the mercy of their parish when their father commits a murder and their mother is imprisoned because she is too inhibited to speak up for herself at the trial. Their experiences show most adult members of their village in a bad light: only the school-teacher, Habrecht, who is himself ostracised, shows kindness towards Pavel; Milada is adopted by the local baroness for her own selfish reasons. The rural setting is similar to that of Keller's *Romeo and Julia auf dem Dorfe* (1876). In its vivid portrayal of the way a community can scapegoat an individual, it points forward to the work of two twentieth-century Austrian writers, Max Frisch (*Andorra*, 1962) and Friedrich Dürrenmatt (*Der Besuch der alten Dame*) (*The Visit*) (1956). The criticism of bigoted religion is also fearless, especially with regard to the nuns who systematically browbeat Milada by suggesting that through her self-denial, atonement can be made for her father's double crime: he commits suicide in jail. She is also encouraged to think that by refusing to see her much-loved brother, he, too, will be helped. By using redemption as a theme, Marie Ebner-Eschenbach might have intended an allusion to Chateaubriand's *René* (1802), though in that story, René's sister is an adult who enters a convent of her own free will, to atone for her love for her brother. While Chateaubriand describes the austerity of convent life with a certain prurience, most of the women writers discussed in this book – especially Eugenie Marlitt, Louise Otto-Peters and Marie von Ebner-Eschenbach – mention convents with a tone of displeasure, possibly because any unpleasantness which takes place is inflicted by women on other females; the exception is Ida von Hahn-Hahn, who values the convent as a place of retreat.

---

[71] Marie von Bunsen, 'Marie von Ebner-Eschenbach – unsere erste Schriftstellerin,' in *Die Frau*, I, 1893, 33. Cited in Rose, *The Guises of Modesty*, p. 18.

[72] Edith Toegel, 'Entsagungsmut', in *Forum for Modern Language Studies*, 28, 2, 1992, pp. 140–149, p. 142.

The criticism of the aristocracy is as telling in this story as is the exposure of the bitterly small-minded malice of the peasants in the village. The whole tragedy of Milada's death comes about because the baroness, who, as representative of the local nobility in the story, is someone who ought to know better, refuses to take both brother and sister under her wing. She rejects Pavel in the full knowledge of the destitution he will undergo as a child of the parish: '[c]hildren whose education is paid for by the parish cannot tell A from Z after twelve years'.[73] Meanwhile, Milada is brought up in the lap of luxury until the pious baroness decides that Milada must go to the convent school for a 'proper' education; the village school is not good enough, and Pavel attends it. The baroness wants Milada to forget her brother and her lowly origins. At the convent, Milada's unfortunate family history is used as a weapon to torment her. The lack of *noblesse oblige* on the part of the baroness eventually exacts its toll, since Milada, deprived of Pavel and overwhelmed by the sense of her own guilt which is inculcated in her by the nuns, pines to death in the convent. As indicated, the vicious nature of such religious indoctrination approximates to child abuse, and is portrayed in every sense as realistically as the child abuse at Lowood School in Jane Austin's *Jane Eyre* (1847), where bullying similarly purports to be religious zeal. While the reader is constantly aware of the desperate plight of the siblings, for whom separation itself is the worst form of cruelty, constant references to the children's mother are also made throughout the novel. This unhappy woman's wasted life is an important sub-theme in the text.

In addition, Habrecht's clandestine attempts to study natural science provide strong hints that science is at a turning point, and one can surmise that Moritz von Ebner-Eschenbach, who devoted himself to the study of natural science in his retirement, had influenced his wife's interest in this area. Like Elizabeth Gaskell's Job Legh in *Mary Barton*, Marie von Ebner-Eschenbach's Habrecht shows that it is not a prerogative of the wealthy to be excited by the new discoveries in the natural sciences. Typically, the narrow-minded Catholic priest upbraids the teacher for his interest in science, whereas the reader comes to view the dogmatic practice of religion in the novel as not much better than hocus-pocus. The teacher has been branded as a dabbler in witchcraft for having had an experience of 'death', and then coming back to life after three days. Such comas and near-death

---

[73] Marie von Ebner-Eschenbach, *Gesammelte Werke*, ed. by Edgar Groß, 9 vols, Munich 1956–1961, 6, *Das Gemeindekind*, p. 13.

experiences are, of course, well-documented nowadays and are not confused with death itself, though the person in question often feels, like Habrecht, that they have died and indeed, gone to heaven before being resuscitated.[74] The comparison between the teacher's recovery from his coma – in his coffin! – and the resurrection of Christ after three days, gives the reader a strong clue that the teacher is the true Christian in this novel; his very name, meaning 'In the Right', shows the authorial stance.

Marie von Ebner-Eschenbach's wit and irony should not be seen as despair, but as clear-sightedness in highlighting human foibles. From her standpoint as a Catholic,[75] she exposed religious zealotry amongst Catholics just as Eugenie Marlitt exposed the hypocrisy of a similar faction of neo-pietists from her standpoint as Protestant. I have 'dropped names' in this evaluation of Ebner-Eschenbach in order to underline the point that, at her best, Marie von Ebner-Eschenbach is a writer of the first rank whose work can be legitimately compared with that of other leading writers of the day. Her contemporaries recognised her achievements, especially her refusal to descend to sentimentality and pathos.[76] Though not inspirational in the way that Rahel was to other women writers, women academics have found her a rich source for their critiques.[77] Her writing reaches a standard of excellence not attained by Eugenie Marlitt or Ida von Hahn-Hahn, though as mentioned, some of her work is of a markedly lower standard than her best (not a unique thing in a writer). Like Eugenie Marlitt and Ida von Hahn-Hahn, she was enormously popular in her day, though it goes without saying that the readers of all three novelists were predominantly women.

---

[74] Ebner-Eschenbach, *Das Gemeindekind*, p. 148.

[75] For further discussion see Eda Sagarra, 'Marie von Ebner-Eschenbach and the tradition of the Catholic Enlightenment' in *Austrian Studies*, 2, 1991, pp. 117–131 *passim*.

[76] Albert Soergel, *Dichtung und Dichter der Zeit. Eine Schilderung der deutschen Literatur der Zeit*, Leipzig, 1911, p. 449.

[77] For example, Karoline Demant, 'Marie von Ebner-Eschenbach's Kindergestalten', PhD Diss., Vienna, 1922 and Gertrud Gerber, 'Wesen und Wandlung der Frau in den Erzählungen Marie von Ebner-Eschenbachs', PhD Diss., Göttingen, 1945. Religious studies include Sister M. Rosa, *Catholic Atmosphere in Marie von Ebner-Eschenbach: Its Use as a Literary Device*, Washington, 1936. These are just samples of the wealth of early critical enquiry from women inspired by Marie von Ebner-Eschenbach.

Hedwig Dohm. Reproduced with kind permission of the Bildarchiv preußischer Kulturbesitz.

5

THE WOMAN QUESTION

Feminism and Nationalism

The work of J. G. Fichte has made the topic of early German nationalism controversial, though in the hands of many writers it was innocuous enough, if one considers the work of Kleist or Eichendorff or the blandly moral contributions of the women writers whose work appeared in the collection *Iduna. Schriften deutscher Frauen* (1820), amongst them, Fanny Tarnow. By the end of the century, the neutral term 'nation' had given way to the term *Volk*, and nationalism itself had developed into an automatic genuflection towards the concept of German superiority. Within the context of early German feminism, a certain nationalism, or love of one's country, is common currency. Louise Otto-Peters' libretto for Wendelin Weißheimer's opera *Theodor Körner* (1872) deals with an overtly patriotic theme, since it treats the historical event of the liberation of German territory at the battle of Leipzig in 1813, the context for the heroic death of the poet Körner in 1813. The *Vorspiel* ends with a predictable call to arms – 'Germany must win or go under',[1] and the second act goes out to a chorus of Luther's hymn, 'A mighty fortress is our God'. The scene shifts from Vienna to Leipzig, reminding us of the traumatic defeat suffered by Austria at the hands of Prussia at the battle of Königgrätz in 1866. In the same year, Louise Otto-Peters founded the Allgemeiner Deutscher Frauenverein (General German Women's Association), generally agreed to mark the beginning of the women's movement in Germany.

[1] Louise Otto-Peters, *Theodor Körner. Oper*, Munich, 1872, p. 12.

The Legal Position of Wilhelmine Women

The history of German feminism is paradoxical in that the curve of development went backwards rather than forwards. The demands of the 1848ers have already been discussed in Chapter Three; and it would have been logical for the charitable reforms instigated to have continued alongside women's intellectual and social emancipation. What actually happened, as Richard Evans has outlined in his path-breaking work *The Feminist Movement in Germany 1894–1933* (1976),[2] was that the statute of 1851 (the *Vereinsgesetz*, repealed only in 1908), which forbade women from attending political assemblies, was simply one of a number of repressive measures which were passed in the wake of the failed revolution. In spite of the reforms in Prussia early in the nineteenth century, the *Preussisches Allgemeines Landrecht* of 1794 (Prussian Civil Code), a highly authoritarian and patriarchal code, was still in place, and had been adapted by most German states as the century wore on, with Prussia mushrooming to prominence until the foundation of the Reich in 1871 rationalised what was already *de facto*: Prussian hegemony in Germany. Evans comments on the essentially feudal nature of German society under Bismarck:

> It was indeed highly anomalous for one of the world's richest and most rapidly expanding industrial societies to be ruled by an elite whose source of wealth and power, ideology and whole outlook were essentially pre-industrial.[3]

Evans points out that it was not a matter of the king (from 1871, Kaiser) doing as he liked: he was 'in reality an instrument of a wider ruling class: the Junkers, the land-owning aristocracy of Prussia.'[4] The Junkers, in turn, dominated the army and the rest of the Establishment. Amongst this class, the male view of a woman's role as helpmeet to her husband and moral educator of her children was virtually unchallenged. It goes without saying that the position of working women was given scant consideration.

The final draft of the *Bürgerliches Gesetzbuch*, the Civil Code which in 1896 replaced the antiquated *Allgemeines Gesetzbuch* (though it officially came into force only on 1 January 1900), was not a great improvement for the legal status of women in the Reich, something which Marie Stritt, amongst others, had

---

[2] Richard Evans, *The Feminist Movement in Germany*, London, 1979, p. 11.
[3] Ibid., p. 7.
[4] Ibid., p. 4.

foreseen. In 1898, Stritt addressed the BDF[5] General Meeting held in Hannover, with the following remarks:

> It is almost two years since the new Civil Code was agreed and promulgated in the German Reich, and since the heated battles fought by German Campaigners for Women's Rights to acquire a worthier position for women within the Code. True, these battles resulted in a few notable achievements, but regarding the most emphatic demands of the campaigners, and in spite of the support of so many right-thinking and humane men, the end result was a *defeat* for us.[6]

In 1890, the first draft of the Family Law section of the Code had been set out for comment; this was followed by a second draft. Sera Proelß and Marie Raschke duly tore it to bits, section by section,[7] whilst Adele Gamper rightly pointed out that it lacked all originality.[8] Lily Braun, anticipating the defeat of the feminists' aspirations, delivered a polemic in 1895 whereby she called for women's full rights as a matter of basic human rights within modern society:

> We demand a thorough-going change in the civil code, which restricts women more severely in Germany than in any other country.
> We demand the application of the principles of a modern state – of general human rights – for the other half of humanity, women.[9]

Braun was not alone in thinking that the effect of the new Code was more punitive towards women in Germany than in other countries. Cäcilie Dose and Alma Kriesche, who had also attended the General Meeting of the BDF (6 October 1898) and who were in the process of writing a commentary on the new Code, were asked by the Assembly to draw up a wider report into the situation of women in other countries. The details of their findings are extremely telling. France, Spain and Italy are seen to have fair laws as a direct result of the Code Napoleon; Austria and Sweden appear in a good light compared to Denmark, where the married

5   The Bund Deutscher Frauenvereine (Federation of German Women's Associations) was founded in 1894; its first President was Auguste Schmidt.
6   Marie Stritt, *Das bürgerliche Gesetzbuch und die Frauenfrage. Vortrag gehalten auf der Generalversammlung des Bundes deutscher Frauenvereine in Hamburg im Oktober, 1898*, Frankenberg, 1900, p. 3.
7   Sera Proelß and Marie Raschke, *Die Frau im neuen bürgerlichen Gesetzbuch. Eine Beleuchtung und Gegenüberstellung der Paragraphen des Entwurfes eines bürgerlichen Gesetzbuchs für das deutsche Reich (2. Fassung) nebst Vorschlägen zur Änderungen derselben im Interesse der Frauen*, Berlin, 1895, *passim*.
8   Adele Gamper, 'Die Zukünftige Stellung der deutschen Frau im Recht', no. 9 of *Lose Blätter im Interesse der Frauenfrage*, Dresden, 1895, p. 4.
9   Lily von Gizycki (Braun), *Die Bürgerpflicht der Frau*, Berlin, 1895, p. 23.

woman has a legal status no better than a child or servant;[10] even
Russia, like England (*sic*) and the United States, is praised for the
rights afforded to women.[11] Not surprisingly, Germany is held to
have a poor record on women's rights compared to other
countries. What rankled in particular with the writers of the survey
was that German husbands still had the right to dispose of property
brought into the marriage by their wives (Paragraph 1,395),
though working women now had the right to their own earnings.
There was even a Paragraph (1,356) which stated that the wife had
a duty to work in the home *and* in her husband's business (my
italics), if this was appropriate to their matrimonial circumstances –
a fact which explains much of the 'moral majority' atmosphere
encompassing the role of housewife in Wilhelmine Germany, since
it was actually viewed as a legal duty. In general, the law was as
patriarchal as the one it succeeded, with the father retaining 'the
right and the duty to care for the person and property of the child'
(Paragraph 1,626), and with all apparent reforms for the most part
being merely window-dressing. In some important areas, notably
divorce, the position for women had worsened.[12]

Louise Otto-Peters 1819–1895

Louise Otto was born in Meissen, the daughter of a state-
employed lawyer and the grand-daughter (on her mother's side)
of a painter employed by the royal porcelain concern in Meissen.
The family were culturally sophisticated and politically liberal.
Louise had three older sisters and enjoyed a happy home life.
The family supported the political events of July 1830, which in
Meissen involved the Saxon Parliament's revocation, in 1831, of
the process of legally viewing women as wards; up to this point,
women had needed a male guardian for every transaction, since
a woman's signature did not count in law. A widow had not been
allowed to carry on her deceased husband's business, even if it
had been jointly run. One result of the new law was that married
women had a right to their own property. Hedda Zinner, whose
novel *Nur Eine Frau* (1984) is a literary biography of Louise Otto-
Peters and follows her film of that title (made in 1958), points out
that Herr Otto, a well-regarded lawyer who had fought for this

---

[10] Cäcilie Dose and Alma Kriesche, *Die Stellung der Frau und Mutter im Familienrecht
der außerdeutschen Staaten und nach den Bestimmungen des Neuen Bürgerlichen
Gesetztbuches für das Deutsche Reich*, Frankenberg, 1900, p. 15.

[11] Dose and Kriesche, *Die Stellung der Frau und Mutter*, pp. 16-24.

[12] Evans, *The Feminist Movement in Germany*, p. 13f.

law to be repealed, explained it to his daughter in terms of what it would mean for her as a woman: '[n]ow the world is open to you Louise, my child, the whole world.'[13] Though the world was not quite ready for such optimism, Louise Otto was able to profit from the encouragement of her father, whose favourite she was; sometimes he called his youngest daughter a boy, to tease her. He made Louise party to his political ideas at an early age, something that was highly unusual at the time, even in such an enlightened family. The death of her parents and an older sister in 1835 (when Louise was just seventeen) and of her fiancé, the writer Gustav Müller, in 1841, were hard blows for Louise Otto and her other two sisters, neither of whom had reached the age of majority (i.e., twenty-one). The three girls nevertheless decided to live together in a country setting as idyllic as it was daring.[14] After the loss of her fiancé, Louise Otto began her to make her first literary attempts.

From the internal evidence to be found in Louise Otto's substantial early novel *Schloß und Fabrik* (1846), she must have read and been inspired by Engels' *Die Lage der arbeitenden Klasse in England* (*The Condition of the Working Class in England*) (1845 – first published in English in 1887). *Schloß und Fabrik* was at first banned for its overtly radical political content, but after Louise had appealed to the censor, it was published with a number of pages excised, notably those most overtly dealing with Communism and the state repression of subversive activity. For many years, the novel was believed to have vanished, though after the partition of Germany following the Second World War, it was regarded as part of the East German socialist heritage, and profiled in Zinner's film *Nur eine Frau*. Shortly after the *Wende*, Johanna Ludwig unearthed a copy of the first edition in Bochum and, by consulting the censorship files, has managed to reconstruct an unexpurgated edition which was brought out in 1996. The novel still has political interest and is well written on the whole, though Louise Otto – still only twenty-six at the time of writing – occasionally allows in a gushing tone which suggests inexperience rather than lack of talent. There are sections where too much is made of a description of the scenery, or of a meaningful glance, and there is the occasionally jarring description of frantic activity, with characters rushing in or out of rooms. There are also so many coincidences that these become

---

[13] Hedda Zinner, *Nur eine Frau*, Berlin, 1984, p. 21.

[14] Renate Möhrmann,'Bio-Bibliographischer Anhang' in *Frauenemanzipation im deutschen Vormärz. Texte und Dokumente*, Stuttgart, 1978, p. 254.

farcical. However, the dialogue is convincing and the authorial tone of gentle satire to mock both the outmoded values of the aristocracy and the gauche social climbing of the *nouveau riche* comes off splendidly.

Louise Otto does not make the mistake of trying to impose her critique of industrialisation onto a city – Germany had no industrial cities comparable to Manchester. Instead, she sets her story in an unnamed mountainous region of Germany where the pleasant countryside, much enjoyed by the Hohenthal family of the country estate, mocks the wretched operatives in the nearby mill who can rarely enjoy it. The daughter of the stately home, Elisabeth Hohenthal, and the daughter of the mill-owner, Pauline Felchner, have been educated together in an exclusive boarding school and have sworn to do charitable deeds whenever they can. For Pauline, wretchedness is all around her and she is only able to take palliative measures against it because of her father's tyrannical belief that the workers will take advantage if they are treated softly. The children in particular suffer from the long hours in the mill, and there is a plea thoughout the book that they should be educated properly. Felchner does not actually pay starvation wages, but any operatives who meet with misfortune find there is no safety net of charitable relief. The descriptions of the plight of the suffering poor are similar to those found in Elisabeth Gaskell's *Mary Barton* (1848) and Charles Dickens' *Hard Times* (1854) of the same period or Zola's *Germinal* (1885) of several decades later.

In these social novels, authorial sympathy with the sufferings of the industrial workers is intimately linked with authorial fear of violence: the ultra-radicals – as yet there was no distinction to be made between socialists or Communists – are invariably spoken of in tones of condemnation, and the brutalised workers are seen as prey to the *agent-provocateur* and worker-agitator. In *Schloß und Fabrik*, Wilhelm, swayed by a half-understood Communism as Étienne Lantier will be in *Germinal*, supersedes the moderate Franz Thalheim as leader of the hands, though the latter is not ostracised to the extent that Stephen Blackpool is under similar circumstances in *Hard Times*. As in all the novels of social change mentioned above, Louise Otto, through her mouthpiece Pauline, urges concessions for the workers out of enlightened self-interest as well as out of sheer pity for the suffering poor, and in order to avoid bloodshed. The potential dangers of the workers' propensity to rely on the demon drink to assuage their despair is a salient theme, one also found repeatedly in Engels, though he was, incidentally, much more prone to comment on the loose morality of the workers than Louise Otto.[15] Engels was, of course, convinced that revolution was the only answer to industrial strife;[16] his collaboration with Marx was about to begin with the publication of the *Communist Manifesto* in 1848. Louise Otto, like other authors of social novels, hopes that 'crazy Communism' ('der wahnsinnige Kommunismus')[17] will not be heeded and revolution will be avoided. Eventually, since the voice of reason is manifestly not heeded, in *Schloß und Fabrik* as elsewhere, the worst happens: the mill-workers erupt in a torrent of machine-breaking.[18]

Though Louise Otto cannot have known that her novel would be the first of a series on similar themes in Britain, there is the common denominator of Engels. Engels had visited England when he wrote *The Condition of of the Working Class in England*, though he never guessed at the time that he would spend the rest of his life there (from 1850 to 1895). His book was written in German and published in Germany in 1845, with a postscript 'An English Strike', published in *Das Westfälische Dampfboot*, in January/February 1846. In addition, in August 1845, the first volume of the *Rheinisches Jahrbuch zur sozialen Reform* was published, only to be swiftly banned. The publishers were instructed to recall the books, but in Leipzig, the contraband volume went the rounds, and its readership included Louise Otto and her circle. Included in the volume were articles by Engels, Moses Heß, Hermann Semmig and Karl Grün. The subject matter was the suffering of the poor in Germany, though the volume also contained the 'Adresse der deutschen Arbeiter in London an Johannes Ronge'. Louise Otto maintains the cross-channel link in *Schloß und Fabrik*, referring specifically to Felchner's newly acquired English machines, the pride of his factory, imported complete with a hapless English engineer to explain their workings. With the machines comes trouble, reminding us that one only had to say 'Manchester' in Germany in 1846 to conjure up industrial unrest, strikes and Communist plots, but there was also plenty of trouble closer to home. The uprising of the Silesian weavers had been brutally put

---

[15] Friedrich Engels, *The Condition of the Working Class in England*, trs. and ed. by W. O. Henderson and W. H. Chaloner, Oxford, 1971, p. 111: '[t]hey are deprived of all pleasures except sexual indulgence and intoxicating liquors.'

[16] Engels, *The Condition of the Working Class in England*, p. 294: 'The only possible outcome of this state of affairs is a great revolution, and it is absolutely certain that such a rising will take place.'

[17] Otto-Peters, *Schloß und Fabrik*, ed. by Johanna Ludwig, Leipzig, 1996 [1846], p. 248. The phrase is used by Gustav Thalheim, who conveys the authorial opinion on political matters in the novel.

[18] Otto-Peters, *Schloß und Fabrik*, p. 297.

down in 1844, and the police had gunned down Protestant
protesters when the heir-apparent to the Saxon throne, the strict
Papist Prinz Johann, appeared in Leipzig on 12 August 1845.
Louise Otto personally witnessed the aftermath of this 'Leipziger
Gemetzel'[19] (Leipzig massacre), the German equivalent of
Manchester's Peterloo (1819). The Leipzig massacre was inspired
by religious rather than social disquiet, which will be further
discussed below, but there were plenty of reports of brutality
towards the industrial poor which no doubt shocked Louise Otto,
as did accounts of the harsh treatment of the striking railway
constructors near Minden in July 1845, who were violently forced
back to work on a viaduct.[20]

As with the other novels of social realism already mentioned,
Schloß und Fabrik has a good deal of love interest, which is skilfully
interwoven into the plot. Elisabeth falls in love with the radically
minded Graf Jaromir Szariny, and Pauline falls in love with her
father's head operative at the mill, the trusty Franz Thalheim,
who is ultimately unable to stem the revolutionary tide which is
whipped up in the men. The aristocratic pair, happily engaged at
the end of the story in spite of initial parental opposition to their
match, are seen to survive, indicating that the higher orders can
and will evolve, but Pauline and Franz die in a hail of bullets fired
by police who have come to stop the rioting hands from
ransacking Felchner's property. The dramatic climax of the novel,
culminating in their death, delivers a timely warning to
industrialists that if they wish to keep their wealth (and here, the
destruction of Felchner's 'treasure', Pauline, is intended as a
salutory lesson), then change must come. Although Pauline
perishes, hers was the voice of reason and hers is the moral
victory. The portrayal of two politically interested women, one
from the aristocracy and one from the bourgeoisie, is thus both
affirmative in terms of women's emancipation and timely in terms
of what was really going on in the Germany of the *Vormärz*.
However, there is also a disappointment for feminists in the
negative portrayal of Amalie Thalheim, the estranged wife of
Gustav Thalheim (formerly a teacher of Elisabeth and Pauline at
their boarding school). She is accused of almost ruining at least
two lives – those of her husband and of Jaromir, her former fiancé
– and is portrayed as full of self-inflicted resentment and

---

[19] Indeed, Louise Otto had interrupted a journey to stay with relatives at nearby
      Gohlis, and wrote a poem about the massacre dated the same day (12 August
      1845) entitled 'Vom Dorfe'.
[20] Johanna Ludwig, editorial *Nachwort, Schloß und Fabrik*, p. 361.

bitterness without there being any investigation into why she should come to this pass. If she is as wicked as the authorial voice suggests, and as ugly as the other women (such as Aurelie) testify, how can it be that the attractive Szariny, decades earlier, was devastated when she broke off her engagement to him in order to marry the rising liberal Gustav Thalheim? This contradictory characterisation, at least, justifies Christine Otto's remark that the novel is one of Louise Otto-Peters' least informative on the position of women.[21] However, the portrayal of Pauline and Elisabeth must be used to offset this criticism.

From 1843, Louise Otto contributed to the journals and periodicals *Vaterlandsblätter, Unser Planet, Wandelsturm* and *Leuchtturm* under the *nom de plume* Otto Stern for the sake of good form, but abandoned the pseudonym in favour of her own name in 1845. She used her maiden name for all her fictional work, continuing to publish as 'Louise Otto' even after her marriage in 1858.[22] The radical tone set in *Schloß und Fabrik* continued in her collection of poems in 1847, *Lieder eines deutschen Mädchens*, and in her editorial articles in the journal she published from 1849 to 1851, the *Frauen-Zeitung*. Though many of the contributions from her other collaborators seem tame, dated, contradictory or even reactionary today, the publication itself was a landmark and was viewed as such by contemporaries, both admirers and detractors. In fact, the success of this publication, which was hailed by revolutionary groups such as the Arbeiterverbrüderung (Workers' Brotherhood), founded in 1848, is to be gauged by the determination of the authorities to have it suppressed.[23] In the final edition, Louise Otto-Peters made her *adieu* to her readers as follows:

> It [the reason for the closure] is contained in Paragraph 12 of the Prussian Civil Code: responsibility for the editorship of a newspaper can only lie with male residents of the Kingdom of Saxony'.[24]

Clearly, Louise Otto-Peters saw her place as belonging to the 1848 revolutionary movement; in particular during this period, she

---

[21] Christine Otto, *Variationen des 'poetischen Tendenzromans'. Das Erz hlwerk von Louise Otto-Peters*, Pfaffenweiler, 1995, p. 255.

[22] Since Louise herself in her long widowhood laid emphasis on being known as Louise Otto-Peters, it has become customary amongst her admirers to use her full name, though all her literary works referred to in this section appear in libraries under the name 'Louise Otto'.

[23] See Ute Gerhard, Elisabeth Hanover-Drück and Romina Schmitter, eds, *'Dem Reich der Freiheit werb' ich Bürgerinnen'. Die Frauen Zeitung von Louise Otto*, Frankfurt am Main, 1980 [1849-1852], p. 30.

[24] Louise Otto-Peters in *'Dem Reich der Freiheit werb' ich Bürgerinnen'*, ed. by Gerhardt, Hanover-Drück and Schmitter, p. 331.

tried to organise working women to demand better conditions and, according to Cordula Koepcke, was remarkably successful.[25] Her writing also reflects these efforts, with her poem 'Die Klöpplerinnen' ('The Lacemakers') becoming as popular as would the song in Hauptmann's *Die Weber* (*The Weavers*) (1892).[26] Christine Otto has drawn attention to Louise Otto-Peters' connection with the liberally-minded 'German Catholics', who encouraged the aspirations of the 1848'ers, and thereby indirectly fostered the early women's movement, since 40% of the membership of the groups comprising freethinkers and 'German Catholics' were women.[27] Christine Otto refers to the leader of the 'German Catholics', Johannes Ronge, as a 'contemporary media star'[28] who had Louise Otto-Peters' full support; in particular, she agreed with the rejection, by the 'German Catholics', of Papal supremacy.[29] During this period of revolutionary upheaval, Louise met the writer and political rebel August Peters, the son of a weaver; they became engaged in 1849, but Peters was arrested for his political activity and condemned to death. He was imprisoned until 1856. It was not until 1858 that they were able to marry; tragically, Peters was to die in 1864 after a long illness. Henriette Goldschmidt remarked, in a public address in 1868, that Louise Otto, having lost her parents at a young age, was now completely bereft.[30] It is to her credit that the bereaved Louise gathered her forces to found the Allgemeiner Deutscher Frauenverein in Leipzig in 1866; she was President of this association, with Auguste Schmidt, until her death in 1895. In 1866, the first journal of the association, *Neue Bahnen*, was published with Louise Otto-Peters and Auguste Schmidt as its editors. This was immediately swamped with enquiries from women trapped in unhappy marriages, mostly asking about their legal status.[31]

As already noted, Louise Otto-Peters' early writing, chiefly poetry and plays, showed a predilection for nationalism which was part and parcel of the revolutionary climate of the 1840s, putting her in company with men such as Herwegh, Kinkel,

[25] Cordula Koepcke, *Frauenbewegung zwischen 1800 und 2000. Was sie war, was sie ist und was sie werden soll*, Gerabronn and Ansbach, 1979, p. 41.

[26] Ibid., p. 38.

[27] Otto, *Variationen des 'poetischen Tendenzromans'*, p. 286, n. 51.

[28] Ibid., p. 288.

[29] Ibid., p. 287.

[30] Henriette Goldschmidt, *Vortrag gehalten im Frauen-Verein zu Leipzig am 15. Juli 1868*, Leipzig, 1868, p. 16.

[31] Ilse Nagelschmidt and Johanna Ludwig, eds, *Louise Otto-Peters. Politische Denkerin und Wegbereiterin der deutschen Frauenbewegung*, Dresden, 1996, p. 31.

Freiligrath, Blum and Müller. As Ruth-Ellen Boetcher Joeres points out in her discussion of Louise Otto's short story *Drei verhängnißvolle Jahre* (1867), 'German women were indeed joining the ranks of writers in far greater numbers than ever before by the 1840s and 1850s.[32] Boetcher Joeres is at pains to point out the methods by which a woman writer deals with her subject matter differently from a man; for example, scenes of battle are dealt with at one remove.[33] It must be stressed that Louise Otto-Peters' creative work is markedly different in character from her political work. In general, her social critique came to focus on the campaign for women's emancipation, as Clara Zetkin pointed out:

> She wanted to put into practice in and through herself the dream she had had in the 1840s: full equality for her sex; full equality for workers. She thought the likeliest routes to success were through education, culture and organisation.[34]

With unflagging energy, Louise Otto-Peters published titles such as *Das Recht der Frauen auf Erwerb* (1866), *Frauenleben im Deutschen Reich* (1876), *Das erste Vierteljahrhundert des Allgemeinen Deutschen Frauenvereins* (1890), *Der Genius des Hauses* (1869), *Der Genius der Menschheit* and *Der Genius der Natur* (1870).

In *Frauenleben im Deutschen Reich*, Louise Otto-Peters devotes a lengthy section to the 'Frauenfrage', arguing first that it is to be placed 'close beside the social question'.[35] She recapitulates the achievement of the women's movement in making 'even the philistine'[36] aware that some women had to earn their daily bread and would need training – she specifically mentions the new jobs for saleswomen and in post and telecommunications, as well as the openings for women in schools: the routes to teaching posts were, for the Kindergarten, Fröbel's training, and for girls' schools, the *Lehrerinnenseminar* (which both Hedwig Dohm and Franziska zu Reventlow pursued). Posts as nursemaid and governess were becoming less and less sought-after.[37] She restates her former defence (made thirty years earlier) of the seamstresses against whom abuses were rife. These abuses were ignored by the women in genteel society, who used the services of these

[32] Ruth-Ellen Boetcher Joeres, '1848 from a Distance: German Women Writers on the Revolution', *Modern Language Notes*, 97, 1982, pp. 590–614, p. 591.

[33] Ibid., p. 599.

[34] Clara Zetkin, *Zur Geschichte der proletarischen Frauenbewegung Deutschlands*, Frankfurt amd Main, 1971, p. 159.

[35] Louise Otto-Peters, *Frauenleben im deutschen Reich. Erinnerungen aus der Vergangenheit mit Hinweis auf Gegenwart und Zukunft*, Leipzig, 1876, p. 154.

[36] Ibid., p. 156.

[37] Ibid., p. 157.

women but were deaf to any plea for better working conditions
for them.[38] She argues – with every justification – that things had
improved in the intervening years because of the efforts of the
women's movement. With some amazement she recounts that in
the United States, such progress had been made that women
could attend university in some areas and were already going
into professions such as dentistry.[39] In Britain, too, universities
had begun to open their doors to women students, but this would
not take place in most regions of Germany until after the turn of
the century. The document is thus a historical signpost,
rehearsing previous campaigns and looking to the future, as
the title indicates; indeed, the work ends with a utopian view of
equal rights for both sexes. It was not Louise Otto-Peters'
purpose to advocate total equality or even female superiority;
a woman's aesthetic sensibility should not be ignored. She
therefore suggested that girls should be encouraged to take up
cultural and aesthetic occupations in the home to broaden the
provision they received at school. Naturally, this was something
which many girls in homes such as her own already enjoyed, but
by the same token, no amount of publicity was going to convert
narrow-minded bourgeois housewives such as Hedwig Dohm's
mother, to whom culture, for a girl, was not just a waste of time,
but downright suspect. It should be noted that the qualities
assumed to belong naturally to the female sex were not
challenged by Louise Otto-Peters.

Though best known for her feminist works, Louise Otto-Peters
was a prolific writer and was capable of writing light-hearted and
entertaining stories which are very little known and not at all
tendentious. Typical of these are the stories contained in *Kunst
und Künstlerleben* (1863). They are not overtly feminist in any way,
though a close reading does indeed deliver a feminist message.
The first story, 'Paul Flemming: Eine literarisch-historische Skizze
aus dem 17. Jahrhundert', is set in 1627 in an austere boys'
boarding school, St Asra, during the Thirty Years' War, when
Saxony was fighting as a Protestant state. Paul Flemming, a youth
of eighteen, is unjustly accused of pressing his attention on the
headmaster's daughter, and of writing a poem for her. Harsh
punishment awaits him, but the twenty-year-old daughter Siderie
placates her father by agreeing to an arranged marriage with a
man she scarcely knows; her only stipulation is that the poem
must be sung at her wedding. The historical Paul Fleming later

---

[38] Ibid., p. 159f.
[39] Ibid., p. 161.

became a prominent baroque poet. The fictional account of Paul Flemming's schooldays provides a focus for what is really a tale of renounced love. Though the story is told from Flemming's perspective, there is a shift towards the female protagonist at the very end in the brief description of Siderie's arranged marriage. Given the horrors which could ensue from such marriages, this leaves the reader with a feeling of discomfort, which was no doubt Louise Otto-Peters' intention.

In the final story of the collection, 'Eine weibliche Ahasver', the feminist critique is more prominent in that a bourgeois woman's prejudice towards actresses is scrutinised and criticised. Dr Bornhöfer has broken his engagement to an opera singer, Florentine Müller, but still loves her; a series of unbelievable coincidences lead her to take shelter in his summer residence, and the upshot is that he declares his undying love and asks her to marry him: he will divorce his wife. Florentine, however, is no marriage-breaker; though she still loves Bornhöfer, she makes a show of solidarity with his wife Klara, having first instructed the latter about her shortcomings. Amongst these was her *hubris* in marrying a man who was already promised to another woman, even if she was 'just an artist'.[40] Given the period in which Louise Otto-Peters was writing, the conventional end to this story is to be expected, although, as these pages show, some women, such as Fanny Lewald and Helene Böhlau, did actually marry men who had to extricate themselves from their marriages in order to do so. In a way, then, literature often lagged behind life in this respect, and indeed, the conventional nature of the creative writing of many unconventional women under discussion in this book is a recurrent feature.

Louise Otto-Peters' tale *Nebeneinander* was written as a lightweight *Reiselektüre* (traveller's reading matter); the two-volume first edition had highly incongruous titillating front covers. However, we see creeping in here and in later stories a much more critical stance towards the behaviour of unscrupulous men who are prepared to seduce women and thus ruin those women's lives. The story itself involves the feud between neighbouring aristocratic families, settled in predictable fashion by a marriage which is a love match rather than a marriage of convenience, in spite of the best efforts of the sister of the eventual bride-to-be. This negative portrayal of a young woman is paralleled by the portrayal of a much more evil and calculating imposter, Baron Nicola, who has made it his speciality to seduce other men's wives

---

[40] Louise Otto-Peters, *Kunst und Künstlerleben. Novellen*, Bromberg, 1863, p. 215.

away from them. In *Zerstörter Friede* (1866), a man is forced to acknowledge the consequences of his actions, which amount to the ruination of a young woman's life, even though he had made no attempt to actually seduce her. Indeed, the opposite is true: Leon Sander attempts to persuade Marianne, the daughter of the village innkeeper, that he does not love her and that she should not reject her (unofficial) fiancé on his account. Marianne runs away to a convent, the falsely pious regime of which is described with the same authorial disapproval as is found in Marie von Ebner-Eschenbach's *Das Gemeindekind*. The savagery of the nuns aside, the point which emerges is that Marianne probably avoids imprisonment by fleeing to the convent, since 'as a daughter of an innkeeper she knew very well that nobody could travel without some sort of legitimate reason.'[41] The insight provided by this remark is a timely reminder that unhappy people (of either sex) could not just run away from trouble with impunity. (Even today, no German sets out on a journey without his or her personal papers.) Leon Sander becomes engaged to an artist, Aloise, but she becomes the protectress of Marianne and breaks off her engagement. Years later, Leon, now the secretary of a duchess, visits the convent and is rebuked by Marianne for his earlier lack of feeling, though she now wishes him well. At the end of the story – in Rome – Aloise wishes to board a boat, but the man who offers her a helping hand is Sander: recoiling in shock, she falls from the step into the water, where she is struck by the boat's wheel. Sander's attempt to save her ends with them both perishing. The destruction mentioned in the title, which specifically refers to the potential for destruction which men have for women, is thus amply borne out in this story.

Apart from the many unbelievable coincidences (which are standard fare for novels of the period), the novel is well-written and the construction is particularly successful: in each of the three sections ('Im Bade', 'Eine Geächtete', 'Eine Künstlerin'), the story is told from a different point of view. This gives an astonishingly fresh perspective and is well carried through. The only thing that is not quite believable is the original premise: that reckless male flirtation is just as potentially harmful as actual seduction. Marianne tells another novice, Anna (expelled from the convent for staying out for an afternoon without prior permission), that she fears men because they are the destroyers of women's peace. Leon's excuse – that he never gave Marianne any reason to fall for him – is treated as weak and invalid, since the result of his

---

[41] Louise Otto-Peters, *Zerstörter Friede*, Jena, 1866, p. 74.

actions forced Marianne into a cloistered life and her mother to an early grave. Quite apart from that, his lack of forethought has wrecked his own chances of future happiness. The artist Aloise, who takes responsibility for Marianne's welfare, is shown to be a caring, independent woman who cannot respect a man like Sander. The sub-text of the novel, as in the story 'Eine weibliche Ahasver', makes the strong claim that artistic women are not automatically immoral, as society brands them to be, but often the most educated and compassionate women in society. Moreover, with their earned wealth, they are frequently in a position to help other women financially, an important feature for middle-class women readers in the 1860s, whose domestic role usually precluded them from earning money themselves.

Louise Otto-Peters did not write an autobiography, and indeed, she scarcely had time: Sophie Pataky's end-of-century *Lexikon deutscher Frauen* (1898) contains a list of her many novels, plays and other pieces of creative writing, all virtually unknown in Britain.[42] The same source lists numerous entries (over thirty-six novels consisting mainly of pious stories for young girls) by the now unknown Clara Cron (1823–1890). We should also be asking questions about writers such as Anna Croissant-Rust, now consigned to oblivion. Louise Otto-Peters wrote a profusion of historical tales and novels such as the three-volume *Nürnberg. Kulturhistorischer Roman aus dem 15. Jahrhundert* (1883). One very readable historical novel, *Gräfin Lauretta* (1884), is set in the thirteenth century. If one excludes the publications written to polemicise the women's movement, the chief of which have been cited above, the arithmetic is as follows: over forty full-length novels or books of stories, several volumes of poetry, several plays and librettos for operas. There is no collected edition of these works and indeed, the Louise Otto-Peters Gesellschaft in Leipzig (founded in 1993) is in the process of seeking to amass copies, which are scattered virtually at random in libraries throughout Germany, a measure of the neglect of Louise Otto-Peters' work. As pointed out above, the creative writing stands on its merits; in terms of characterisation and structure there is much to recommend it, although the plots sometimes demonstrate weaknesses common to writers of the period. The conventional endings, where lovers bow to social codes, are no more unusual than those found in male writers of the period, such as Theodor

---

[42] Sophie Pataky, *Lexikon deutscher Frauen*, 2 vols, Berlin, 1898, I, p. 109f. The British Library copies of *Kunst and Künstlerleben* (1863) and *Nebeneinander* (1864) were brought to me in October 1996, still uncut.

Fontane. The mere fact that such a prolific creative German writer could remain so unknown is itself a comment on the value hitherto placed on nineteenth-century women's writing.

Hedwig Dohm, 1831–1919

Unlike Louise Otto-Peters, Hedwig Dohm had an unhappy childhood, chiefly because she felt that her mother did not love her. As she was the fourth child and first daughter of a large family (her mother, Henriette Wilhelmine Schleh, gave birth to eighteen children, the first when she was still only eighteen years old), Hedwig Schleh's early experiences bear some similarity to those of Fanny Lewald: both came from Jewish families which had converted to Christianity for political reasons, with the result that religious awareness was completely lacking in the household. Furthermore, the constant upheaval in such a large family – which must have made the premises feel more like a boarding house or small hotel than a home – were not a conducive atmosphere for a teenage girl with dreams of becoming a writer; Hedwig Dohm had decided to be a writer at the age of eleven. This aspiration was entirely out of line with the cultural impoverishment in the home in general and the lack of encouragement of Hedwig's intellectual development in particular. Part of Hedwig Dohm's desire to marry was inspired by her wish to leave home, since her mother had regarded it as axiomatic that her eldest daughter should be used as nursemaid, and should leave school at fifteen, whereas her sons were expected to complete their studies. However, Hedwig did manage to attend the *Lehrerinnenseminar*, though she did not actually teach because she married Ernst Dohm in 1853, at the age of twenty-two. He was the chief editor for the political-satirical publication *Kladderadatsch*, and encouraged his wife's literary attempts. Their son was born in 1854 but died in infancy; they had four daughters, Gertrud, Else, Maria and Eve, all of whom were strong personalities in their own right. Gertrud was the mother of Katja Pringsheim, who married Thomas Mann. Hedwig Dohm clearly overcame her early social inadequacies and even had her own *jour fixe* at her home in Berlin, where the intellectuals of the day would gather.[43]

Like Louise Otto-Peters, Hedwig Dohm's early literary attempts were dramatic pieces which were actually well received,

---

[43] Heike Brandt, *'Die Menschenrechte haben kein Geschlecht'. Die Lebengeschichte der Hedwig Dohm*, Weinheim, 1995, p. 29.

though it must be said that a play such as *Der Seelenretter* (1875), with its plot hinging on mistaken identity (a tactic also employed in the comedy *Die Ritter vom Goldenen Kalb*, [1879]), gives little indication of the feminist potential which would gradually unfurl in Dohm's work, beyond criticising women's own refusal to seek education; this is indicated in the bored and frivolous Lotte's opening remark, in *Der Seelenretter*, in which she refers to her brother, who is reading a book, '[m]y God, he's got his nose in a book again!'.[44] The delineation of Lotte as bored and boring is retracted later in the play. As with Louise Otto-Peters, the literary works by Hedwig Dohm are less robustly emancipatory than her polemic work, and indeed, almost undermine the message of the latter. This prompts Singer to comment:

> When faced with the entire breadth of Hedwig Dohm's work, modern scholars have been perplexed by the contradiction between the positive, radical and witty political essays and the depressing, frustrating fates of the female protagonists in the fiction.[45]

The 'modern' critics Singer has in mind are Philippa Reed[46] and Boetcher Joeres,[47] though the difference in tone was already noted by Dohm's contemporaries, such as Sophie Hoechstetter.[48] Perhaps one should speak of realism rather than ambiguity, since Dohm gives an accurate portrayal of the situation for women as it pertained at the time, whereas the rather upbeat nature of her polemical works is used precisely because she seeks to overturn that situation. That said, Gaby Pailer has recently brought out a study of the fictional work of Hedwig Dohm in which she seeks to ascertain the authorial intention from within the text, stating her intention as follows:

> I try to show, in the following [study], that Dohm's texts playfully set cultural norms and images against one another.[49]

---

[44] Hedwig Dohm, *Der Seelenretter*, Berlin, 1875, p. 5.

[45] Sandra Singer, *Free Soul, Free Woman? A Study of Selected Works by Hedwig Dohm, Isolde Kurz and Helene Böhlau*, New York, Washington D.C./Baltimore, Bern, Frankfurt am Main, Berlin, Vienna and Paris, 1995, p. 23.

[46] Philippa Reed, *'Alles, was ich schreibe, steht im Dienst der Frauen'. Zum essayistichen und fiktionalen Werk Hedwig Dohms (1833–1919)*, Frankfurt am Main, Bern, New York and Paris, 1987, *passim*.

[47] Ruth-Ellen Boetcher Joeres, 'The Ambiguous World of Hedwig Dohm' in *Gestaltet und Gestaltend. Frauen in der deutschen Literatur*, pp. 255–276, *passim*.

[48] Singer, *Free Soul, Free Woman?*, p. 23.

[49] Gaby Pailer, *Schreibe, die du bist! Die Gestaltung weiblicher Autorschaft im erzählerischen Werk Hedwig Dohms*, Pfaffenweiler, 1994, p. 13, n. 21.

Pailer's study is particularly strong in tracing the influence of Nietzsche within the literary works.

Hedwig Dohm wrote what has been regarded as a 'trilogy' of novels dealing with emancipatory issues involving three women in succeeding generations. The first in the trilogy, *Schicksale einer Seele* (1899), was actually written second; if this is overlooked, the trilogy deals with three women at the turn of the century, one in her sixties (Marlene in *Schicksale einer Seele*), one in her forties (Sibilla in *Sibilla Dalmar*, 1896) and one in her twenties (Christa in *Christa Ruhland*, 1902). *Schicksale einer Seele* has been widely interpreted as containing autobiographical elements,[50] especially concerning Marlene's relationship towards her mother, who has no sympathy whatsoever for her dreamy child; furthermore, she is the victim of low-level sexual abuse at school, where the 'Schreiblehrer' (writing teacher) and piano teacher press themselves uncomfortably close to Marlene.[51] The oppressive atmosphere Marlene encounters at home and at school is continued in her married life, when her playwright husband mocks and bullies her as well as betraying her with any available woman, including their own cook. He ridicules Marlene's attempts to educate herself, which gives an indication that Walter is not to be confused with Ernst Dohm, who encouraged his wife's literary attempts, though like Walter, he appears to have made his wife unhappy with his many extra-marital affairs during the thirty years of their marriage.[52] The birth date of Marlene having been given as 1833, many readers took this to be the real birth date of Hedwig Dohm; the result being that Hedwig Dohm's eightieth birthday was celebrated two years too late.[53]

Schicksale einer Seele is written entirely in the first person and is presented as a series of letters sent to her platonic friend Arnold. When Marlene marries – on a cold day which alienates her as it did Henriette Herz – she is at first glad to escape from home, but her naivety (she serves chocolate soup to her husband as a delicacy),

---

[50] As Pailer points out (*Schreibe, die du bist!*, p. 63), this impression was encouraged by Dohm's early biographer, Adele Schreiber, who perpetuated the mistake over Dohm's birth date in *Hedwig Dohm als Vorkämpferin und Vordenkerin neuer Frauenideale*, Berlin, 1914. The only autobiographical piece we have by Hedwig Dohm is 'Kindheitserinnerungen einer alten Berlinerinnen' in *Als unsere große Dichterinnen noch kleine Mädchen waren. Selbsterzählte Jugenderinnerungen von Ida Boy-Ed, Hedwig Dohm, Enrica von Handel-Mazzetti, Charlotte Niese, Clara Viebig, Hermine Villinger, L. Westkirch*, Leipzig, 1912, pp. 17–57.

[51] Hedwig Dohm, *Schicksale einer Seele*, Munich, 1988 [1899], p. 50.

[52] Singer, *Free Soul, Free Woman?*, p. 45.

[53] Ruth-Ellen Boetcher Joeres, 'Hedwig Dohm: Leben und Werk', afterword to *Schicksale einer Seele*, pp. 333-335, p. 334, n. 2.

coupled with a rather chaotic incompetence regarding household matters and ignorance on literary topics, provokes the contempt of her husband. His vindictiveness is only shown later, when he puts about the invented story that Marlene herself has had a relationship before her marriage. Marlene's attempt to read the classics fails not so much through boredom[54] as through lack of guidance. She is often reliant on a dream world which is sometimes preferable to the real world – a factor in her earlier failure to react to her cousin Erich's attempt to propose to her. Her early attempts at writing show the distinct influence of Bettina,[55] and her preferred reading includes the escapist novels of Ida Hahn-Hahn and Eugenie Marlitt. But even without prompting, Marlene is able to test the ideas of Schopenhauer in polite society: people who, as she knows, admire Schopenhauer, laugh at his ideas when she conveys them as though they are her own, and this provides her with proof that she is being marginalised because she is a woman:

> Aha, I thought, it does not depend on what is said but on who says it, and perhaps how it is said.[56]

Marlene is educated on how to cope with her situation by the mannish divorcée, Charlotte, who bears all the hallmarks of the New Woman: manly clothes and fat cigars, though her supposed lesbianism is left in doubt, since she prefers to die rather than live through her son's reaction to her former husband's slanderous sexual slurs. Singer assumes that the character of Charlotte is meant to be that of a lesbian, and sees Marlene's rejection of Charlotte as 'reinforcing the negative image of lesbianism by emphasising the unnaturalness of such a sexuality',[57] whereas Charlotte is portrayed as horrified by the very suggestion that she should be accused of being a lesbian. I would prefer not to get tied up in present-day arguments on politically correct attitudes to 'otherness'; it is far more important to remember that *all* radical feminists around the turn of the century were tarred with the same brush regarding the accusation of lesbianism.[58]

Although Marlene manages to become emotionally bilingual in society, with 'romanticism in my heart and a singing, ringing scepticism, cold and questioning, in my head',[59] she is not able to

---

[54] Boetcher Joeres, 'The Ambiguous World of Hedwig Dohm', p. 258f.
[55] See the letter to Walter on p. 87, Dohm, *Schicksale einer Seele*.
[56] Dohm, *Schicksale einer Seele*, p. 134.
[57] Singer, *Free Soul, Free Woman?*, p. 38f.
[58] See Diethe, *Nietzsche's Women: Beyond the Whip*, Berlin and New York, 1996, p. 41ff.
[59] Dohm, *Schicksale einer Seele*, p. 176.

resolve her married difficulties, and merely drifts away from her husband, who sends her to Rome on account of a lung malady after the mysterious wasting illness and death of their daughter, Traut. In Rome, Marlene comes close to accepting Catholicism, but at the very end of the novel she has become a disciple of Helena, a theosophist, and is about to depart for India with her. Helena is taken to represent Madame Helena Petrowna Blavatsky, who founded the Theosophical society in New York in 1875. With the President of the society, Henry Steel Olcott, she travelled to India to govern the society from there. Both converted to Buddhism. Singer points out that there were racial elements in theosophy around the turn of the century which were already feeding into anti-Semitism and colonialism; however, the burden of her comment is that too little appreciation has been given to the encouragement such a society offered to women, since it did not make distinctions on grounds of gender.[60] Of course, the society owed much to Schopenhauer's dissemination of ideas on Indian philosophy and culture during the first half of the nineteenth century.

At the time Dohm was writing her major novels, Nietzsche's ideas, and especially those contained in *Also sprach Zarathustra* (*Thus Spoke Zarathustra*) (1883–1885) were becoming well known. The influence of Nietzsche will be discussed more fully in the next chapter. The important point to grasp in dealing with a radical feminist like Hedwig Dohm is that many of Nietzsche's central tenets were construed as favourable to women, in spite of his consistent attack on feminists, especially those who wished to be educated or creatively productive: on this, Hedwig Dohm disagreed strongly. She contradicted the argument which rested on the fact that women's achievements throughout the history of culture had been inferior to those of men, writing in *Die wissenschaftliche Emancipation der Frau* (1893):

> Surely most thinking people will agree with me that such achievements prove nothing without a thorough consideration of the social, political and historical circumstances under which they were produced … it would really be even more of a wonder if women's achievements had not lagged behind those of men.[61]

In *Die Antifeministen* (1902), she took issue with women who agreed with Nietzsche that a woman should not strive for professional or creative recognition, especially Ellen Key, Laura Marholm and

---

[60] Singer, *Free Soul, Free Woman?*, p. 43f.
[61] Hedwig Dohm, *Die wissenschaftliche Emancipation der Frau*, Berlin, 1893, p. 60f.

Lou Salomé, the three women who were most prominent in upholding this view. Hedwig Dohm found Lou Salomé's stance particularly irritating and inconsistent, in view of the fact that Lou herself was a successful writer:

> She rejects it as the most personal ambition, as the absolute peak of selfish individualism, if a woman wants to reach a certain stage of development ... instead of finding contentment in her own sphere as a woman in general, happy to be a single droplet in the ocean of womanhood.[62]

Nevertheless, Hedwig Dohm, in common with many feminist women such as Helene Stöcker, seized on the message of the *Übermensch* that the individual had to take on the task of creating his own identity. The phrase from Pindar, 'become who you are', was often used by Nietzsche,[63] and was used with regard to Lou Salomé in a letter written at the end of August, 1882. It would also become Hedwig Dohm's favourite motto. She agreed with Nietzsche's basic premise, that the most important knowledge we can have is self-knowledge,[64] and in fact this was an insight which informed all her literary work form the mid-1890s, nowhere more so than in the short story *Werde, die du bist!* (1894).[65] Hedwig Dohm's discomfort regarding eroticism is placed centre-stage in this story: an old woman, so old as to be completely beyond any erotic impulses – she is fifty-four (!) – suddenly has a sexual passion aroused in her by a young doctor whom she has met by chance; the encounter makes her realise that this is the one man meant for her, but of course, he is entirely out of reach because of her age. At the end of the novel she has passed beyond this passion, but Boetcher Joeres has remarked that this ending jars with the rest of the story.[66] Certainly one can say that the attempt to portray woman's emancipation as somehow linked to a freedom from sexual desire is controversial within feminist discourse, but not inconsistent with Hedwig Dohm's view of the right of the

---

[62] Hedwig Dohm, 'Reaktion in der Frauenbewegung', *Die Zukunft*, 1899, pp. 279–291, p. 286. Compare n. 57, Chapter 6, in this volume.

[63] Friedrich Nietzsche, *Joyful Wisdom*, translated by Thomas Common, New York, 1973 [1882], III, 270, p. 209.

[64] Friedrich Nietzsche, *On The Genealogy of Morality*, ed. by Keith Ansell-Pearson and trs. by Carol Diethe, Cambridge, 1994 [1887], Preface, p. 3.

[65] Hedwig Dohm, *Wie Frauen Werden. Werde, die du bist! Novellen*, Breslau, 1894.

[66] Ruth-Ellen Boetcher Joeres, 'Die Zähmung der alten Frau: Hedwig Dohms "Werde, die du bist"', in *Der Widerspenstigen Zähmung. Studien zur bezwungenen Weiblichkeit in der Literatur vom Mittelalter bis zur Gegenwart*, ed. by Sylvia Wallinger and Monika Jonas, Innsbruck, 1986, pp. 217–227.

individual woman to be herself, as the following comment in *Die Antifeministen* makes clear:

> It is irrelevant whether I am a man, a woman or neuter, sexuality is a
> private affair – above all, I am I, a definite individuality, and my value
> as a human being rests on this individuality.[67]

The theme recurs in *Plein Air* (1891), where Hedwig Dohm was likewise unable to square the demands of eroticism with the quest for freedom. Here, an adulterous couple whose life has become impossible decide, in Schopenhauerian despair, to commit suicide in the sea. In the other two novels in the 'trilogy', *Sibilla Dalmar* and *Christa Ruhland*, the female protagonist struggles to assert her individuality in a society which insists on seeing her only in relation to a man.

This pursuit and development of the self informs Hedwig Dohm's quest for woman's equality, which she pursued through the following writings: *Was die Pastoren von den Frauen Denken* (1872), *Der Jesuitismus im Hausstande* (1873), *Die wissenschaftliche Emancipation der Frau* (1874), *Der Frauen Natur und Recht. Zwei Abhandlungen über Eigenschaften und Stimmrecht der Frauen* (1876) and *Die Mütter. Beitrag zur Erziehungsfrage* (1903). She was a member of the Verein für Stimmrecht, an honourary member of the Verein Frauenwohl and on the founding committee of the Deutsche Frauenverein Reform. She was also a member of the executive committee of the Bund für Mutterschutz, where she worked alongside that convinced 'Nietzscheanerin', Helene Stöcker. During the war, she was a pacifist; she died a year after women had been granted the vote in Germany.

Helene Böhlau, 1856–1940

The child of Catholic parents, Helene Böhlau used her native Weimar as the setting for a series of 'nice, harmless stories'[68] with which she established her reputation, though as we shall see, her credentials as proto-feminist can be asserted in relation to several major novels written in the 1890s. The *Ratsmädelgeschichten* (1888) are set in the Weimar of Goethe's day and revolve around two sisters, Röse and Marie, the 'Ratsmädel', who play all sorts of pranks but are generally lovable; their father has another

---

[67] Hedwig Dohm, *Die Antifeministen. Ein Buch der Verteidigung*, Berlin, 1902, p. 335.

[68] Josef Becker, *Helene Böhlau. Leben und Werk*, PhD Diss., Zurich, 1988, p. 1.

daughter, their stepsister, by an earlier marriage, who becomes a nun. The mother of the 'Ratsmädel' was modelled on Böhlau's own great-grandmother, and a portrait of her appears as frontispiece in later editions of the work. In the largely autobiographical novel *Isebies* (1911), the eponymous heroine, who is closely modelled on Helene Böhlau herself in many respects, is virtually ungovernable as a young child by all except her grandmother, Gomelchen (a corruption of *Großmutter*), or 'Frau Mutter', as her son-in-law, Isebies' father, calls her. She is the Röse of the earlier tales in old age: cheerful, mobile and good-humoured. Through her eyes, we see many assumptions challenged. In this way, the aura of the *Ratsmädelgeschichten* is maintained in the later *Isebies*. At the very beginning of *Isebies*, when a cow has its calf removed and bellows in grief, the suggestion is made that animals are superior to humans,[69] a topic which Böhlau herself had dealt with in a school essay. According to *Wie die Enkelin der Ratsmädel zum Blaustrumpf wurde*, the actual title for the essay was 'Die Vorzäge des Menschen vor dem Tiere'[70], but Böhlau decided to turn this the other way round, to 'Die Vorzäge des Tieres vor dem Menschen', only to be met with scorn from her teacher. Her childhood sympathy with dumb animals never left her, and the theme of man's inhumanity, and especially the 'beastly' behaviour of some men towards women, is a pervasive factor in her work. The precocious Isebies (alias Böhlau) sums it all up in the words 'I do not like people', declaring that 'animals are preferable in every way'.[71] Isebies adores her grandmother, however, and the stories which her grandmother tells of Weimar in the heyday of Goethe and his family, including his grandchildren, Alma and Walter, have a resonance with the discussion of Alma's death, which represented such a tragic loss for Ottilie Goethe. 'Frau Mutter' Gomelchen surmises that Alma's untimely death spared her an impossible life, as she would not have been able to settle to her womanly duty: '[s]ince for us women, the highest things are denied, that is probably why she died'.[72] Helene Böhlau herself, though she loved her grandmother deeply, did not share this fatalistic view of a woman's duty.

Helene Böhlau's father owned the Böhlau printing press, which still exists in Weimar today, and she had two younger sisters. Having spent a turbulent childhood, certainly in comparison with

---

[69] Helene Böhlau, *Isebies*, Munich, 1911, p. VII.
[70] Helene Böhlau, 'Wie die Enkelin der Ratsmädel zum Blaustrumpf wurde' in *Ratsmädelgeschichten*, Stuttgart, 1897, p. 150.
[71] Böhlau, *Isebies*, p. 21.
[72] Ibid., p. 29.

what was expected of well-bred young ladies of the day, she passed through the religious experiences so common amongst adolescents, having been sent to a country Pastor and his wife to be prepared for her first communion. Helene Böhlau's religious devotion is described in ecstatic terms: '[m]y soul demanded to feel itself at the pinnacle of life,'[73] she recounts, but she herself was anything but bigoted, as her steady advocacy for the vulnerable in general and for Jews in particular makes clear. She was only twenty-three when, in 1882, her first collection of stories, with the simple title *Novellen*, appeared, amongst them the masterly novelle *Salin Kaliske*, written as early as 1879, which deals sympathetically with Judaism. In *Isebies*, we find an enthusiastic description of the Friday night supper enjoyed by the Lewin family (but only after Isebies, a 'Goj', has lit the seven-branched candle-stick). Yet though she seeks to be even-handed towards the Jews, Helene Böhlau cannot resist making Isebies wonder whether the meal itself, so carefully prepared, is not an imposition on the wife. Frau Lewin is clearly exhausted as she sits listening to her husband regale her with Solomon's *Song of Songs*:

> What other people on earth has such a praise of woman and gets the husband to sing it? ... the evening before the Sabbath is wonderful with the Jews, ceremonious and full of mystery, but what a lot of work Frau Lewin has every week to prepare everything and cook it so that it smells so fragrantly.[74]

By 1882, Böhlau had met and fallen in love with Friedrich Hellwig Arnd, her mentor, whose wife refused to divorce him, though she appears to have first given, and then withdrawn, her tacit permission for their affair, and indeed Josef Becker asserts that Therese Arnd had a 'slightly sadistic trait'.[75] In *Isebies*, the parallel situation is conveyed through the Dohrn couple; in real life, as in the novel, the lovers were forced to journey to the East, where Arnd converted to Islam so that he could divorce his wife without her consent. Thus it was under Islamic law that Helene Böhlau married Omar al Raschid Bey in Constantinople in 1886. The marriage itself occasioned much scandal, and prior to it there was a good deal of heart-searching. Böhlau's own relationship towards her husband was to become a common theme in her works, though the story *Herzenswahn* (1888), which depicts a rather similar growth of passion between an older mentor and a young woman, introduces a note of hysterical

[73] Böhlau, 'Wie dei Enkelin der Ratsmädel zum Blaustrumpf wurde', p. 158.
[74] Böhlau, *Isebies*, p. 60f.
[75] Becker, *Helene Böhlau*, p. 38.

longing on the part of the girl which is not really resolved, for the man involved is her uncle and therefore could never marry her. Arnd/Raschid Bey was able to circumvent bigamy by the ruse of changing religion; Böhlau, for her part, had to square her Catholicism with the fact that the man she had married was divorced (not even that, to some critics). In spite of these difficulties, the marriage was extremely happy, with Omar Raschid Bey fulfilling simultaneously the role of 'friend, teacher and husband'.[76] They had one son, who, ironically in view of the liberalism and tolerance of his parents,[77] became a National Socialist, as did Böhlau's sister, Mia Vollert. Omar Raschid Bey spent most of his time at work on his *magnum opus*, which Helene Böhlau published in 1912, a year after his death, with the title, *Das hohe Ziel der Erkenntnis. Aranada Upanishad*.

Though she was never an active campaigner for women's rights, Helene Böhlau's work shows a lively participation in the issues surrounding the discussion of women's emancipation, and, as shown in the title of the autobiographical essay *Wie die Enkelin der Ratsmädel zum Blaustrumpf Wurde*, she clearly viewed herself as a 'Blue Stocking'. Indeed, though she had little formal academic training, her husband's tuition can be viewed as a highly effective substitute: he tutored his wife on Schopenhauer and, from the internal evidence of the works, both were familiar with Nietzsche's ideas as well. Helene Böhlau later expressed how astonished she was at her own success, since she had appeared to be so poorly equipped to achieve anything as a young girl.[78] The description of her lamentable progress at school makes this only too clear: she even loathed Kindergarten.[79] At all times, Helene Böhlau makes a deliberate attempt to invite the reader to revalue certain assumptions. She does not make snide comments about women who want to have a career, but she does point out the difficult path they will have to tread. Thus she acknowledges women's right to educational and career opportunities; in the broad sense, one can detect a constant engagement with issues involving the question of women's emancipation. It is a reflection of the conservatism of the day that Helene Böhlau was construed as being radical in her comments on women's subjection, when today it is more likely that the reader will feel that she has pulled

[76] Böhlau, 'Wie die Enkelin der Ratsmädel zum Blaustrumpf wurde', p. 135.

[77] Helene Böhlau's 'motto' after the title page of Zillmann's *Helene Böhlau. Ein Beitrag zu ihrer Würdigung*, Leipzig, 1918, is: 'The only thing on earth which makes the heart peaceful and happy is being good to one another'.

[78] Böhlau, 'Wie die Enkelin der Ratsmädel zum Blaustrumpf wurde', p. 159.

[79] Ibid., p. 136.

her punches. For example, in the short story *Glory, Glory Halleluja* (1898),[80] sexism is gently rebuked rather than attacked. The 'woman question' is treated much more energetically in the novels *Das Recht der Mutter* (1896), *Der Rangierbahnhof* (1896) and *Halbtier!* (1899). In *Das Recht der Mutter*, the feminist dimension is at its strongest: here, the myth of Romantic love is debunked, and a woman's desire to keep her child, even if that child is illegitimate, is viewed as 'heilig' (sacred).

In *Der Rangierbahnhof*, the male protagonist, Friedel, is an artist who, as his name implies, would like peace and quiet. He leaves his noisy but well-run lodgings adjacent to the railway shunting yard (the comforts appear to have included free sexual use of the landlord's daughter, which causes him a feeling of vague disturbance), only to find that he has landed in an equally disturbing mental shunting yard. In his new lodgings, his landlady, Frau Kovalski, an artist's widow, presides over a neurotic family, the most sane of whom, Olly, is a pretty young woman and an artist in her own right. Friedel and Olly are soon married. As the plot develops, Olly is shown to have true artistic genius. Böhlau is clearly split over the delineation of this character; on the one hand, Olly's ineptitude in simple tasks such as cooking meals is shown to be negligence of almost criminal proportion (in fact, the Civil Code of 1900 would enshrine such wifely duties in law, as discussed above); on the other hand, Olly is a gifted artist with a mission to paint. Böhlau, herself a gifted writer, knew about the demands of domesticity on the creative artist from first-hand experience. There is therefore both sympathy and censure for the young and incompetent housewife Olly, with censure seemingly gaining the upper hand before Olly's fatal illness sets in. Olly appears to be shallow and indeed, narcissistic:

> She put her hands together and looked into the mirror. The light was soft and golden. 'What a gorgeous creature!', she said, and was quite taken up by the contemplation of her own reflection.[81]

Later in the story, Olly's maturity is signalled by her recognition that she has acted selfishly in the past. At all times, the reader is aware that the woman whom the hero should have married, his childhood companion Anna, is waiting in the mountains, though she has to wait until the very last page of the novel for her

---

[80] The title of the novella is in English in the original; it was first published in the collection Böhlau, *Schlimme Flitterwochen* (1898).

[81] Helene Böhlau, *Der Rangierbahnhof* in Helene Böhlau, *Gesammelte Werke. Romane und Erzählungen in 5 Bänden*, II, Weimar, 1929, p. 87.

patience to be rewarded. Nevertheless, it is Anna's model which sets the standard for what a woman's role should be in this work.

No stronger hint at Olly's unsuitability as a wife could be given than her horror at finding herself pregnant, not because she feels physically unequal to what lies ahead, though that is a factor, but chiefly because she will not be able to paint.[82] Helene Böhlau, like Dickens in *David Copperfield* (1850), kills off her version of the immature child-bride before the irregular meals and general chaos of the household take their toll, and thus shies away from a sustained depiction of the conflicts attendant upon the 'doppelte Belastung' so familiar now to working wives and mothers. The death of Olly therefore skirts the real issues. Neither Dora nor Olly are ready for marriage: they both need to grow up. In Olly's case, the self-knowledge she gains merely shows her what a trap she has fallen into. Like the carp which she buys for Christmas lunch but cannot bear to kill, she has been 'hooked'. When the artist Köppert, a misogynist who makes an exception in Olly's case because he recognises her genius, hears that Olly has released the carp, his reaction is 'that sounds like something out of Marlitt'.[83] Though intended as a reprimand regarding sentimentality, one does well to remember the values Eugenie Marlitt outlined in *Goldelse*: freedom of mind, simplicity, cheerfulness, all qualities stifled in the general ambience of the Kovalski family. Though Helene Böhlau tries to portray Olly as one of a new breed, she gives the reader continual hints that this new breed will be sterile. The incongruous style of Olly's wedding dress, coupled with her predilection for wearing long white dresses in daily life, arouse suspicion that all is not well with the marriage from the outset, as well as providing a subliminal image of a death shroud.

Though a feminist reader will cavil at the assumption that art and domesticity cannot co-exist, the era under discussion abounded with examples which could be cited to prove Böhlau right: in 1907, Paula Modersohn-Becker would die soon after the birth of her daughter, having painted in wild energy, as though she knew she did not have long to live. Olly is therefore a more realistic creation than one might at first credit. It is at this level that the novel works best: Köppert's half-baked attempts to mutter quotes from Schopenhauer are characteristically indistinct, as indeed they should be in a novel where the actual message is that life goes on, strong and uncomplicated, the

---

[82] Ibid., p. 99.
[83] Ibid., p. 152.

further away one is from the city and life-sapping demands made by art. Of course, Böhlau's undermining of Schopenhauer at this juncture is a subtle method of denying his argument that women could be talented, but not geniuses.[84] Whilst the mention of Schopenhauer's stance towards art prefigures Thomas Mann's major theme that art weakens the artist, a theme borne out by Olly's terrible sickness and death, the life-affirming aspects of the novel indicate a knowledge of Nietzsche's *Lebensbejahung*, a knowledge which had deepened by the time *Halbtier!* was written. Böhlau ironically ascribes yea-saying to the most negative character in *Der Rangierbahnhof*, Frau Kovalski,[85] thus side-stepping Nietzsche in the same way that Kant[86] is dismissed. In like manner, a potentially interesting aspect of the novel – the realisation by Olly and Köppert that they are in love – is swiftly circumvented so that the real test of Nietzschean ideas of freedom is not attempted. Singer suggests that Köppert brings out the erotic potential in Olly, which is then sublimated into art,[87] but he also indirectly hastens her death in so doing. Juxtaposed to this dangerous creativity is the superficial artistic dilettantism of Friedel, who likes his comfort and is going bald; however, the novel depicts his attitude, and that of Anna, as one of health. Ultimately, then, bourgeois patriarchal society, with all its banality, is affirmed in contrast to the weakening shunting yard of artistic creativity.

The message of *Halbtier!* is completely different. Instead of having a good-natured but inadequate man as hero, the novel portrays a series of men behaving badly towards women. These women, though constantly referred to in animal terminology, show themselves to be true, kind and warm when they are not crushed by male brutality. The novel indicates a knowledge of Nietzsche's *Also sprach Zarathustra* at first or second hand – for example, the patriarchal writer, Dr Frey, whose daughter Isolde is the protagonist, is greeted by his friends with 'Grüß Gott, Übermensch!'.[88] Nietzsche's opinion of women as fundamentally domestic creatures is taken at face value and shown to be a hollow and false stance towards woman's work. Nietzsche's anxiety for the race not to become degenerate by levelling down is ignored

---

[84] Gisela Brinkler-Gabler, 'Perspektiven des Übergangs. Weibliches Bewußtsein und frühe Moderne' in *Deutsche Literatur von Frauen*, II, pp. 169–205, p. 177.

[85] Böhlau, *Der Rangierbahnhof*, p. 110: '[s]he [Olly] could not get a saying of her mother's out of her head: "every 'no' is bad luck, every 'yes' is good luck"'.

[86] Köppert gives a lengthy description of why Kant is a '*Julklapp*' on pp. 146–147, Böhlau, *Der Rangierbahnhof*.

[87] Singer, *Free Soul, Free Woman?*, p. 79.

[88] Helene Böhlau, *Halbtier!*, Berlin, 1900 [1896], p. 67.

or probably not known about; his absurdly insulting reference to women as cows[89] finds its way into the novel in order to be soundly refuted by the society *grande dame*, Mrs Wendland. This outspoken woman (who is convincingly foreign, making mistakes in German, especially with her prepositions!), declares that '[a]lle deutsche Frauen sind Kühen' [*sic*] ('all German women are cows'),[90] the reason being that German men give women far too much provocation to be tolerated, and should resist being bullied. Mrs Wendland continues:

> I admire German women for not losing their patience. I would take a bomb and throw it at my husband's nightgown and at the nightgowns of all men who philosophise and speak about women.[91]

This, and constant references towards women as mere animals throughout the novel in contexts in which they are anything but that, invites the reader to speculate that this is a novel fundamentally concerned with female emancipation. Isolde Frey has become a successful artist after an early infatuation with the artist Henry Mengersen. The latter decides to marry Isolde's sister Marie instead of Isolde, largely to spite Isolde because of her independent ways. He proceeds to bully and ignore Marie, just as Frey has bullied his wife throughout her marriage. A successful writer with a second life led on the level of polite society, Frey has behaved as a stingy and petty tyrant in the home. Early in the novel, Frey decides that Isolde cannot study to be a teacher because he does not want her to turn into a Blue Stocking:[92] he gives no consideration to the question of how she will earn her living in later life if she chooses not to marry. Frey's wife has long since sunk to the level of weary obedience. Cowed into making every economy she can, neither she nor her daughters eat meat whilst Frey is away for a week, though the younger son has his daily chop. When Frau Frey inherits her brother's fortune, Frey disposes of it as he thinks fit, just as the law permits him to do. It has pained the protagonist, Isolde, to observe the mute suffering of her mother under this steady pressure.

Helene Böhlau's point is that German men, in particular, frequently behave with either unthinking harshness or cynical cruelty towards their wives. The novel documents a veritable

---

[89] Friedrich Nietzsche, *Thus Spoke Zarathustra*, I: 'Of the Friend', trs. by R. J. Hollingdale, Harmondsworth, Penguin, 1969, p. 84: '[w]oman is not yet capable of friendship; women are still cats and birds. Or, at best, cows.'

[90] Böhlau, *Halbtier!*, p. 72.

[91] Ibid., p. 76.

[92] Ibid., p. 208.

catalogue of insults and injustices towards women, with only one happily married woman, Lu Geber. 'Frau Lu' has had many difficulties to overcome, and these are reminiscent of Helen Böhlau's own difficulties in her relationship with Arnd, which must at times have seemed insuperable. Arnd's pet name for Helene was 'Lu', which strengthens the case for a biographical interpretation of this character,[93] though the name 'Frau Lu' reminds one not a little of Lou Salomé ('Frau Lou' to her friends). However, Frau Lu in the novel has a young son, whilst Salomé's own marriage remained unconsummated. In Mengersen's callous treatment of Marie, who for her part is soon so worn down by difficult pregnancies that she can no longer protest, we clearly see that he is the brute, though he treats Marie as 'something brutal – a body and no more'.[94] When Frey dies on Christmas Eve and his heavy body is carried into the house, we are told that he is 'like an animal that has fallen into a giant barrel of wine or syrup'.[95] As the novel draws to its close, Isolde is disgusted by the fact that her brother Karl has deserted a girl whom he had seduced (both she and her child subsequently die). The final straw comes when Mengersen tries to force himself on Isolde, explaining that he now regrets having married Marie. Isolde is so revolted by her importunate brother-in-law that she shoots him, ironically with a little revolver which he himself had given her to protect herself on her walks. As Singer says, the novel ends without any discussion of guilt, crime and punishment of the type found in a similar situation in Hardy's *Tess of the D'Urbervilles* (1891), where Tess is hanged for murder;[96] however, Singer wrongly assumes that Isolde remains alive at the end of the novel, whereas the text makes it clear that she commits suicide.[97] Before this, Isolde glories in the sense of having avenged herself (and her sister too, her mother ... all German women) for the injustices received in the past: '[s]he felt herself to be the representative figure of the eternally oppressed woman, the woman driven mad, the slave of all peoples'.[98]

The final vision of Isolde as she ecstatically greets the dawn is not, as with Thomas Hardy's Tess, set in a context of pathetic fallacy with nature (Tess bowed and broken, like the empty plain), but in a Nietzschean context whereby we realise that she has seized the

---

[93] Becker, *Helene Böhlau*, p. 127.
[94] Böhlau, *Halbtier!*, p. 233.
[95] Ibid., p. 183.
[96] Singer, *Free Soul, Free Woman?*, p. 90.
[97] Böhlau, *Halbtier!*, p. 358f : '[s]o, she ran to death? Yes, with outstretched arms. No, she did not creep towards it.'
[98] Böhlau, *Halbtier!*, p. 359.

initiative and become the *Übermensch* in her own right. Zillmann comments that 'the whole [novel] is full of reflections and passionate dithyrambs in the style of Zarathustra, quite unlike anything else written by Helene Böhlau'.[99] Indeed, it is her strongest statement in favour of women's emancipation. As so many emancipated women were to do, Böhlau has co-opted Nietzsche's principal idea of the possibility of creating one's own destiny by making it apply to women, though she was not sufficiently committed to women's emancipation to take the idea further, hence Isolde's suicide at the end of the novel. However, unlike Olly in *Der Rangierbahnhof*, art has not bowed Isolde down: on the contrary, she is exultant at the close of the novel, as though taking her own life were her final creative act. Not surprisingly, the novel was controversial amongst contemporary critics.[100] Even campaigners for female equality asked why Böhlau had deemed 'such a gruesome deed and suicide' necessary.[101] The deliberate refusal, on Helene Böhlau's part, to give the reader a glimpse of the consequences of this act, in which a man has been shot by a woman, reversing the usual image of man as hunter, again forces one to comment that Helene Böhlau raises issues of importance for the woman question, only to abandon them as too difficult to sustain.[102]

We have, in Helene Böhlau, a writer whose works written before the turn of the century portray women who are in their element in two different milieux: that of historical Weimar, and that of the wider world of work and creativity; in the case of the latter, we find that women who have creative ability and aspire to recognition of their talents are torn by inner conflicts whereby their sexual desires frequently undermine such aspirations, a dilemma which can be observed in both *Der Rangierbahnhof* and *Halbtier!*. Böhlau can be described as radical in these novels and in *Das Recht der Mutter*; in the latter especially, the conditions in society which, enshrined in the Civil Code, continued to impose unfair restrictions on women, are attacked. However, after the turn of the century, a more conservative note begins to creep in. Böhlau, herself a mother (Becker even speaks of her as a mother to both her son and her husband[103]), now seems to approve of the self-denying mother's role and supports the role of woman as

---

[99] Friedrich Zillmann, *Helene Böhlau. Ein Beitrag zu ihrer Würdigung*, Leipzig, 1918, p. 130.

[100] The details are in Becker, *Helene Böhlau*, p. 64ff.

[101] 'E. L.' 'Halbtier' in *Die Frauenbewegung*, V, 18, 15 September 1899, p. 155f.

[102] Zillman in *Helene Böhlau. Ein Beitrag zu ihrer Würdigung*, also deplores the weak ending – and in general finds much fault with the novel (e.g., p. 131).

[103] Becker, *Helen Böhlau*, p. 166.

man's helpmeet. As Becker has shown, whether Böhlau liked it
or not, her stress on motherhood as woman's defining function
played straight into the hands of the National Socialists, though
her attempt to accommodate herself to the new regime went little
further than her effort to prove that her husband had not been a
Jew. Becker points out that although there is a slightly more
'German' consciousness in Böhlau's writing of the 1930s, her
frequently positive portrayal of Judaism in her earlier writing
(one thinks of *Isebies*, *Salin Kaliske* and *Kers Judenlied*[104]) was hardly
likely to endear her to the new regime.[105] The problematic nature
of Böhlau's relationship towards the National Socialists was,
however, just one factor which has led to her subsequent neglect:
her popularity had been in decline from the turn of the century
onwards, and indeed, as Becker notes, '[i]t is almost as if she had
outlived herself'.[106]

---

[104] Ker had fathered Kristine's illegitimate child in Böhlau's *Des Recht der Mutter*;
the final version of the poem *Kers Judenlied*, an appendage to the novel, tells of
Sulamith's love for a shepherd, which, though initially proscribed, is finally
permitted.
[105] Becker, *Helene Böhlau*, p. 111.
[106] Ibid., p. 118.

Louise Andreas-Salomé. Reproduced with kind permission of the Stiftung Weimarer Klassik.

6

IN NIETZSCHE'S SHADOW

Nietzsche and Feminist Issues at the End of the Century

It was seen in Chapter Five that feminists of all persuasions were made nervous by the recidivist nature of the new Civil Code, in particular where it made an impact on the lives of women. The more radical amongst the feminists deplored the new Code because it did little to help the unmarried mother – usually, though not always, from the lower classes. Conservative feminists saw the Code though a middle-class prism. Other factors which played a role were the new sciences of eugenics and sexology. The chief campaign which preoccupied feminists at the turn of the century was the campaign for the abolition of state regulation of prostitution, strongest in Berlin, where it was led by Anna Pappritz. This movement was a reaction to the law promulgated in 1892, the *Lex Heinze*, which in effect ratified state control over prostitution.[1] The *Lex Heinze*, which also brought in repressive measures for art and press censorship, did not finally become law until 1900. Radical feminists in Hamburg, Germany's 'Amsterdam', chief amongst them Gustava Lida Heymann, tried to attack legalised prostitution through the moral argument that men ought to have the same high moral principles as women. The Hamburg radicals encountered much hostility from moderate feminists in the town, and the campaign was correspondingly high-profile, though this did not make it any more successful, in spite of public unease over what was perceived to be

---

[1] See Harrad Schenk, *Die feministische Herausforderung. 150 Jahre Frauenbewegung in Deutschland*, Munich, 1988 [1980], p. 33.

rampant prostitution. Richard Evans writes: '[w]hat was new about the problem in the late nineteenth century was that it appeared to contemporaries to be both large-scale and endemic'.[2]

The radical Helene Stöcker caused a controversy in the Berlin abolition movement comparable to that occasioned by Heymann in Hamburg, with Maria Lischnewska supporting her against Anna Pappritz, who had the backing of Minna Cauer. The factional nature of the German women's movement would become even more pronounced in the first decade of the twentieth century, when the efforts of Stöcker to promote the *neue Ethik* (new ethics) movement, which acknowledged woman's right to enjoy sexual satisfaction, ran directly counter to those of 'moderates' such as Helene Lange, the tireless if somewhat arrogant campaigner for girls' education,[3] who viewed Stöcker as a sexual libertine. Stöcker, for her part, argued that sexual abstinence was, or could be, harmful to the individual's health. Stöcker had come by these ideas as a direct result of her research into Nietzsche's philosophy, which she assiduously promoted[4] from the beginning of the twentieth century until 1933, when she fled from Germany in fear of political persecution. This fear was entirely justified, since the Nazis destroyed the papers which she had been forced to leave behind in her flat.[5]

Helene Stöcker was just one of a group of active feminist writers who were attracted by Nietzsche's ideas at the end of the nineteenth century in the belief that these ideas liberated women as individuals; Lily Braun was another. Ignoring Nietzsche's petulant strictures against the emancipation of women on the grounds that this would ultimately lead to a social and cultural weakening, they paid homage to him for his blueprint of the self-created person whose morality would no longer depend on the lies of philistine priests. Nietzsche made it not just possible, but plausible, for such women to challenge the values by which they were marginalised, and these included religious values. Nietzsche in *Die fröhliche Wissenschaft* (*Joyful Wisdom*) (1882) had also criticised the practice of keeping the facts of life from women so

---

[2] Richard Evans, 'Prostitution, State and Society in Imperial Germany' in *Past and Present*, 70. February 1976, pp. 106–129, p. 108.

[3] Helene Lange was founding President of the Allgemeiner Deutscher Lehrerinnenverein (General German Teachers' Association) from 1890 until her death in 1930. The Association itself was dissolved in 1933.

[4] Helene Stöcker was the chief instigator behind the Bund für Mutterschutz (a society to help the unmarried mother) from 1905 until 1910; she was editor of its journal *Die neue Generation*.

[5] Evans, *The Feminist Movement in Germany, 1894–1933*, London, 1976, p. 262f.

that their bridal night was often a traumatic event,[6] and he said that it was nonsense to suggest that women did not have sexual impulses. One can understand why Braun and Stöcker looked to Nietzsche for inspiration, ignoring the other point he made – and this is central – that a woman is out for one thing only in sexual intercourse: to be made pregnant. By a strange twist, Nietzsche's insistence on woman's maternal destiny put him within the camp of the 'moderate' feminists, though the latter were much more cautious about whether Nietzscheanism was 'a good thing'.[7]

The Nietzschean debate on woman's domestic destiny took place within a cultural climate in which some avant-garde literature spoke of the battle of the sexes as a favoured topic, whilst other avant-garde literature gravitated towards a Dionysian atmosphere of orgiastic sexuality. The flash points occurred in Berlin and Munich. In Berlin, where the Hart brothers held a late-nineteenth century equivalent of the salon, the works of Ibsen and Nietzsche were avidly scanned for liberalising ideas within a society in which all sorts of 'alternative' lifestyles were being tried: one thinks of the *Freikörperkultur* (nudism) and various vegetarian and eugenic societies. Berlin was also the centre of the nascent science of sexology, led by the pioneering work of Magnus Hirschfeld. In Munich, the poets round Stefan George in the artistic quarter of Schwabing led a Nietzsche-inspired Dionysian lifestyle. They dubbed themselves *die Kosmiker* ('the Cosmics') and dabbled in cosmology and other semi-occult practices. They also adapted Nietzsche's ideas regarding the emergence of genius after their own fashion by arguing that a nation sometimes gets the equivalent of a rush of blood to the head (a *Blutleuchte*). Nietzsche's theory of Dionysian abandonment had been the most recent German *Blutleuchte*. Though George himself kept aloof from the most outlandish antics of the *Kosmiker*, he played a central role in distorting the picture of Nietzsche's life and work, as Steven Aschheim has pointed out: 'Nietzsche was made into a Germanic legend, his life and thought transmuted into a nation-saving prophetic myth'.[8]

The political precepts of the left-wing philosopher Otto Groß, who argued that the social and political development of society

6   Friedrich Nietzsche, *Joyful Wisdom*, II: 71, 'On Female Chastity', trs. by Thomas Common, New York, 1973, p. 71. [Original translation pub. 1910.]

7   Helene Lange argues that Nietzsche's ideas endanger family life: 'Feministische Gedankenanarchie' (1908) in *Kampfzeiten. Aufsätze und Reden aus vier Jahrzehnten*, 2 vols, Berlin, 1928, II, pp. 1–8, p. 1.

8   Steven E. Aschheim, *The Nietzsche Legacy in Germany 1890–1990*, Berkeley, Los Angeles and Oxford, 1992, p. 77.

could only be achieved if individuals released their erotic potential,[9] were somewhat paradoxically seized upon by the Schwabing Bohemians to justify their own profoundly right-wing views. However, Groß shared with the Schwabing Bohemians an admiration for J. J. Bachofen, a private scholar in Roman Law (and inspiration to Nietzsche when the latter was in Basle), whose notion that an ancient matriarchy pre-dated patriarchy was derived from his study of the grave inscriptions of antiquity. His theory was postulated in *Das Mutterrecht* (1861). The myth of matriarchy was, as Sombart has pointed out, profoundly conservative, 'bound up with the past, esoteric and elitist'.[10] By delving into Greek antiquity to justify hetaeric sexuality, and linking this to an elitist view of woman in society, the fused figure of whore/*grande dame* was applauded, and found her incarnation in women such as Franziska zu Reventlow or Alma Mahler.[11] The Schwabing group believed in, and practised, free love, and in general sought to live up to their own idea of what a heathen Dionysian orgy entailed. It goes without saying that the group were diametrically opposed to the demands of the feminists, of whatever persuasion. Though purporting to be Nietzschean in the ecstatic mode made fashionable by Rudolf Pannwitz, the group would have no doubt horrified Nietzsche, not least by its anti-Semitic overtones. Since the second-in-command, after Stefan George, was the Jewish poet Karl Wolfskehl, there was, understandably, an undercurrent of tension, and this rose to the surface in 1904. The most prolific writer in the group was Ludwig Klages, and the most anti-Semitic by far was Alfred Schuler. Franziska zu Reventlow was the token woman.

Gabriele Reuter 1859–1942

Gabriele Reuter was born in Cairo into a wealthy German family: her father had his own trading company, and sometimes travelled on business between Dessau in Germany and Egypt. Reuter herself spent long periods of the formative years of her childhood and adolescence in Egypt, then part of the German Empire. In her autobiography, *Vom Kinde zum Menschen* (1921), the sections which describe her life in Egypt are entitled 'Von den Eltern und dem

---

[9] Nicolaus Sombart, 'Gruppenbild mit zwei Damen', in *Merkur*, 30, 10, October 1976, pp. 972–990, p. 978.

[10] Ibid., p. 980.

[11] Ibid., p. 980.

Kinde' and 'Orientbilder'. The autobiography itself, which only deals with Gabriele Reuter's life up to the age of thirty-six, is divided into two parts, *Das Buch des Kindes*, which goes up to early adolescence, and *Das Buch des Mädchens*, which is twice as long as the preceding section and deals with Reuter's experiences from the age of fourteen to thirty-six (during the years 1873 to 1894). As Gabriele Rahaman points out, it is remarkable that a woman of sixty-two should speak of herself at the age of thirty-six as a 'Mädchen',[12] though, as Reuter's works demonstrate, woman's position of tutelage in Wilhelmine patriarchal society justified the use of the term. Though men have called grown women 'Kind' throughout the literature discussed in this book, they do so programmatically in Reuter's fiction, and the use of the term in *Vom Kinde zum Menschen* is deliberate, especially as the end result is to be – with Nietzsche's assistance – the fully fledged person or 'Mensch'. It is therefore no surprise that Bettina von Arnim, that other fully mature 'Kind', is mentioned in the autobiography,[13] the first section of which establishes a genealogy for Gabriele Reuter as woman writer.

Though she was 'at home' in the exotic milieu of Egypt for much of her youth, there were several years in her early childhood when, together with her mother and brothers, Gabriele Reuter stayed in Dessau while her father managed his business in Egypt, returning home on visits. From the 1890s, she lived in Weimar. Rahaman describes Gabriele Reuter's relationship with her father as less problematic than that with her mother, though her father prevented her from pursuing her first choice of calling, the theatre; his death marked 'the end of childhood'.[14] It also spelled out a drastic change in social status and, as Faranak Alimadad-Mensch has pointed out, Reuter resolved her identity crisis by taking up writing as a means of earning a living.[15] Her attitude to her work was to change, since Reuter was to discover a real calling in her writing. This would involve her overcoming a trait in her personality which tended towards the excessive effusions so characteristic of romanticism and which was criticised by her aunt, Elisabeth Behmer (the wife of her mother's brother), of whom she was inordinately fond.[16] Reuter herself defended this

---

[12] Gabriele Rahaman, 'Problems of Female Identity in Selected Works by Isolde Kurz and Gabriele Reuter', PhD Diss, University of London, 1994, p. 114.

[13] Gabriele Reuter, *Vom Kinde zum Menschen. Die Geschichte meiner Jugend*, Berlin, 1921, pp. 13 and 19.

[14] Rahaman, *Problems of Female Identity*, p. 127.

[15] Faranak Alimadad-Mensch, 'Gabriele Reuter. Porträt einer Schriftstellerin', PhD Diss., Bern, 1984, p. 51.

[16] Reuter, *Vom Kinde zum Menschen*, p. 237.

romantic tendency as part of the artistic impulse driving her to write, though she admitted that such 'exaltations' could be 'unhealthy and dangerous'.[17] She was attracted to the ideas of Max Stirner, who, in *Der Einzige und sein Eigentum* (*The Ego and His Own*) (1845), argued in favour of the right to egoism. She applauded her friend John Henry Mackay's rejection of socialism and Communism and was, like him, attracted by the 'right to egotism' advocated by Stirner; in her appendix to Mackay's novel *The Anarchists* (1891), she wrote, '[w]ho has ever quite overcome his own self?'.[18] Possibly it was this propensity to reject socialism for its weakening effect on the individual which attracted her to the circle of Nietzsche admirers in Weimar in the early 1890s, even when Nietzsche, himself insane, was still resident in Naumburg.

From Weimar, Gabriele Reuter made several trips to Naumburg, where she visited Nietzsche's house on several occasions, the first in the company of her friends Fritz Kögel and Rudolf Steiner, who wanted to read from the manuscript of Nietzsche's *Der Antichrist* (*The Anti-Christ*) (eventually published 1894), which they fully expected to be banned.[19] At the time the manuscript was in Franziska's safe keeping: Elisabeth had dissuaded her mother from burning it. On this visit, Reuter did not meet Nietzsche, though he could be heard in the next room making noises 'like a captured animal',[20] but she often visited Elisabeth after that. However, Elisabeth was not in the house when Franziska took Gabriele Reuter to see Nietzsche in person. Nietzsche was obviously very upset at being disturbed and, in *Vom Kinde zum Menschen*, Reuter gives a graphic account of her reaction to Nietzsche – 'I stood trembling at the power of his gaze', she writes.[21] Thomas Mann, who greatly admired Reuter in any case, paid her the ultimate compliment of copying from her when he incorporated this description into his novel, *Doktor Faustus* (1947).[22] Nietzsche's works were already becoming known and discussed, especially amongst Weimar intellectuals; often the only

---

[17] Ibid., p. 237.

[18] Gabriele Reuter, Appendix to John Henry Mackay's *The Anarchists: A Picture of Civilization at the Close of the Nineteenth Century*, trs. by George Schumm, Boston, 1891, p. 302. The novel examines social conditions with an indignation reminiscent of Friedrich Engels in *The Condition of the Working Class in England* (1845).

[19] Reuter, *Vom Kinde zum Menschen*, p. 457.

[20] Ibid., p. 456.

[21] Ibid., pp. 458f.

[22] See Helmut Kreuzer, 'Thomas Mann and Gabriele Reuter. Zu einer Entlehnung für den "Doktor Faustus"', *Neue deutsche Hefte*, 10, 1963, pp. 108–119 *passim*.

text available to the group was Nietzsche's manuscript, from which Fritz Kögel would read. Reuter emphasises the importance of these readings for herself and for the group:

> We were a small group of people passionately devoted to truth ... We all enjoyed the feeling of having left bourgeois society behind and landed in the realm 'beyond good and evil'.[23]

Reuter was not able to see much more of Elisabeth Förster-Nietzsche, with whom she had become friendly, for several years, as she had to nurse her sick mother, and moved to Munich upon publication of *Aus guter Familie* in 1895.

Gabriele Reuter herself was overjoyed at the reception of *Aus guter Familie* by the reading public; it rapidly became a best-seller and was into its fifth edition by 1897, though the critics tended to be less appreciative than her readers.[24] Most commonly, the novel was taken to be a *Tendenzroman*,[25] sacrificing style for ideological content, in this case a realistic portrayal of the wrongs suffered by German *höhere Töchter* towards the end of the century. Up to this point in her life, Reuter had not taken any active part in the women's movement. She knew members of the Verband Frauenbildung Frauenstudium in Weimar, but had never felt that their cause was directly relevant to her; she herself did not feel educationally marginalised. However, in Munich, the women's movement was more active, and Reuter herself, once she was a single mother, felt more directly involved. She took part in the campaign against the excesses of the new Civil Code, mentioned in Chapter Five, but with time came to realise that 'art is a strict goddess – demanding the entire person'.[26] She felt that the politically engaged writer would not be able to avoid making propaganda, and became convinced that her own writing would suffer if she were to join the struggle on behalf of the feminists. She therefore adopted the position of observer. Another aspect of her stance towards feminism comes out most closely in the powerful novel *Das Tränenhaus* (1909); she does not hold out any hope for feminism until women like the vulnerable young Toni's mother take a more humane attitude towards girls who get into trouble. Female solidarity is therefore the only solution to the problem of the double standard, and the strength to fight for a place in the modern world must come from women rather than

[23] Reuter, *Vom Kind zum Menschen*, pp. 447 and 451.
[24] Rahaman in *Problems of Female Identity* gives an excellent summary of contemporary reactions to *Aus guter Familie*, pp. 25–29.
[25] Rahaman, *Problems of Female Identity*, p. 28.
[26] Reuter, *Vom Kinde zum Menschen*, p. 462.

be borrowed from men. Though feminists might well feel that Reuter lets men off rather lightly, in theory at least (in practice, the novels give graphic portrayals of men's unacceptable behaviour towards women), she was never hostile to the efforts of the feminists in the way Franziska zu Reventlow and Lou Salomé would turn out to be.

The success of *Aus guter Familie* went beyond any of Reuter's hopes: 'I had arrived at last', she wrote. With this new self-confidence went a determination to live an independent lifestyle; thus, when she gave birth to her daughter Lili under circumstances similar to those shown in *Das Tränenhaus*, she did not feel the need to marry the father of her child. Though Reuter remains reticent on the subject, it can be conjectured that Cornelie Reimann's fate in the novel is similar to the reversal in fortune Reuter herself experienced. Cornelie has been a successful writer of non-fiction (her works include *Beiträge zur Psychologie der Frau* and she is in the process of writing *Der Seelenzustand des modernen Kulturweibes*), but she is now despised as an unmarried mother; nevertheless, she feels that '[h]aving an illegitimate child has given a new legitimacy to her life'.[27] In addition, Cornelie is also able to set a standard of female solidarity which exemplifies Reuter's own position as discussed above. All her fellow inmates in the 'house of tears' depart the wiser through her kindness and insight. However, the position of wise woman is achieved at the expense of a despair verging on suicide, in which Cornelie loses her belief in God.[28] The subsequent (difficult) birth of the child is all the more triumphant. Gabriele Reuter herself, like Cornelie in the novel, exulted in the birth of her child and regarded this as her most important achievement: 'mother love' was, as she said at the beginning of *Vom Kinde zum Menschen* in her dedicatory poem to Lili, the inspiration for her 'dreams, work and writing';[29] Reuter also speaks of the 'sacred wealth of sorrows and happiness' which she passes on to her daughter. Rahaman points out that this gives a framework to the first part of the autobiography, which deals with the legacy which Gabriele Reuter herself received from her ancestors, especially women who had had literary success.[30] It is noteworthy that the three women whose works are examined in this chapter all agreed with Nietzsche's pronouncement that

---

[27] Georgia A. Schnieder, *Portraits of Women in Selected Works of Gabriele Reuter*, Frankfurt am Main, Bern, New York and Paris, 1988, p. 80.

[28] Gabriele Reuter, *Das Tränenhaus*, Berlin, 1928 [1909], p. 63: 'Kein Gott war im Himmel'.

[29] Reuter, *Vom Kinde zum Menschen*, dedicatory poem 'An Lili'.

[30] Rahaman, *Problems of Female Identity*, p. 116.

maternity was woman's destiny; even Lou Salomé, who herself remained childless, subscribed to this view. A salient feature in Reuter's writing is her attack on mothers who abuse their children in some way; she herself had no compunction in revealing that she had had a difficult relationship with her own mother.[31] She had a strong affection for her brothers.

If Nietzsche's ideas on freedom inspired Gabriele Reuter to insist upon freedom for herself, the fate of Agathe Heidling in *Aus guter Familie* demonstrates what happens when that freedom is denied. Agathe, in seeking a religion which will answer her desire for new values, visits an evangelical sect, the *Jesubrüder*,[32] but these visits are forbidden by her father when he finds out about them. All her other attempts to find a pathway for herself through the suffocating conventionality of Wilhelmine Germany are similarly blocked. Reuter's receptivity, during the 1890s, to Nietzschean principles of self-overcoming and *amor fati* produced a detectable change within her writing. The early novels are placed in exotic settings, for example, Egypt in *Glück and Geld* (1888) and Argentina (where one of her brothers now lived) in *Kolonistenvolk* (1891); the plots in these early novels tend to be morally conventional in tone.[33]

In contrast, *Aus guter Familie* is set in middle-class Germany. After repeated discouragements, Agathe is unable to react to the chance of becoming independent when it presents itself; she thus fails to respond to offers of help from her cousin Martin, since he is a socialist. Socialism (illegal in Germany from 1878 until 1890) is anathema to Agathe's father, an employee of the Prussian state, with whom Agathe still lives. In addition, Agathe is patently dishonest with herself, saying repeatedly that she does not love Martin until she makes the final, confrontational admission that she does love him, which instigates her nervous breakdown. Reuter shows how, at every stage, Agathe is prevented from 'becoming who she is', to the extent that she is so mad at the end of the novel that she even gives the impression of being content

---

[31] Reuter in *Vom Kinde zum Menschen*, p. 442, speaks of the resentment she had to fight when nursing her mother and trying to write *Aus guter Familie* at the same time. 'I would often look at the quiet, pale face of my mother and think, "she has won ... she has me all to herself"'.

[32] Gabriele Reuter, *Aus guter Familie*, Berlin 1895, p. 216ff.

[33] Johnson writes of Reuter with reference to *Glück und Geld*: '... she remained within the Christian conventions expected of proper bourgeois women writers ...'. Richard L. Johnson, 'Gabriele Reuter: Romantic and Realist', in *Beyond the Eternal Feminine: Critical Essays on Women and German Literature*, ed. by Susan L. Cocalis and Kay Goodman, Stuttgart, 1982, pp. 225–244, p. 227.

with the sort of life she had feared and despised in her youth. With sublime irony, Reuter speaks of the 'success' of the doctors in having brought about her 'cure'. Richard Johnson comments: '[t]he two years of baths, sleeping tablets, shock treatments, massage and hypnosis are her punishment and corrective. Her will is broken'.[34]

The works written after *Aus guter Familie* often depict a determination on the part of the protagonist to live a free life, whatever the cost; the refusal to be true to oneself can only lead to the type of collapse we see with Agathe Heidling or to the creeping illness of Frau Bürgelin, whose refusal to have a cancerous growth removed from her face, because she fears the operation will spoil her looks, will ultimately reduce her to a red-eyed, cowering cripple.[35] Frau Bürgelin has been a 'substitute patriarch' to her two sons, faithfully upholding the name of the father even in his absence (see n. 35, Introduction to this volume). Gabriele Rahaman gives an alternative interpretation for the way mothers can act against the interests of themselves and their daughters in an article which leans heavily on Theweleit's argument that *Entlebendigung* is 'a subconscious process at the heart of all relationships involving power'.[36] Here, Rahaman argues that woman's bodies are no longer their own within the Prussian military ethos, citing *Aus guter Familie* as 'the perfect "Entlebendigungsroman"'.[37] The Lacanian dialectic inherent in the 'name of the father' is seen when Frau Heidling, against her better judgement, beats her daughter because that is the accepted paternalistic punishment for little girls who stay out late. Since the disobedience was occasioned by Agathe's horrified reaction at hearing the facts of life,[38] the link between sexuality and the prohibitive '*non* du père' has been established early in the novel.

Agathe's desperate desire to find a husband, expressed in the novel throughout as a hysterical *idée fixe*,[39] is not quite as strong as the inhibition which causes her to refuse to kiss Raikendorf just

---

[34] Richard Johnson, 'Men's Power over Women in Gabriele Reuter's *Aus guter Familie*', in Marianne Burkhard, ed, *Gestaltet und Gestaltend. Frauen in der deutschen Literatur*, Amsterdam, 1980, pp. 235–253, p. 250.

[35] Gabriele Reuter, *Frau Bürgelin und ihre Söhne*, Berlin 1899, p. 326.

[36] Gabriele Rahaman, 'Gabriele Reuter's *Aus guter Familie* in the Light of Klaus Theweleit's Concept of "Entlebendigung"' in *German Life and Letters*, 44, 5, October 1991, pp. 459–68, p. 459.

[37] Rahaman, 'Gabriele Reuter's *Aus guter Familie* in the Light of Klaus Theweleit's Concept of "Entlebendigung"', p. 461.

[38] Reuter, *Aus guter Familie*, p. 31.

[39] Ibid., p. 216.

after he has proposed to her. The match is doomed, since Agathe's dowry has been spent on her brother Walter's gambling debts – to save the family name – but the reader feels that the total collapse might have been averted if she had granted that kiss. Agathe's inability to overcome her sexual inhibitions guarantees that she will remain a mere onlooker whilst her friend Eugenie, blessed with sex appeal, becomes a self-confident wife and mother in her marriage to Walter (whose seduction of a servant has parallels with the incident described in Böhlau's *Halbtier!*, discussed in Chapter Five). Eugenie's shallow behaviour, and complicity in acting as intermediary between the morally dubious Adrian Lutz[40] and Agathe, build up a wall of resentment in Agathe. It is no accident that Agathe, at the onset of her frenzied nervous breakdown, tries to strangle Eugenie, nor is it an accident that, at the close of the novel, Eugenie and Walter, who promised Frau Heidling that Agathe would always have a home with them, are looking out for an institution which will take Agathe when her father dies, since they do not want a person with a history of mental disease in their home – and Agathe, at forty, could still have a long life ahead of her: a very empty long life. Perhaps Gabriele Reuter intends us to draw a comparison with the fate of Nietzsche, who was nursed by his mother and then by his sister during the eleven years of mental insanity which preceded his death, in 1900, at the age of only fifty-six.

Gabriele Reuter was sceptical about the possibility of happiness within marriage and her work often reflects this. Rather than counselling celibacy, she advocates more humane divorce laws. The unfairness of divorce towards the married woman is shown graphically in *Ellen von der Weiden* (1900). Here, Ellen tells her husband that she is in love with another man, Uglandy. As this coincides with her discovery that she is pregnant, her husband refuses to believe that she has not been unfaithful to him and divorces her with extreme callousness, especially as Ellen is innocent of the charge. After the birth of her baby she discovers the strength within herself to carry on, even though she realises she has grown apart from Uglandy. She explains her new-found sense of personal freedom to her friend Jacobus, her ex-husband's brother, in terms reminiscent of Zarathustra's *amor fati*: 'I pity you if you know nothing about

---

[40] Lutz has a daughter by the actress Daniel; it is characteristic of Reuter that she should invert Wilhelmine values, so that this social outcast (as actress and single mother) is shown in a positive light and the refusal of Lutz to acknowledge paternity for his child is portrayed as disgraceful.

the ecstasy of suffering. – Just to be able to say: "I will" – and not "I can" – that sums it all up'.[41] This function of the will is fundamental to the life-affirmation of the *Übermensch*: '[t]o redeem the past and to transform every "it was" into an "I wanted it thus!" – that alone do I call redemption! Will – that is what the liberator and bringer of joy is called: thus I have taught you, my friends!'[42]

Nietzsche's insight into 'the phenomenon that pain begets joy' is already detectable in his early work *Die Geburt der Tragödie (The Birth of Tragedy)* (1872).[43] As though to underline the Nietzschean message, at the end of the novel the much-abused Ellen rejoices to see her son, who has never smiled, laughingly trying to catch hold of the beams of sunlight which stream through the open window. The image, which conjures up Zarathustra's ecstatic reaction to the dawn, also evokes the similar but much more pessimistic scene at the end of Ibsen's *Ghosts* (1881).

In her comments on what constitutes happiness, Reuter counts sensual pleasure as a constituent of happiness which she then couples with freedom: it is invariably to be enjoyed outside marriage rather than within. This is shown in the novel *Liselotte von Reckling* (1903), where the married couple have a physically satisfying honeymoon. In fact, it is almost too good: the prudery inculcated by Wilhelmine bigotry works its poison when the child conceived on the honeymoon is miscarried. The shame of the wife Liselotte is matched by the restlessness of her husband Lorenzo, who seeks companionship with a woman philosopher, the early twentieth-century thinking man's version of a *femme fatale*. In the short story 'Five O'Clock' (the title is in English) (in *Frauenseelen* [1902]), Reuter portrays, with considerable psychological skill, the thoughts which go through a woman's mind now that her husband is dead. She is free – free! – for her young lover, but he fails to visit her.[44] At last she admits the truth to herself – that she misses the man who seemed to be such a brake on her freedom when she was married to him. In an essay which Gabriele Reuter wrote for the periodical *Nord und Süd*, she commented that too few people give sufficient thought to the links between happiness and freedom: '[h]ow few free

---

[41] Gabriele Reuter, *Ellen von der Weiden*, Berlin, 1904 [1900], p. 275.

[42] Friedich Nietzsche, *Thus Spoke Zarathustra*, trs R. J. Hollingdale, Harmondsworth, 1969 [1883–1885], II: 'Of Redemption', p. 161.

[43] Friedrich Nietzsche, *The Birth of Tragedy*, trs. by R. J. Hollingdale, Harmondsworth, 1967, p. 40.

[44] Gabriele Reuter, 'Five O'Clock' in *Frauenseelen*, Berlin, 1910 [1902], p. 109.

people there are today, though so much is spoken about freedom in every way... it should not be freedom *from what*, but freedom *for what*:[45] a notion for which she gave the credit to Nietzsche.

Lou Andreas-Salomé, 1861–1937

Lou Andreas-Salomé was born in St Petersburg into a German-speaking family; her father was of Huguenot extraction and her mother was of mainly German descent. One of the most important of her early experiences was her breach with formal religion; this happened spontaneously, but the matter was further complicated because the pastor who prepared her for confirmation, Gillot, fell in love with her. This followed a course of stringent lessons in philosophy, theology and history, which had begun with the determined breaking of her will, and with a relentless attack on her tendency to give her imagination free rein. This trait had developed because Lou Salomé felt alienated from the social whirl of balls and formal festivities which belonged to the aristocratic society into which she had been born. The seventeen-year-old Lou had approached Gillot through her own initiative;[46] his lessons were brilliantly effective when one considers Lou's later intellectual achievements, though it must be said that they were less successful if measured in formal religious terms. In her subsequent life, Lou retained a neurosis in her sexual life which she herself referred back to Gillot; she also formed an unorthodox concept of religion, after much struggle, outlined in *Im Kampf um Gott* (1885).

In 1880, Lou Salomé went to Zurich for a year to study theology as a *Hörerin*, which meant that she attended lectures without presenting herself for examination. However, she fell ill and was forced to discontinue her studies, but not before she had caught the attention of Gottfried Kinkel,[47] who procured for her an introduction to Malwida von Meysenbug, then resident in Rome. Meysenbug, it will be recalled, took great pleasure in being hostess to intelligent young people, and she invited Nietzsche to meet Lou Salomé in Rome in 1882. Another guest was Paul Rée, who, unbeknown to Nietzsche, had already proposed to Lou Salomé without success. The big event for Lou Salomé that year was, however, not the weeks spent with

---

[45] Gabriele Reuter, 'Die Erziehung zum Glück', in *Nord und Süd*, 32, 1910, pp. 45–67, p. 55.

[46] Angela Livingstone, *Lou Andreas-Salomé*, London, 1984, p. 24.

[47] Cordula Koepcke, *Lou Andreas-Salomé. Leben – Persönlichkeit – Werk. Eine Biographie*, Frankfurt am Main, 1986, p. 52.

Nietzsche at Tautenberg in August 1882, with a hostile Elisabeth as chaperone, but the preceding visit to Bayreuth, where Lou had been welcomed into the Wagner circle with considerable *éclat*, no doubt making Elisabeth Förster-Nietzsche, who was trying to retain her position in the group though Nietzsche himself was distancing himself from it, thoroughly jealous. Whatever Nietzsche said about Lou later, and some of it was vitriolic, he found her to be the person who was most receptive to his ideas, and he clearly wished to establish her as some sort of disciple. The extent of his failure can be seen in Salomé's book on Nietzsche, *Friedrich Nietzsche in seinen Werken*, which appeared in 1894. Though this was path-breaking in that it was the first full-length treatise on Nietzsche's works, there is far too much emphasis on the literal meaning of what Nietzsche wrote, without an appreciation of his originality:[48] Salomé presumes that Nietzsche had a system, whereas this was precisely what he studiously avoided. Nevertheless, some of her psychological insights are profound, in the same way that her observations on Ibsen in her first scholarly work, *Henrik Ibsens Frauengestalten* (1891), are psychologically astute. Clearly, even before she had met Freud in 1911,[49] she had a propensity for psychology, which she found a joy from her first encounter with it,[50] and it is not surprising that she became a proficient practitioner of psychoanalysis through her collaboration with Freud from 1912 until her death.[51]

The failure of Nietzsche's attempt to come close to Lou Salomé in Tautenberg can, in large measure, be laid at Elisabeth's door; nevertheless, as in the affair with Gillot, Lou Salomé clearly had difficulties of her own in relating to intelligent men. The upshot of the whole *fracas* was that instead of Nietzsche being included in Lou Salomé's plan for a *ménage à trois* that winter, she and Rée departed for Paris together. Nietzsche was left feeling bereft and bemused as to what had gone wrong. Subsequently, Lou would live in a platonic relationship with Rée in Berlin and Vienna for three years, until she met Andreas in 1886; they were married in June 1887. Rée was as devastated as Nietzsche had been over his

---

[48] See Livingstone, *Lou Andreas-Salomé*, p. 95ff.

[49] According to her memoirs, Lou Salomé met Freud at the Psychoanalytical Congress in Weimar Society in 1911. On the strength of this, she determined to study under Freud and went to Vienna in 1912 for that purpose.

[50] Livingstone, *Lou Andreas-Salomé*, p. 149.

[51] A full account of Lou Salomé's engagement with psychoanalysis can be found in Biddy Martin, *Woman and Modernity: The (Life)Styles of Lou Andreas-Salomé*, New York, 1991, pp. 191-229.

sudden abandonment in favour of Andreas; Lou, for her part, had merely swopped one platonic lover for another, since she never allowed Andreas to consummate their marriage. In 1897, after ten years of marriage, she finally surrendered her virginity to the young Rilke, then twenty-one; Lou Salomé was thirty-six. Rilke proceeded to become emotionally dependent on Lou, so that Mackey[52] has argued that she took up psychoanalysis to help him overcome his crises, one of which was actually caused by their break-up. Lou Salomé became a member of Freud's circle, and her later works include many posthumous essays on the topic of psychoanalysis. After her affair with Rilke, which had ended by early 1901, Lou Salomé had several other lovers, though the greatest challenge to her marriage came in the person of Georg Ledebour, whom she met in 1891. To her consternation, he immediately detected the fact that she was still a virgin.[53]

Although, in her theoretical work, Lou Salomé argues in favour of woman's destiny as mother, she nevertheless feared motherhood herself because of the brake it would place on her intellectual life. Her stance is not unusual for the time: the emergence of independent women had not been followed by the emergence of reliable birth control methods, which in any case were still shrouded in mystery and viewed by many as immoral. Though speculation is rife about whether or not she ever had an abortion, or whether she just miscarried, she was certainly pregnant at least once by Zemek (Friedrich Pineles). Apparently, she took a protective interest in Marie, her husband's daughter by the housekeeper. Though one ought not to pry into another woman's marriage, we are entitled to view as inconsistent some of the instructions she laid down for other women but manifestly failed to follow herself, such as her recommendation for women to follow their maternal calling. Her principal point was that women should exult in their biological destiny: they should not try to emulate men. Radical feminists such as Hedwig Dohm took exception to Lou Salomé's anti-feminism, as discussed in Chapter Five, in particular to her crushing remarks on the folly of women who wish to pursue a career.[54] Dohm also objected to her disparagement of women who wish to write as a profession,

---

[52] L. S. Mackey, *Lou Salomé, inspiratrice et interpr te de Nietzsche, Rilke et Freud*, Paris, 1959, p. 140.

[53] Ledebour recognised that Salomé was 'still a girl' even when told she was married. See Lou Andreas-Salomé, *Lebensrückblick. Grundriß einiger Lebenserinnerungen*, ed. by Ernst Pfeiffer, Frankfurt am Main, 1979 [1951], p. 208.

[54] Lou Andreas-Salomé, 'Der Mensch als Weib' in *Die Erotik. Vier Aufsätze*, Frankfurt am Main and Berlin, 1986, p. 29.

something which it is impossible not to view as hypocritical, since she took herself seriously as a writer. Her official pronouncement on the matter was that writing should not be more than a pleasant hobby for women.[55]

Lou Salomé's definition of femininity is found in several essays, 'Der Mensch als Weib' (1899), 'Gedanken über das Liebesproblem' (1900), 'Die Erotik' (1910) and 'Psychosexualität' (1917). The first three essays form a coherent argument. Lou Salomé takes issue with the low evaluation of woman's role in society by showing that in nature, the female of the species is usually the independent one. She argues that woman is less differentiated than man, but adds that precisely this is her strength: she has her *Heimat* around her like a snail, and is thus still connected to the 'all encompassing, infinite whole'.[56] Woman is in harmony with her surroundings through her biology. Thus, Salomé refuses to be drawn on the issue of equality, since it does not apply. Woman, through her biological functioning, lives a 'sexually heightened life' even in areas which lie beyond the usual bounds of 'feminine and motherly' functions, Salomé's euphemism for intercourse and childbirth. Clearly, Salomé's reading of Wilhelm Bölsche's *Das Liebesleben in der Natur* (1898–1901) had led her to draw certain conclusions about female physiology which she then makes applicable to women's lives in general: all women.

It is not just the content of Salomé's remarks which make them uncomfortable reading for a feminist: there is also the matter of style. Salomé cloaks her comments in tones of hushed mystique.[57] Her vision (which infuriated Hedwig Dohm) was that woman should be content to be a 'drop in the ocean' of life.[58] In Lou Salomé's defence, one can say that she wished to avoid the label of mannishness (in other words lesbianism) which had been attached to women who campaigned for 'the cause'. The influence of Nietzsche's elitist ideas is also apparent. In addition, Lou appears to have convinced herself that a woman did not need to actually give birth to children in order to be 'maternal', and thus in touch with 'the all'; her biology made sure that she was in tune with nature. Such harmony cast a radiance all around

---

[55] Lou Andreas-Salomé, 'Ketzereien gegen die modernen Frau', in *Die Zukunft*, 7, 26, 1888/1889, pp. 237–240, p. 239.

[56] Andreas-Salomé, 'Der Mensch als Weib', p. 9.

[57] See Carol Diethe, 'Lou Andreas-Salomé and Female Sexuality', in *German Women Writers 1900–1933: Twelve Essays*, ed. by Brian Keith-Smith, New York, Ontario and Lampeter, 1993, pp. 25–40.

[58] Andreas-Salomé, 'Der Mensch als Weib', p. 36f.

a woman so that all she had to do to exert the beneficial effect of motherliness (whether matron or not) was simply to be, to exist.

In her novel *Ruth* (1895), Lou Salomé gives a fictionalised account of her relationship with Gillot (Erik in the novel). The only departure from the broad biographical outline is that Erik is an atheist. He has carefully looked after his invalid wife for many years, but when he falls in love with Ruth, he tells his Klare-Bel that he can no longer love her. He does this in an unkind manner, though one could ask whether there is actually a kind way of conveying this type of information. The rejection itself, just after Klare-Bel has relearned to walk and has indicated to her husband that sexual relations could now resume, is extremely well written, without bathos, and informative in terms of plot, since the sexual deprivation on the part of Erik has been guessed at by the reader throughout the novel. We have seen him stroking Ruth's hair and sitting her on his lap, as Gillot did with Lou, and he gives her the pet name *Liebling*.[59] Clear-sighted as her name suggests, Klare-Bel leaves her husband so that the way is free for him to propose to Ruth. He does so, ironically, just after his own son Jonas has proposed to her, and it is doubly ironic that part of Ruth's reason for rejecting Erik is that he has been unkind to Klare-Bel. The novel also raises questions about the role of the wife and mother and about the 'New Woman'; given Lou Salomé's sustained attack on the feminists, it is somewhat surprising to be presented with two young 'moderns', Ruth herself and Frau Römer, with her bobbed hair and admiring husband, Professor Römer. However, we are informed that Frau Römer's activities are only connected with charitable concerns – soup kitchens – and then only in a very small way.[60] Almost as a side issue, Ruth apparently enrols at Heidelberg University as *Hörerin*, although we are told nothing about the lectures she attends, and there is no authorial recognition that this new and radical departure had been largely brought about by the efforts of the feminists.

Lou Salomé's own stance towards the married woman is made clear through the actions of the invalid Klare-Bel. Having staked her whole life on her husband and children, she experiences nothing but a void within herself when she realises that her husband no longer loves her, hence her flight into religion. Lou

---

[59] Lou Andreas-Salomé, *Ruth*, Stuttgart 1897 [1895], p. 75: 'Erik, who was much better at understanding others than himself, never guessed how strongly a youthful, demanding desire rose up in him, concealed beneath the cloak of the pedagogue.'

[60] Andreas-Salomé, *Ruth*, p. 170.

herself would applaud the selfless affection which Klare-Bel has towards her family, but she would also argue that woman is autonomous and must find her strength within herself. An important feature of the plot is that Erik made a terrible mistake by marrying Klare-Bel whilst he was still a student. The birth of Jonas put paid to all his projects and hopes; after the accident, the men in the family have to perform the tasks which rightfully belong to the woman of the house. The family is thus inherently out of balance. Lou Salomé's skill in anticipating Freud's perception of the re-channeling of sexual libido is shown in the delineation of the efforts made by Erik to be the most rigorous teacher in town, and Jonas to be the best scholar in class. The competition between the two of them for Ruth's love (though Jonas is unaware that his father is a direct rival) prefigures Freud's theories on the Oedipal complex. Lou Salomé is less skilful in showing the inner life of Klare-Bel, though in fairness it should be said that the inner life of her nubile eponymous heroine is the centre of her study. What can be said is that the effects of Klare-Bel's injury and her subsequent sterility underline the cautionary tale which is here set out, since the propensity for motherhood, or at least the general attitude of motherly care, is crucial for Lou Salomé.

In the novella *Fenitschka*, 1898, the influence of Nietzsche on Lou Salomé is clearly visible. The story depicts a young woman who resists seduction by a man (an incident apparently derived from real life, when Wedekind tried to force himself on Lou Salomé in Paris in 1894).[61] The Nietzschean influence is traced through the ages of the protagonists, with Fenitschka just at the age she was when she met Nietzsche in 1882. In addition, the marriage proposal in the story could allude to Nietzsche's putative proposal to Salomé, which made her angry and defensive. Though Nietzsche later tried to explain away the matter of whether or not he had proposed to Salomé (he put it as a matter of being 'prepared to do the right thing' if people were to gossip about himself and Lou[62]), Salomé herself had thought he had proposed and acted with righteous indignation, as though he had not been treating her as an intellectual but had had his own, all-too-human agenda. With Lou Salomé, men who proposed were usually punished, and this is the case in Fenitschka: not Max Werner, the would-be seducer, but Fenitschka's lover, is the culprit in the novella. Max thinks that

---

[61] Martin, *Woman and Modernity*, p. 178.
[62] See Diethe, *Nietzsche's Women: Beyond the Whip*, pp. 49-61.

erotic love and marriage can go together, and is disabused of this view by being persuaded to overhear Fenitschka rejecting her lover because he has proposed marriage. The 'Peeping Tom' component in this *dénouement* reminds the reader of Lou Salomé's repeated attempts to have tripartite relationships with two men at the same time; invariably one or both of the men were hurt. In Berlin, Lou Salomé had attracted the attention of Ferdinand Tönnies, soon to be punished by being made to feel supernumerary in the Rée-Salomé-Tönnies triangle, especially on their trip to the Engadine in 1896, just as Lou Salomé's trip to Russia in 1899 with Andreas and Rilke made Andreas feel the odd one out.

Fenitschka ends with the heroine experiencing a kind of ecstasy following her successful bid for autonomy, complete with an acoustic backcloth of church bells.[63] This epiphany is parallelled at the end of *Ma* (1901), a novel with a similar theme in that a woman rejects her would-be suitor. However, Ma (short for Marianne) is an older woman whose two daughters have left home; she therefore only needs to consider herself. But that self must remain celibate. The lack of ease with sexual matters is also a theme in *Menschenkinder* (1899), a collection of stories which show women seeking to break away from conventional lifestyles. In the first of these stories, 'Vor dem Erwachen', the wife has, like Salomé herself, retained her virginity, though in Edith's case the age of her husband makes this plausible: Klaus Rönnies looks old enough to be her father. Edith is completely wrapped up in her own independence, which is described on a metaphysical level, so that she remains as cold as the snow outside when her old flame, Hans Ebling, tries to seduce her. In 'Eine Ausschweifung' (1898), the affair with Gillot is retraced, though the heroine places less insistence on remaining a child in her relationship with her tutor. Livingstone questions Lou Salomé's motive for blaming her sexual problems on her relationship with Gillot: 'Lou von Salomé declared – to Nietzsche and to Reé, and then no doubt to Andreas (and perhaps to Ledebour) – that her love for Gillot and its disappointment had closed off her love life for ever. But what does this mean?'[64] What it means is that in Lou Salomé's logic, the perfect relationship of spiritual oneness is wrecked when a man offers marriage, thus exposing himself as 'only a man, with nasty

---

[63] Lou Andreas-Salomé, *Fenitschka*, in Fenitschka. *Eine Ausschweifung. Zwei Erzählungen*, Frankfurt am Main, 1982 [1898], p. 97: 'All the bells sang and clanged, "thank you! Thank you!"'

[64] Livingstone, *Lou Andreas-Salomé*, p. 209.

little male desires'.[65] This tortuous reasoning might explain the behaviour of both Salomé and her heroines.

On a less personal level, Salomé provides insights into the actual dynamics of the way the sexes relate to one another which sometimes belies her anti-feminist stance. Brigid Haines writes of the opening scene in *Fenitschka*: '[w]hat comes across forcefully ... is the impossibility for a man of relating to a woman whom he has not categorised sexually.'[66] This is a theme shown even more graphically in the short story *Abteilung 'Innere Männer'*, the second in the collection *Menschenkinder*. In this story, Salomé shows the egoistic narrow-mindedness of Dr Griepenkerl when he decides to 'test' his intended fiancée, Marianne, since a kiss he has witnessed, and believed to be a sign of infidelity, was forced upon her by one of her patients. The stolen kiss makes Marianne 'feel like a whore'.[67] Through her collapse into sickness and death, Lou Salomé delivers a warning to women about the fate which can overtake them if they allow men to dictate the image of their own *persona*.

Franziska zu Reventlow, 1871–1918

Born with the new Reich at a castle near Husum into the Prussian nobility, Fanny zu Reventlow (she renamed herself Franziska when she left home) was a rebel who perceived herself as an outsider, much as did Lou Andreas-Salomé, though in Franziska's case, there was no love lost between herself and her mother. Whether this is the cause or the result of her stormy behaviour at home is not clear. She was sent away to a boarding school for young ladies in Altenburg at the age of just fifteen. On her return home in 1887, having been virtually expelled for rowdy behaviour, Franziska was unable to persuade her parents – or, more precisely, her father, whose decision was final – to let her train as a painter, though she was allowed to attend the course for teacher-training (*Lehrerinnenseminar*) in Lübeck in autumn, 1890. In Lübeck, Franziska zu Reventlow carried on a clandestine affair with Emmanuel Fehling, her brother's friend, chiefly through letters written in great secret, and lover's trysts in Lübeck

[65] Ibid., p. 210.

[66] Brigid Haines, 'Lou Andreas-Salomé's *Fenitschka*: A Feminist Reading', in *German Life and Letters*, 44, 5, October 1991, pp. 416–425, p. 420.

[67] Lou Andreas-Salomé, 'Abteilung "Innere Männer"', in *Menschenkinder. Novellen-cyklus*, Stuttgart, 1899, p. 69.

Cathedral, the *Marienkirche*. They also visited the Ibsen Club in Lübeck together, and Franziska's knowledge of the work of Ibsen and Nietzsche stems from acquaintanceship with this club. A letter to Emmanuel written on 25 February 1891 describes the excitement with which she and her brother Carl ('Catty') read *Thus Spoke Zarathustra*; the incident is related in her autobiographical novel *Ellen Olestjerne* (1912).[68] Four months later she tells Emmanuel that she has acquired *Thus Spoke Zarathustra* on credit (an ominous indication of her future method of purchasing commodities) – 'I *had* to have it'.[69]

In the summer of the following year, just after Franziska zu Reventlow had passed her teacher-training examination, her private correspondence with Emmanuel Fehling was discovered by her mother, who had broken into her daughter's writing desk. An immediate embargo was placed on further letters, whereupon Fehling, who had just begun his career in the army, distanced himself from Reventlow. The letters to Emmanuel Fehling are surprisingly frank, with Reventlow relating mundane details about her life, even to the point of mentioning that she cannot go skating because of her period; but in the same letter, and characteristically, she comments on her whole *Lebensanschauung* when she makes the following statement:

> I will and must be free; it lies deep in my nature, this boundless striving and longing for freedom. The slightest restriction, which others do not even perceive as such, is an unbearable pressure which I cannot stand, and I have to fight and run away from all restrictions, all limitations.[70]

The paradoxical dimension to this correspondence is that Emmanuel Fehling was actually somewhat conservative, though this does not appear to have bothered either of the lovers. Once again, though, a casual remark in one of the letters reveals Reventlow's whole later attitude to life:

> I agree with everything you say, but there is one idea which I cannot come to terms with, namely that procreation is the duty and purpose of marriage. One can say: this is how things are and one has to succumb to the law of nature, but I must say that I do not find that it squares up with my feelings on morality.[71]

---

[68] Franziska zu Reventlow, *Ellen Olestjerne*, in *Gesammelte Werke in Einem Band*, ed. by Else Reventlow, Munich 1925, p. 553.

[69] In Heike Gfrereis, *Franziska zu Reventlow. Jugendbriefe*, Stuttgart, 1994, p. 71.

[70] Undated letter from Franziska zu Reventlow to Emmanuel Fehling, probably 30 or 31 November 1890. In Gfrereis, *Franziska zu Reventlow*, p. 41f.

[71] Letter of 29 November 1890, in Gfrereis, *Franziska zu Reventlow*, p. 41.

This statement, which is important as a yardstick against which to measure Franziska zu Reventlow's later actions, was no doubt fairly shocking for Emmanuel Fehling to read, let alone her conventional mother. What bothered the latter even more was the frequent manifestation of passionate eroticism which makes up a good deal of the text of the letters, but also – worse – there is a clear indication that by summer 1891, Reventlow had been initiated into sex by an older man (referred to as 'der Greis'[72]). The heated style used in parts of the letters to Emmanuel Fehling is similar to that used by Bettina von Arnim in her 'factional' correspondence with Goethe. There is much mention of moonlit nights, dreams, voluptuous longing. As with Bettina, the letters function as a clearing house for Franziska zu Reventlow's own thoughts rather than an actual communication with the loved one:

> Oh, this sinking into the silent night is so holy, in it, you are all mine, and I surround you with my dreams, you dear loved one, sleep sweetly, dream of your true, longing child.[73]

The allusion to herself as 'child' here points to Franziska zu Reventlow's deliberate attempt to copy Bettina and indeed, like Bettina, who gleaned details of Goethe's early life from his mother, Franziska ingratiated herself with Fehling's mother, in the hope, according to Heike Gfrereis, that she would become a member of the Fehling family.[74]

As punishment for her outrageous behaviour, to which the letters discussed above are witness, Franziska zu Reventlow was sent to the equivalent, for her, of Siberia, actually the remote home of a 'country parson', where she was given much love and understanding by the parson's wife. Nevertheless, she escaped from this refuge on her twenty-first birthday, in 1892, and went to Wandsbeck, where she had friends through the network of the Ibsen Club. Here, she met another Ibsen enthusiast, the Hamburg lawyer Walter Lübke, who paid for her to go to Munich for a year (in 1893) to study art. This financial assistance was necessary since Franziska zu Reventlow's parents had disinherited her; the quarrel would remain final, and she was not even allowed past her mother to see her dying father,[75] nor was she summoned to her

---

[72] See letter of 13 June 1891, in Gfrereis, *Franziska zu Reventlow*, p. 69ff.

[73] Franziska von Reventlow to Emmanuel Fehling, 17 January 1891, in Gfrereis, *Franziska zu Reventlow*, p. 59.

[74] Gfrereis, *Franziska zu Reventlow*, p. 23.

[75] The priest was given the message to pass on from her mother: 'Go away, you are not welcome here any more' (du hast hier nichts zu suchen). In *Franziska zu Reventlow. Autobiographisches*, ed. by Ellen Reventlow, Frankfurt am Main and Berlin, 1986, p. 75.

dying mother.[76] In 1894, Franziska zu Reventlow married Lübke, and 'played at being a lawyer's wife in Hamburg' for a year;[77] in 1895, Walter allowed her to return to Munich to finish her art studies. She returned home pregnant by an artist in Munich; before she had told Walter, she had a miscarriage from which she was ill for over half a year. She finally told Walter about her promiscuity, knowing that it would mean the end of the marriage. She left the hospital completely alone and in despair at the turn her life was taking; her depression lasted until the New Year, when she notes in her diary:

> Why do I experience life so wonderfully intensely if I have many [partners]? – I always have the feeling that I actually belong to them all. And then there is always the terrible catastrophe of thereby losing the one who loves me. Why are love and eroticism so completely separated in me?[78]

Walter divorced Franziska zu Reventlow in 1897. In *Ellen Olestjerne*, the marriage of Reinhard and Ellen has a similar scenario, except that Ellen is already pregnant (by the painter Henryk) when she marries Reinhard.

By the spring of 1897, Franziska zu Reventlow realised to her great joy that she was pregnant, and her son Rolf was born on the first of September. It is not overstating matters to say that she worshipped her child. Her diary for September 1897 records: '[e]verything depends on him, all my love and all my life, and for me the world is wonderful again, with gods and temples and the blue sky above.'[79] Nicknamed 'Bubi', Rolf went everywhere with his mother (though never to school); when he was called up to fight in the war, his mother helped him to desert. Rolf was the single solid point of reference in a life which continued to be characterised by sex with many partners. Perhaps one can point out, without sounding too much like the 'moral majority', that Franziska zu Reventlow was entirely protected by her aristocratic name from campaigners who were trying to 'clean up' the morals of the big cities, and targeting prostitution and illegitimacy. Had she been under-age, her child would have almost certainly been removed from her for adoption, and if she were alive today, Rolf would probably be taken into care. Though Franziska zu

---

[76] Richard Faber, *Franziska zu Reventlow und die Schwabinger Gegenkultur*, Cologne, Weimar and Vienna, 1993, p. 182.

[77] Else Reventlow in her Introduction ('Biographische Skizze') to *Franziska zu Reventlow. Tagebücher 1895–1910*, Munich and Vienna, 1992, p. 16.

[78] In Gfrereis, *Franziska zu Reventlow*, p. 92.

[79] Reventlow, *Franziska zu Reventlow. Tagebücher 1895–1910*, p. 71.

Reventlow was not a prostitute in the sense of earning her living through selling sex, she did extract money from any source possible, including her lovers – though often enough they were even more broke than she was. Even so, this was *fin-de-siècle* Germany, in moral matters often more Catholic than the Pope. The fact that Franziska zu Reventlow was able to continue her promiscuous lifestyle unmolested by the police (who were sharply proscriptive towards acknowledged prostitutes) shows two things: the magic wand of aristocratic descent in Wilhelmine Germany, and the permissiveness of the Schwabing district of Munich.

As discussed already, the Schwabing area of Munich was the centre of a hedonistic Bohemian lifestyle in which Franziska zu Reventlow now fully participated. Naturally, Munich also had an active feminist movement, but the 'cosmic' circle to which Reventlow belonged, who despised Wilhelmine respectability in all its manifestations, also viewed the feminists as proto-lesbians who were trying to make women more manly; the attempts by feminists to clean up sexual morality by arguing that men should be more chaste was laughed at.[80] Franziska zu Reventlow herself wrote a short essay on the feminists, 'Viragines oder Hetëren?', in which she outlined her position. She believed that women were out of place in the universities as well as in the work place. In contrast to a male student who revels and carouses and makes love as part and parcel of his pathway to a professional career, the female student 'does not drink, does not make love, she just lives in and for her work and does not count as a woman any more'.[81] The career world belongs to men: '[i]t is the man who gets the job which suits him by nature, he is the dominant one everywhere, the active one, in all walks of life, in all professions.'[82] In this sense, Franziska zu Reventlow simply uttered a broad 'amen' to everything Nietzsche had said on the subject, but added her own comment that the position of women who were forced to work for their daily bread was a scandal and should be the object of the feminists' concerns.[83] It is highly ironic that, in spite of her many occupations which she was forced to undertake in order to feed herself and Bubi, she never actually saw herself as a working woman.

---

[80] Regina Schaps, 'Tragik und Erotik – Kultur der Geschlechter: Franziska Gräfin zu Reventlows "modernes Hetärentum"' in Wolfgang Lipp, ed., *Kulturtypen, Kulturcharaktere. Träger, Mittler und Stifter von Kultur*, Berlin, 1987.
[81] In Gfrereis, *Franziska zu Reventlow*, p. 123. The extract from the essay, which first appeared in *Zürcher Diskussionen* in 1899, is found on pp. 123–125.
[82] In Gfrereis, *Franziska zu Reventlow*, p. 125.
[83] Ibid., p. 125.

Confirmation that Nietzsche was on everyone's lips in the 'cosmic' community can be found in Franziska's novel *Herrn Dames Aufzeichnungen* (1913). This gives a suitably witty account of the chaotic lifestyle of the *Kosmiker*, where a hedonistic and Dionysian lifestyle is *de rigeur*. All that belongs to the bourgeois world of Moloch is 'Molochistic' and outlawed. The novel is a *roman à clef*[84], providing valuable insights into the *Kosmiker* circle; key figures are Hallwig (Klages), Delius (Schuler) and Professor Hofmann (Wolfskehl). As Szély has shown, Maria and Susanna both represent Franziska zu Reventlow, with Maria representing the affair with Klages (from August 1899 until the end of 1902) and Susanna representing Reventlow at the time of her relationship with 'Such', Bogdan von Suchocki, from September 1902. Maria therefore documents an earlier period in the life of Reventlow, when she was deeply involved with the *Kosmiker*, whilst Susanna represents the later *ménage à trois* with Such and Franz Hessel, from the end of October 1903 until the end of May 1906. Maria is criticised by the *Kosmiker* for her affairs with bourgeois men, dubbed 'tin soldiers' in the novel; actually, though it is not clearly stated in the novel, the men are beginning to quarrel over her. In real life, Klages was jealous that Franziska was having a relationship with Wolfskehl at the same time.

Though Richard Faber sees Franziska zu Reventlow's 'lived hedonism'[85] as a precondition for a heightened pitch of vitality, Szély points out that the appointment of Reventlow to the position of high priestess of hetaerism actually had the effect of restricting her freedom: 'Franziska zu Reventlow was flattered to be admired and honoured as a hetaera, but she regretted seeing her hitherto spontaneous libertine way of living increasingly being seen as an artificial hetaerism under the expectations of the *Kosmiker*'.[86] The novel describes parties and the Fasching carnival, which in Wahnmoching (Schwabing) are construed as portents of a 'Dionysian age',[87] everyone having read their Nietzsche, but its main event is the threatened attempt on Hofmann's life by Hallwig, reminding readers of the real-life quarrel between Klages and Wolfskehl in 1904. Franziska zu Reventlow makes it

---

[84] Johannes Szély, *Franziska Gräfin zu Reventlow. Leben und Werk*, Bonn, 1979, pp. 79–81.

[85] Richard Faber, *Männerrunde mit Gräfin. Die 'Kosmiker' Derleth, George, Klages, Schuler, Wolfskehl und Franziska zu Reventlow*, Frankfurt am Main, Berlin, Bern, New York, Paris and Vienna, 1994, p. 186.

[86] Szély, *Franziska Gräfin zu Reventlow*, p. 133.

[87] Franziska zu Reventlow, *Herrn Dames Aufzeichnungen*, in Franziska zu Reventlow, *Gesammelte Werke in einem Bande*, p. 788.

abundantly clear in the novel, through the character of Dr Sendt (based on Paul Stern), that she does not approve of the anti-Semitism of Hallwig and Delius. The latter is shown to be on the brink of insanity, arguing that Martin Luther was a Jew. In real life, Schuler was even madder, believing himself to be the reincarnation of a Roman legionary.

To keep track of Franziska zu Reventlow's sexual partners[88] is only the task of this study in so far as her tempestuous need for sex informs her literature: for instance, Klages was influential in encouraging Franziska zu Reventlow to write her major work, *Ellen Olestjerne*. Whether Franziska zu Reventlow was actually happy with her lifestyle is something that the novels do not really reveal, though the hetaeric lifestyle is praised in *Ellen Olestjerne*: '[t]here was such a voluptuousness in feeling mistress over one's own body'.[89] The letters and diaries say more. In 1899, she visited Greece with Albrecht Hentschl (Adam), naturally at his expense. Though they had agreed to have an affair based on 'free love', Franziska zu Reventlow was somewhat troubled when Hentschel married in 1901. In March of that year she writes: 'I have had too little love in my life, and who needed it more than me?'.[90] It was sometimes hard for her to realise that men whom she had hurt, such as her husband Walther, did not want to remain friends. In *Ellen Olestjerne*, Ellen reflects 'Henryk, Mutter, Reinhard, none of them know what love is. They are hard'.[91] The loneliness of such reflections was made infinitely worse through Reventlow's incapacity to deal with money. This reached such a pitch that in 1909 she had to leave Munich in order to flee from her creditors. In Tessin, Franziska zu Reventlow married the Baltic Baron Rechenberg-Linten; Rechenberg senior only realised that this was a marriage of convenience just before his death, whereupon he disinherited his son. Nevertheless, when her husband died, Franziska zu Reventlow had a considerable sum which she put in the bank in Locarno, only to hear – in 1914 – that the bank itself (centred in Tessin) had gone bankrupt. Again and again in her diaries there is reference to the pressure she is under to earn money; however, no sooner did she have the hard-won

---

[88] The details are in Faber, *Franziska zu Reventlow und die Schwabinger Gegenkultur*, pp. 130–176 ('Große Lieben Franziska zu Reventlows').

[89] Reventlow, *Ellen Olestjerne*, p. 674.

[90] Reventlow's diary entry for 30 March 1901, in *Franziska zu Reventlow. Tagebücher 1895–1910*, ed. by Else Reventlow, Munich and Vienna, 1992, p. 183.

[91] Reventlow, *Ellen Olestjerne*, p. 697.

[92] Franziska zu Reventlow, *Der Geldkomplex*, in *Gesammelte Werke in einem Bande*, p. 909.

cash in her hands than it flowed out again. She inherited 8,000 Marks from her mother in 1905, but by the following year this had been spent.

Though Franziska zu Reventlow's stance towards money appears to have been informed by the studied indifference of the aristocrat, it was also typical of the relationship of the bohemian towards money; it must be faced that she could have lived a much less stressful life if she had been able to sort out her financial affairs. In her last work of any significance, *Der Geldkomplex* (1916), she laughs at her own incapacity to deal with money by diagnosing it as a Freudian neurosis which can, ostensibly, by cured by psychoanalysis in a special sanatorium. However, the first-person narrator of the story finds that money, not the lack of it, is the cure for her nervous condition: she finds gambling a relaxation: '… you see nothing but money and feel nothing but money and that is just what I was in need of'.[92] At the end of the novel, the main character loses all her money in a bank failure, but shrugs off the disaster with a flippancy characteristic of the literary characters in Wahnmoching, where one word could be used to end all discussion: 'Mirobuk!'. In playing poker with her own life, Franziska zu Reventlow made that, and not her writing, her creative work of art; and what could be more Nietzschean?

NDICATIVE BIBLIOGRAPHY

bibliography is not exhaustive; where possible, the collected works been cited, otherwise the main works are cited in every case, and as secondary sources as exist or as many as was practicable, there being e variation in the material available. Articles are not included in the graphy; relevant details are given in the footnotes to the chapters.

INDIVIDUAL WRITERS

Andreas-Salomé, Lou

Primary Works:

as-Salomé, Lou, (alias 'Henri Lou'), *Im Kampf um Gott*, Berlin, 1885.
Henrik Ibsen's Frauen-Gestalten, Berlin, 1892.
Friedrich Nietzsche in seinen Werken, Vienna, 1894.
Ruth, Stuttgart, 1895.
Fenitschka. Eine Ausschweifung. Zwei Erzählungen, Stuttgart, 1898.
Menschenkinder. Novellencyklus, 1899.
Ma, Stuttgart, 1901.
Im Zwischenland, Stuttgart and Berlin, 1902.
Die Erotik, Frankfurt, 1910.
Rainer Maria Rilke, Leipzig, 1928.
Lebensrückblick. Grundriß einiger Lebenserinnerungen, ed. by Ernst Pfeiffer, ankfurt am Main, 1975 [1951].

Secondary Sources:

, Rudolph, *Frau Lou: Nietzsche's Wayward Disciple*, Princeton, 1968.
ke, Cordula, *Lou Andreas-Salomé. Leben, Persönlichkeit, Werk*, Frankfurt am ain, 1986.
stone, Angela, *Lou Andreas-Salomé*, London, 1984.
y, Ilona Schmidt, *Lou Salomé, inspiratrice et interpréte de Nietzsche, Rilke et ud*, Paris, 1968.
, Biddy, *Woman and Modernity: The (Life)Styles of Lou Andreas-Salomé*, Ithaca d London, 1991.

EPILOGUE

It is astonishing to note that literary examples of nervous or psychosomatic illness such as that encountered in Reuter's *Aus guter Familie* are as frequent in the works of women writers at the end of the century as they were at the beginning, indicating that women throughout the century were dependant on men for an evaluation of their own identity, though the authorial position has become much more critical of such an attitude. Male characters are portrayed as harsh judges of women's morality, no doubt because they were in real life: upon a kiss (in Lou Salomé's story *Abteilung 'Innere Männer'*), or lack of one (in Gabriele Reuter's *Aus guter Familie*), a woman's whole fate can hang. Only the most brazen woman, such as Franziska zu Reventlow, could challenge the assumptions about the respectable woman's need to preserve her virtue, and even she adhered to what can be called the ideology of motherhood, which dominated women's perception of their role in society in spite of the new sciences of psychoanalysis and sexology. These were about to overturn many assumptions dear to the German middle class, such as the assumption that children are without sexual desire.

Several important features of German cultural life became more reactionary rather than less as the century drew to its close. As has been shown, the new Civil Code contained little to relieve the repression of women; in addition, the banning of socialism from 1878 until 1890 meant that socialist feminists such as Clara Zetkin and Lily Braun were taboo to the moderates, who in their turn opposed the efforts of the radicals, such as Hedwig Dohm and Helene Stöcker. They, as we have seen, drew much from the

arch anti-feminist Nietzsche. Such paradoxes, a[n] splits in the feminist movement in Germany, wo[uld] hamper progress until the removal of the *Reich*[...] 1908 resulted in the BDF being flooded by mod[...] hitherto held back from any political activity. [...] nature of the German feminist movement after G[...] became its president in 1910 placed it on a pat[h...] lead it very close to collaboration with the Nation[...]

Anti-Semitism was another feature of Germa[n] political life which was as pronounced at the end [of] it was at the beginning. The earlier, harmless vie[w] a 'people' such as the Saxons or the Prussians b[...] insistence on the German *Volk* as sole constituen[t] blinkered concept which excluded other nationa[l...] the Jews, not even a nation at that time, doubly su[...] target of bitter anti-Semitism from such historia[n] This occurred in spite of the acknowledged cult[...] the Germans owed to the Jews, dating from the [...] Mendelssohn onwards. The anti-Semitism portra[yed] zu Reventlow in *Herrn Dames Aufzeichnungen* so[...] note for what was to come. It is also signific[ant] conversions of Jews to Christianity had not alway[s] as those of Henriette Herz and Rahel Varnhage[n] century. Many Jewish women, such as Fanny Lew[...] Dohm, found that conversion to Christianity [...] spiritual limbo, and the result was unfamilia[r] Judaism or Christianity. What nobody could an[...] conversion would not be recognised as a qualifica[...] nationality under the National Socialists.

What does change by the end of the century is [...] no longer prepared to be the instigators of man[...] instead self-consciously use their writing as a p[...] own self-knowledge, even if they need a ma[...] husband or lover), or the influence of a male th[...] be made manifest. The influence of some wome[n] von Varnhagen, Bettina von Arnim and Malwida [...] has remained seminal, though the other wom[...] these pages have not – yet – become sufficiently [...] such an influence. The effects of two wars, [...] division of Germany and, finally, reunification, h[...] the natural process of influence, but there now [...] determined *Putsch* to make up for lost time, a[...] works amply demonstrate.

Arnim, Bettina von

Primary Works:

Arnim, Bettine von, *Werke und Briefe*, 4 vols, ed. by Wolfgang Bunzel, Ulrike Landfester, Walter Schmitz and Sibylle von Steinsdorff, Frankfurt am Main, 1986–1995.

Secondary Sources:

Arnim, Hans von, *Bettina von Arnim*, Berlin, 1963.

Bäumer, Konstanze, *Bettine, Psyche, Mignon*, Stuttgart, 1986.

—— and Hartwig Schultz, *Bettina von Arnim*, Stuttgart and Weimar, 1995.

Böttger, Fritz, *Bettina von Arnim. Ein Leben zwischen Tag und Traum*, Berlin, 1986.

Drewitz, Ingeborg, *Bettine von Arnim. Romantik, Revolution, Utopie*, Düsseldorf and Cologne, 1969.

Hirsch, Helmut, *Bettine von Arnim*, Reinbek bei Hamburg, 1987.

Liebertz-Grün, Ursula, *Ordnung im Chaos. Studien zur Poetik der Bettine Brentano-von Arnim*, Heidelberg, 1989.

Schormann, Sabine, *Bettina von Arnim: die Bedeutung Schleiermachers für ihr Leben und Werk*, Tübingen, 1993.

Seidel, Ina, *Die Dichterin der Deutschen*, Stuttgart, 1944.

Weißenborn, Birgit, *Bettina von Arnim und Goethe. Topographie einer Beziehung als Beispiel weiblicher Emanzipation zu Beginn des 19. Jahrhunderts*, Frankfurt am Main, Bern, New York and Paris, 1987.

Wyss, Hilde, *Bettina von Arnims Stellung zu der Romantik und dem jungen Deutschland*, Bern and Leipzig, 1935.

Böhlau Helene

Primary Works:

Böhlau, Helene, *Gesammelte Werke*, 4 vols, Weimar, 1927.

——, *Gesammelte Werke*, 5 vols, Weimar, 1929.

Secondary Sources:

Becker, Josef, 'Helene Böhlau. Leben und Werk', PhD Diss., Zürich, 1978.

Singer, Sandra, *Free Soul, Free Woman? A Study of Selected Works by Hedwig Dohm, Isolde Kurz and Helene Böhlau*, New York, Washington/Baltimore, Bern, Frankfurt am Main, Berlin, Vienna and Paris, 1995.

Zillmann, Friedrich, *Helene Böhlau. Ein Beitrag zu ihrer Würdigung*, Leipzig, 1918.

Dohm, Hedwig

Primary Works: (Literary)

Dohm, Hedwig, *Christa Ruhland*, Berlin, 1902.

——, *Der Seelenretter*, Vienna, 1876.

——, *Die Ritter vom goldenen Kalb*, Berlin, 1879.

——, *Plein Air*, Berlin and Stuttgart, 1891.

——, *Schicksale einer Seele*, Berlin, 1899.

——, *Schwanenlieder. Novellen*, Berlin, 1906.

——, *Sibilla Dalmar. Roman aus dem Ende dieses Jahrhunderts*, Berlin, 1896.

——, *Sommerlieben. Freiluftnovellen*, Berlin, 1910.

——, *Vom Stamm der Asra*, Berlin, 1876.

——, *Wie Frauen werden/ Werde, die du bist!*, Breslau, 1894.

Primary Works: (Political)

——, *Der Frauen Natur und Recht*, Berlin, 1876.
——, *Der Jesuitismus im Hausstande*, Berlin, 1873.
——, *Der Mißbrauch des Todes*, Berlin-Wilmersdorf, 1917.
——, *Die Antifeministen*, Berlin, 1902.
——, *Die Mütter*, Berlin, 1903.
——, *Die wissenschaftliche Erziehung der Frau*, Berlin, 1874.
——, *Erziehung zum Stimmrecht der Frau*, Berlin, 1909.
——, *Was die Pastoren von den Frauen denken*, Berlin and Leipzig, 1872.

Secondary Sources:

Brandt, Heike, *'Die Menschenrechte haben kein Geschlecht'. Die Lebensgeschichte der Hedwig Dohm*, Weinheim, 1995.
Meißner, Julia, *Mehr Stolz, ihr Frauen! Hedwig Dohm – eine Biographie*, Düsseldorf, 1987.
Pailer, Gaby, *Schreibe, die du bist! Die Gestaltung weiblicher 'Autorschaft' im erzählerischen Werk Hedwig Dohms*, Bamberg, 1994.
Reed, Philippa, *'Alles, was ich schreibe, steht im Dienst der Frauen'. Zum essayistischen und fiktionalalen Werk Hedwig Dohms (1833–1919)*, Frankfurt am Main, Bern, New York and Paris, 1987.
Schreiber, Adele, *Hedwig Dohm als Vorkämpferin und Vordenkerin neuer Frauenideale*, Berlin, 1914.

Droste-Hülshoff, Annette von

Primary Works:

Droste-Hülshoff, Annette von, *Sämtliche Werke*, ed. by Clemens Heselhaus, Munich, 1966.
Schulte-Kemminghausen, Karl, ed., *Die Briefe der Annette Droste-Hülshoff*, 2 vols, Darmstadt, 1968.

Secondary Sources:

Heselhaus, Clemens, *Annette von Droste-Hülshoff. Werk und Leben*, Düsseldorf, 1971.
Lavater-Sloman, Mary, *Annette von Droste-Hülshoff. Einsamkeit und Leidenschaft*, Munich, 1981.
Maurer, Doris, *Annette von Droste-Hülshoff. Ein Leben zwischen Auflehnung und Gehorsam/Biographie*, Bonn, 1982.
Mare, Margaret, *Annette von Droste-Hülshoff*, London, 1963.
Nettesheim, Josefine, *Die geistige Welt der Dichterin Annette von Droste-Hülshoff*, Münster, 1967.
Reuter, Gabriele, *Annette von Droste-Hülshoff*, Berlin, 1905.
Schücking, Levin, *Annette von Droste-Hülshoff. Ein Lebensbild*, Hannover, 1862.
Sichelschmidt, Gustav, *Allein mit meinem Zauberwort. Annette von Droste-Hülshoff. Eine Biographie*, Düsseldorf, 1990.

Ebner-Eschenbach, Marie von

Primary Works:

Ebner-Eschenbach, Marie von, *Sämtliche Werke*, 12 vols, Leipzig, 1928.
——, *Gesammelte Werke*, 9 vols, Munich, 1961.
——, *Tagebücher*, ed. by Konrad Polheim and Rainer Baasner, I: 1862–1869, Tübingen, 1989; II: 1871–1878, Tübingen, 1991.

Secondary Sources:

Alkemade, Mechtildis, *Die lebens- und Weltanschauung der Freifrau Marie von Ebner-Eschenbach*, Graz, 1935.

Benesch, Kurt, *Die Frau mit den 100 Schicksalen. Das Leben von der Marie von Ebner-Eschenbach*, Vienna and Munich, 1966.

Bettelheim, Anton, *Marie von Ebner-Eschenbach. Biographische Blätter*, Berlin, 1900.

——, *Marie von Ebner-Eschenbachs Wirken und Vermächtnis*, Leipzig, 1920.

Bramkamp, Agathe C., *Marie von Eschenbach: The Author, Her Time and Her Critics*, Bonn, 1990.

Fussenegger, Gertrud, *Marie von Ebner-Eschenbach oder der gute Mensch von Zdißlawitz*, Munich, 1967.

Necker, Moritz, *Marie von Ebner-Eschenbach nach ihren Werken geschildert*, Munich, 1916.

Rose, Ferrel V, *The Guises of Modesty: Marie von Ebner-Eschenbach's Female Artists*, Columbia SC, 1994.

Wintersteiner, Marianne, *Ein kleines Lied, wie fängt's nur an … Das Leben der Marie von Ebner-Eschenbach. Eine erzählende Biographie*, Heilbronn, 1989.

Fouqué, Caroline de la Motte

Primary Works:

Fouqué, Caroline de la Motte, *Rodrich*, Berlin 1806/1807.

——, *Die Frau des Falkensteins. Ein Roman in zwei Bändchen*, Berlin, 1810.

——, *Die Frauen in der großen Welt. Bildungsbuch bei'm Eintritt in das gesellige Leben*, Berlin, 1826.

——, *Magie der Natur. Eine Revolutionsgeschichte*, Berlin, Frankfurt am Main, New York and Paris, 1989 [1812].

——, *Edmunds Wege und Irrwege. Ein Roman aus der nächsten Vergangenheit*, Leipzig, 1815.

——, *The Castle of Scharffenstein*, in *German Stories Selected from the Works of Hoffmann, de la Motte Fouqué, Pichler, Kruse and Others*, trs. by R. P. Gilles, London, 1826.

Secondary Sources:

Prill, Vera, *Caroline de la Motte-Fouqué* [*sic*], Berlin, 1933.

Wägenbauer, Birgit, *Die Pathologie der Liebe. Literarische Weiblichkeitsentwürfe um 1800*, Berlin, 1996 (on Fouqué/Tarnow).

Wilde, Jean, *The Romantic Realist: Caroline de la Motte Fouqué*, New York, 1955.

Varnhagen, Karl August, *Biographische Portraits nebst Briefen von Koreff, Clemens Brentano, Frau von Fouqué, Henri Campan und Scholz*, Leipzig, 1871.

Goethe, Ottilie von

Primary Works:

Goethe, Ottilie, *Tagebücher und Briefe von und an Ottilie von Goethe*, 5 vols, ed. by Heinz Bluhm, Vienna (1–4, 1962–1966) and Bern, Frankfurt am Main and Las Vegas (5: 1979).

——, ed., *Chaos*, Bern, 1968 [facsimile of 1829–1831].

Secondary Sources:

Barth, Ilse-Marie, *Literarisches Weimar*, Stuttgart, 1971.

Bode, Wilhelm, *Damals in Weimar*, Weimar, 1917.

Gerstenberk, Jenny von, *Ottilie von Goethe und ihre Söhne Walter und Wolf*, Stuttgart, 1901.
Houben, H. H., *Ottilie von Goethe. Geständnisse 1832–1837*, Leipzig, 1923.
Janetzki, Ulrich, *Ottilie von Goethe. Goethes Schwiegertochter*, Frankfurt am Main, Berlin and Vienna, 1983.
Mahngold, Elisabeth, *Ottilie von Goethe*, Cologne and Graz, 1970.
Rahmeyer, Ruth, *Ottilie von Goethe. Das Leben einer ungewöhnlichen Frau*, Stuttgart, 1988.
Zeeman, Dorothea, *Ottilie. Ein Schicksal um Goethe*, Salzburg, 1949.

Hahn-Hahn, Ida von
Primary Works:

Hahn-Hahn, Ida, *Gesamtausgabe*, 21 vols, Berlin 1851 (contains works written 1835–1848).
——, *Gesammelte Werke*, 15 vols (contains works written 1851–1878).
First editions etc. as per dates given in the text.

Secondary Sources:

Geiger, Gerlinde Maria, *Die befreite Psyche. Emanzipationsansätze im Frühwerk Ida Hahn-Hahns (1833–1848)*, Frankfurt am Main, Bern and New York, 1986.
Lüpke, Gerd, *Ida Hahn-Hahn. Ein Lebensbild nach der Natur gezeichnet*, Leipzig, 1869.
Munster, Katrien van, 'Die junge Ida Gräfin Hahn-Hahn', PhD Diss., Graz, 1929.
Oberembt, Gerd, *Ida Gräfin Hahn-Hahn. Weltschmerz und Ultramontanismus. Studium zum Unterhaltungsroman im 19. Jahrhundert*, Bonn, 1980.
Schmid-Jürgens, Erna Ines, 'Ida Gräfin Hahn-Hahn', PhD Diss., Munich, 1933.

Herz, Henriette
Primary Works:

Fürst, J, *Henriette Herz. Ihr Leben und Ihre Erinnerungen*, Berlin, 1850. (Contains brief biography by Herz and sundry essays.)
Schmitz, Rainer, *Henriette Herz in Erinnerungen, Briefen und Zeugnissen*, Leipzig and Weimar, 1984.

Secondary Sources:

Anon., *Schleiermacher und seine Lieben in Briefen der Henriette Herz*, Magdeburg, 1910.
Davies, Martin, *Identity or History? Marcus Herz and the End of the Enlightenment*, Michigan, 1995. (Chapter Three has a large section on Henriette.)
Drewitz, Ingeberg, *Berliner Salons. Gesellschaft und Literatur zwischen Aufklärung und Industriezeitalter*, Berlin, 1965.
Landsberg, Hans, *Henriette Herz. Ihr Leben und ihre Zeit*, Weimar, 1913.

Kinkel, Johanna
Primary Works:

Kinkel, Johanna, *Hans Ibeles in London. Ein Roman aus dem Flüchtlingsleben*, ed. by Ulrike Helmer, Frankfurt am Main, 1991 [1860].
—— and Gottfried, *Erzählungen*, Stuttgart, 1883.

Secondary Sources:

Schulte, J. F., *Johanna Kinkel nach ihren Briefen und Erinnerungs-Blättern*, Münster, 1908. (*Festschrift* to mark the fiftieth anniversary of Johanna Kinkel's death.)

Lewald, Fanny

Primary Works:

Lewald, Fanny, *Gesammelte Werke*, 10 vols, Berlin, 1871 (not complete, in spite of title).

—, *Diogena (Pseudonym). Roman von Gräfin Iduna H...H...*, Leipzig, 1847.

—, *Prinz Louis Ferdinand*, Breslau, 1849.

—, *Erinnerungen aus dem Jahre 1848*, 2 vols., Braunschweig, 1850.

—, *Jenny*, ed. by Ulrike Helmer, Frankfurt am Main, 1988.

—, *Politische Schriften für und wider die Frauen*, ed. by Ulrike Helmer, Frankfurt am Main, 1989.

——, *Meine Lebensgeschichte I: Im Vaterhaus, II: Leidensjahre, III: Befreiung und Wanderleben* ed. by Ulrike Helmer, Frankfurt am Main, I: 1988 II/III: 1989.

——, *The Education of Fanny Lewald. An Autobiography*, trs. and ed. by Hanna Ballin Lewis, State University of New York Press, 1992.

——, *A Year of Revolutions: Fanny Lewald's Recollections of 1848*, trs. and ed. by Hanna Ballin Lewis, Oxford, 1997.

Secondary Sources:

Brochet-Duvillard, Mme, *Deux auteurs contemporains. Quelques pensées sur la vie des femmes*, Lausanne, 1880.

Göhler, Rudolf, *Großherzog Carl Alexander und Fanny Lewald-Stahr in ihren Briefen*, Berlin, 1932.

Rheinberg, Brigitte van, *Fanny Lewald. Geschichte einer Emanzipation*, Frankfurt am Main and New York, 1990.

Schlüpmann, Grete, 'Fanny Lewalds Stellung zur sozialen Frage', PhD Diss., Münster, 1921.

Segerbarth, Ruth, 'Fanny Lewald und ihre Auffassung von Liebe und Ehe, PhD Diss., Münster, 1920.

Steinhauer, Marieluise, 'Fanny Lewald, die deutsche George Sand. Ein Kapitel aus der Geschichte des Frauenromans im 19. Jahrhundert', PhD Diss., Berlin, 1937.

Weber, Martha, 'Fanny Lewald', PhD Diss., Zürich, 1921.

Marlitt, Eugenie

Primary Works:

Marlitt, Eugenie, *Romane und Novellen. Einzige vollständige Gesamtausgabe in 10 Bänden*, Stuttgart, Berlin and Leipzig, circa 1900.

——, *Maienblütenhauch. Die Gedichte*, ed. by Cornelia Brauer, Rudolstadt and Jena, 1994.

Secondary Sources:

Brümmer, Franz, *Eugenie Marlitt. Allgemeine deutsche Biographie*, 52, Leipzig, 1900.

Necker, Moritz, *Eugenie Marlitt. Gartenlaube*, Leipzig, 1899.

Potthast, Berta, 'Eugenie Marlitt. Ein Beitrag zur Geschichte des deutschen Frauenromans', PhD Diss., Bielefeld, 1926.

Meysenbug, Malwida von

Primary Works:

Meysenbug, Malwida von, *Gesammelte Werke*, 5 vols, ed. by Berta Schleicher, Berlin, Stuttgart, Leipzig, 1922.

Vol 1: *Memoiren einer Idealistin*, I and II
Vol 2: *Memoiren einer idealistin*, III, and *Lebensabend eiener Idealistin*
Vol 3: *Gestalten* (Originally *Individualitäten*)
Vol 4: *Kulturbilder* (originally *Stimmungsbilder*)
Vol 5: *Erzählungen* and *Himmlische und Irdische Liebe* (novel) and *Der Segen der heiligen Katharina* (Drama)
——, *Briefe an Johanna und Gottfried Kinkel 1849–1885*, Bonn, 1982.

Secondary Sources:

Meyer-Hepner, Gertrud, *Malwida von Meysenbug*, Leipzig, 1948.
Schleicher, Berta, ed., *Briefe von und an Malwida von Meysenbug*, Munich, 1920.
——, *Malwida von Meysenbug. Ein Lebensbild einer Idealistin*, Berlin, 1915.
——, *Malwida von Meysenbug*, Wedel in Holstein, 1947.
Tietz, Gunther, ed., *Malwida von Meysenbug. Ein Portrait*, Frankfurt am Main, Berlin, Vienna, 1983.
Vinant, Gaby, *Malwida de Meysenbug 1816–1903. Sa vie et ses amies*, Paris, 1932.

Otto-Peters, Louise

Primary Works: (Literary)

Otto-Peters, Louise, *Schloß und Fabrik*, Leipzig, 1996[1847].
——, *Kunst und Künstlerleben. Novellen*, Berlin, 1863.
——, *Nebeneinander*, Altona, 1866.
——, *Zerstörter Friede*, Jena, 1866.
——, *Die Idealisten. Roman*, Jena, 1867.
—— *Gedichte*. Leipzig, 1868.
——, *Theodor Körner. Oper*, Munich, 1872.
——, *Gräfin Lauretta. Historische Erzählung aus dem 14. Jahrhundert*, Leipzig, 1884.
——, *Mein Lebensgesang. Gedichte aus fünf Jahrzehnten*, Leipzig, 1893.

Primary Works: (Political)

——, *Das Recht der Frauen auf Erwerb*, Hamburg, 1866.
——, *Der Genius des Hauses*, Pest, Vienna and Leipzig, 1869.
——, *Der Genius der Menschheit*, Pest, Vienna and Leipzig, 1870.
——, *Der Genius der Natur*, Pest, Vienna and Leipzig, 1870.
——, *Frauenleben im deutschen Reich. Erinnerungen aus der Vergangenheit und Zukunft*, Leipzig, 1876.

Secondary Sources:

Gerhardt, Ute, Hanover-Drück, Elisabeth and Schmitter, Romina, eds, '*Dem Reich der Freiheit werb' ich Bürgerinnen'. Die Frauen-Zeitung von Louise Otto*, Frankfurt am Main, 1980 [1849–1852].
Goldschmidt, Henriette, *Vortrag gehaltem im Frauenbildungs-Verein*, Leipzig, 1868.
Ludwig, Johanna and Jorek, Rita, eds, *Louise Otto-Peters. Ihr Literarisches und publizisitisches Werk*, Leipzig, 1995.
Nagelschmidt, Ilse and Ludwig, Johanna, eds, *Louise Otto-Peters, Politische Denkerin und Wegbereiterin der deutschen Frauenbewegung*, Dresden, 1996.
Otto, Christine, *Variationen des 'poetischen Tendenzromans'. Das Erzählwerk Louise Otto-Peters*, Pfaffenweiler, 1995.

Reuter, Gabriele

Primary Works:

Reuter, Gabriele, *Glück und Geld*, Berlin, 1888.

——, *Aus guter Familie*, Berlin, 1895.

——, *Frau Bürgelin und ihre Söhne*, 1899.

——, *Ellen von der Weiden. Ein Tagebuch*, Berlin, 1904 [1900].

——, *Liselotte von Reckling*, Berlin, 1904.

——, *Ebner-Eschenbach*, Berlin, 1905.

——, *Frauenseelen*, Berlin, 1910 [1902].

——, *Das Tränenhaus*, Berlin, 1909.

——, *Vom Kinde zum Menschen. Die Geschichte meiner Jugend*, Berlin, 1921

Secondary Sources:

Alimadad-Mensch, Faranak, 'Gabriele Reuter. Porträt einer Schriftstellerin', PhD Diss, Bern, 1984.

Rahaman, Gabriele, 'Problems of Female Identity in the Works by Isolde Kurz and Gabriele Reuter', PhD Diss, London, 1994.

Schneider, Georgia, *Portraits of Women in Selected Works of Gabriele Reuter*, Frankfurt am Main, Bern, New York and Paris, 1988.

Reventlow, Franziska zu

Primary Works:

Reventlow, Franziska zu, *Gesammelte Werke in einem Band*, ed. by Else Reventlow, Munich, 1925.

——, *Autobiographisches. Novellen, Schriften Selbstzeugnisse*, ed. by Else Reventlow, Frankfurt am Main and Berlin, 1986.

——, *Franziska zu Reventlow. Tagebücher 1895–1910*, ed. by Else Reventlow, Munich and Vienna, 1992.

Secondary Sources:

Faber, Richard, *Franziska zu Reventlow und die Schwabinger Gegenkultur*, Cologne, Weimar and Vienna, 1993.

——, *Männerrunde mit Gräfin. Die 'Kosmiker' Derleth, George, Klages, Schuler, Wolfskehl und Franziska zu Reventlow*, Frankfurt am Main, Berlin, Bern, New York, Paris and Vienna, 1994.

Fritz, Helmut, *Die erotische Rebellion. Das Leben der Franziska zu Reventlow*, Frankfurt am Main, 1980.

Gfrereis, Heike, *Franziska zu Reventlow. Jugendbriefe*, Stuttgart, 1994.

Szély, Johannes, *Franziska Gräfin zu Reventlow. Leben und Werk*, Bonn, 1979.

Schopenhauer, Adele

Primary Works:

Schopenhauer, Adele, *Haus-: Wald und Feldmärchen*, ed. by Karl Wolfgang Becker, Berlin, 1987.

——, *Tagebuch einer Einsamen*, ed. by H.H. Houben, with illustrations, Munich, 1985.

——, *Tagebücher der Adele Schopenhauer*, 2 vols, Leipzig, 1909.

——, *Anna. Ein Roman aus der nächsten Vergangenheit*, Leipzig, 1845.

——, *Eine dänische Geschichte*, Braunschweig, 1848.

——, *Gedichte und Scherenschnitte*, ed. by H. H. Houben and Hans Wahl, Leipzig, 1920.

Secondary Sources:

Brandes, Anna, 'Adele Schopenhauer in den geistigen Beziehungen zu ihrer Zeit', PhD Diss., Frankfurt am Main, 1930.
Houben, H. H., *Die Rheingräfin. Das Leben der Sibylle Mertens Schaafhausen*, Essen, 1935.

Schopenhauer, Johanna

Primary Works:

Schopenhauer, Johanna, *Gesammelte Werke, 10 vols*, Leipzig and Frankfurt, 1834 [1830/1831].
——, *Jugend und Wanderbilder*, Tübingen, 1958 [1839].

Secondary Sources:

Düntzer, Heinrich, *Goethes Beziehungen zu Johanna und ihren Kindern*, Leipzig, 1883.
Dworetzki, Gertrud, *Johanna Schopenhauer. Ein Charakterbild aus Goethes Zeiten*, Düsseldorf, 1987.
Frost, Laura, 'Johanna Schopenhauer. Ein Frauenleben aus der klassischen Zeit', PhD Diss., Frankfurt am Main, 1905.
H. H. Houben, ed., *Damals in Weimar. Erinnerungen und Briefe von und an Johanna Schopenhauer*, Berlin, 1923.
Kühn, Paul, *Die Frauen um Goethe*, 2 vols, Leipzig, 1911/1912.
Schleucher, Kurt, *Das Leben der Amalia Schoppe und Johanna Schopenhauer*, Munich, 1983.
Schütze, Stephan, 'Die Abendgesellschaften der Hofrätin Schopenhauer in Weimar', in *Weimars Album zur vierten Säcularfeier der Buchdruckerkunst am 24. Juni 1840*, Weimar, 1840.

Varnhagen, Rahel

Primary Works:

Varnhagen, Rahel, *Gesammelte Werke*, 10 vols, ed. by Konrad Feilchenfeldt, Uwe Schweikert and Rahel Steiner, Munich, 1983.
——, *Briefwechsel*, 4 vols, ed. by Freidhelm Kemp, Munich, 1979.

Secondary Sources:

Anon., *Über Rahels Religiosität*, Leipzig, 1836.
Arendt, Hannah, *Rahel Varnhagen: Life of a Jewess*, London, 1957.
Assing, Ludmilla, ed., *Aus Rahels Herzensleben. Briefe und Tagebücher*, Leipzig, 1877.
Gerhardt, Marlis, *Ein jeder machte seine Frau aus mir wie er sie liebte und verlangte. Rahel Varnhagen/Pauline Wiesel, Ein Briefwechsel*, Darmstadt, 1987.
Hahn, Barbara, *'Antworten Sie mir!' Rahel Levin Varnhagens Briefwechsel*, Basle and Frankfurt am Main, 1989.
Hahn, Barbara and Isselstein, Ursula, *Rahel Varnhagen. Die Wiederentdeckung einer Schriftstellerin*, Göttingen, 1987.
Scurla, Herbert, *Begegnungen mit Rahel. Der Salon von Rahel Levin*, Berlin, 1962.
——, *Rahel Varnhagen. Die große Frauengestalt in der Romantik*, Düsseldorf, 1978.
Spenlé, Jean-Edouard, *Rahel. Mme Varnhagen von Ense. Histoire d'un salon romantique en allemagne*, Paris, 1910.

Subotic, Dragutin, 'Rahel Levin und das junge Deutschland. Ihr Einfluß auf die jungen Geister, PhD Diss., Munich, 1914.

Vaughan Jennings, Mrs, *Rahel: Her Life and Times*, London, 1883.

Varnhagen von Ense, Karl August, *Rahel. Ein Buch des Andenkens für ihre Freunde*, ed. by Hans Landsberg, Berlin, 1912 [1833].

Varnhagen, Karl August and Assing, Ludmilla, *Rahel und ihre Freunde. Ein Buch der Erinnerung*, ed. by Albine Fiala, Vienna and Leipzig, 1907.

SECONDARY SOURCES: GENERAL

Barth, Ilse-Marie, *Literarisches Weimar*, Stuttgart, 1971.

Blochmann, Elisabeth, *Das 'Frauenzimmer' und die Gelehrsamkeit*, Heidelberg, 1966.

Boetcher Joeres, Ruth-Ellen and Mayne, Mary Jo, *German Women in the Eighteenth and Nineteenth Centuries: A Social and Literary History*, Bloomington, 1989.

Boetcher Joeres, Ruth-Ellen and Marianne Burkhard, eds, *Out of Line/Ausgefallen: The Paradox of Marginality in the Writings of Nineteenth-Century German Women*, Amsterdam, 1989.

Bovenschen, Silvia: *Die imaginierte Weiblichkeit. Exemplarische Untersuchungen zu kulturgeschichtlichen und literarischen Präsentationsformen des Weiblichen*, Frankfurt am Main, 1979.

Bramsted, Ernest K., *Germany*, New Jersey, 1972.

Brinkler-Gabler, Gisela, *Deutsche Literatur von Frauen*, 2 vols, Munich, 1988.

——, ed., *Deutsche Literatur vom 16. Jahrhundert bis zur Gegenwart. Gedichte und Lebensläufe*, Frankfurt am Main, 1978.

——Burkhard, Marianne, ed., *Gestaltet und gestaltend. Frauen in der deutschen Literatur*, Amsterdam, 1980.

Butler, E. M., *The Tempestuous Prince: Hermann Pückler-Muskau*, London, New York and Toronto, 1929.

Cauer, Minna, *Die Frau im 19. Jahrhundert*, Berlin, 1898.

Cocalis, Susan and Goodman, Kay, *Beyond the Eternal Feminine: Critical Essays on Women and German Literature*, Stuttgart, 1982.

Conrad, Heinrich, ed., *Frauenbriefe von und an Hermann Fürsten Pücker-Muskau*, Munich and Leipzig, 1912.

Dittmar, Luise, ed., *Das Wesen der Ehe*, Leipzig, 1849.

Drewitz, Ingeborg, *Berliner Salons. Gesellschaft und Literatur zwischen Aufklärung und Industriezeitalter*, Berlin, 1965.

Duelli-Klein, Renate *et al.*, eds., *Feministische Wissenschaft und Frauenstudium*, Göttingen, 1982.

Eifert, Christiane and Rouette, Susanne, eds., *Unter allen Umständen. Frauengeschichte(n) in Berlin*, 1986.

Evans, Richard, *The Feminist Movement in Germany, 1894–1933*, London, 1976.

Fout, John, ed, *German Women in the Nineteenth Century*, New York, 1984.

Frederiksen, Elke, *Die Frauenfrage in Deutschland 1865–1915*, Stuttgart, 1981.

Frederiksen, Elke, *Women Writers of Austria, Germany and Switzerland: An Annotated Biographical Guide*, New York, 1988.

Frevert, Ute, *Women in German History: From Bourgeois Emancipation to Sexual Liberation*, Oxford, New York and Munich, 1993 [1986].

Gilbert, Sandra M. and Gubar, Sandra, *The Madwoman in the Attic: The Woman Writer and the Nineteenth-Century Literary Imagination*, New Haven, 1979.

Goetzinger, Germaine, *Für die Selbstverwirklichung der Frau: Louise Aston in Selbstzeugnissen und Dokumenten*, Frankfurt am Main, 1983.

Good, David F., Grander, Margarete and Maynes, Mary Jo, eds, *Austrian Women in the Nineteenth and Twentieth Centuries*, Oxford, 1996.

Goodman, Kay, 'German Women and Autobiography in the nineteenth century: Louise Aston, Fanny Lewald Malwida von Meysenbug and Marie von Ebner-Eschenbach', PhD Diss., Madison, 1977.

Gnüg, H and Möhrmann, R., *Frauen Literatur Geschichte. Schreibende Frauen vom Mittelalter bis zur Gegenwart*, Stuttgart, 1985.

Grab, Walter and Schoeps, Julian, eds, *Juden im Vormarz und in der deutschen Revolution von 1848*, Stuttgart and Bonn, 1983.

Greven-Aschoff, Barbara, *Die bürgerliche Frauenbewegung in Deutschland 1894–1933*, Göttingen, 1981.

Hausen, Karin, ed., *Frauen suchen ihre Geschichte. Historische Studien zum 19. und 20. Jahrhundert*, Munich 1983.

Hummel-Haasis, Gerlinde, ed., *Schwestern zerreißt eure Ketten. Zeugnisse zur Geschichte der Frauen in der Revolution von 1848/9*, Munich, 1982.

Hermand, Jost, *Das junge Deutschland*, Stuttgart, 1966.

Koepcke, Cordula, *Frauenbewegung. Zwischen 1800 und 2000. Was sie war, was sie jetzt ist und was sie werden soll*, Heroldsberg and Nürnberg, 1979.

Kreyßig, Friedrich, *Vorlesungen über den deutschen Roman der Gegenwart*, Berlin, 1871.

Lange, Helene and Bäumer, Gertrud, *Handbuch der Frauenbewegung*, 5 vols, Weinheim, 1980 [1901-1906].

Linnhoff, Ursula, *'Zur Freiheit, oh, zur einzig wahren.' Schreibende Frauen kämpfen um ihre Rechte*, Cologne, 1979.

Menschik, Jutta, *Feminismus. Geschichte, Theorie, Praxis*, Cologne, 1977.

Möhrmann, Renate, ed., *Die andere Frau. Emanzipationsanätze deutscher Schriftstellerinnen im Vorfeld der Achtundvierziger Revolution*, Stuttgart, 1977.

——, ed., *Frauenemanzipation im deutschen Vormärz. Texte und Dokumente*, Stuttgart, 1978.

Morgenstern, Lina, *Die Frauen des 19. Jahrhunderts. Biographische und cultur-historische Zeit- und Charaktergemälde*, 3 vols, Berlin, 1888–1891.

Müller, Klaus-Detlef, *Autobiographie und Roman. Studien zur literarischen Autobiographie der Goethezeit*, Tübingen, 1976.

Nipperdey, Thomas, *Deutsche Geschichte 1800–1860. Bürgerwelt und starker Staat*, Munich, 1983.

Pataky, Sophie, *Lexikon deutscher Frauen*, 2 vols, Berlin, 1898.

Paulsen, W. ed., *Die Frau als Heldin und Autorin*, Berne and Munich, 1979.

Sagarra, Eda, *Am Introduction to Nineteenth Century Germany*, London, 1960.

——, *A Social History of Germany 1648–1914*, London, 1977.

Schenk, Herrad, *Die feministische Herausforderung. 150 Jahre Frauenbewegung in Deutschland*, Munich, 1988 [1980].

Schultz, Hans Jürgen, ed., *Frauen. Portaits aus zwei Jahrhunderten*, Stuttgart, 1981.

Simmel, Monika, *Erziehung zum Weibe. Mädchenbildung im 19. Jahrhundert*, Frankfurt am Main, 1980.

Sveistrup, Hans and Zahn-Harnack, Agnes von, eds, *Die Frauenfrage in Deutschland. Strömungen und Gegenströmungen*, Tübingen, 1969.

Thönnessen, Werner, *Frauenemanzipation. Politik und Literatur der deutschen Sozialdekokratie zur Frauenbewegung*, Frankfurt am Main, 1969.

Wägenbauer, Birgit, *Die Pathologie der Liebe. Literarische Weiblichkeitsentwürfe um 1800*, Berlin, 1996.

Weber, Marianne, *Ehefrau und Mutter in der Rechtsentwicklung*, Tübingen, 1907.

Zinnecker, Jürgen, *Sozialgeschichte der Mädchenbildung. Zur Kritik der Schulerziehung von Mädchen im bürgerlichen Patriarchat*, Weinheim and Basle, 1973.

INDEX

cash in her hands than it flowed out again. She inherited 8,000 Marks from her mother in 1905, but by the following year this had been spent.

Though Franziska zu Reventlow's stance towards money appears to have been informed by the studied indifference of the aristocrat, it was also typical of the relationship of the bohemian towards money; it must be faced that she could have lived a much less stressful life if she had been able to sort out her financial affairs. In her last work of any significance, *Der Geldkomplex* (1916), she laughs at her own incapacity to deal with money by diagnosing it as a Freudian neurosis which can, ostensibly, by cured by psychoanalysis in a special sanatorium. However, the first-person narrator of the story finds that money, not the lack of it, is the cure for her nervous condition: she finds gambling a relaxation: '... you see nothing but money and feel nothing but money and that is just what I was in need of'.[92] At the end of the novel, the main character loses all her money in a bank failure, but shrugs off the disaster with a flippancy characteristic of the literary characters in Wahnmoching, where one word could be used to end all discussion: 'Mirobuk!'. In playing poker with her own life, Franziska zu Reventlow made that, and not her writing, her creative work of art; and what could be more Nietzschean?

EPILOGUE

It is astonishing to note that literary examples of nervous or psychosomatic illness such as that encountered in Reuter's *Aus guter Familie* are as frequent in the works of women writers at the end of the century as they were at the beginning, indicating that women throughout the century were dependant on men for an evaluation of their own identity, though the authorial position has become much more critical of such an attitude. Male characters are portrayed as harsh judges of women's morality, no doubt because they were in real life: upon a kiss (in Lou Salomé's story *Abteilung 'Innere Männer'*), or lack of one (in Gabriele Reuter's *Aus guter Familie*), a woman's whole fate can hang. Only the most brazen woman, such as Franziska zu Reventlow, could challenge the assumptions about the respectable woman's need to preserve her virtue, and even she adhered to what can be called the ideology of motherhood, which dominated women's perception of their role in society in spite of the new sciences of psychoanalysis and sexology. These were about to overturn many assumptions dear to the German middle class, such as the assumption that children are without sexual desire.

Several important features of German cultural life became more reactionary rather than less as the century drew to its close. As has been shown, the new Civil Code contained little to relieve the repression of women; in addition, the banning of socialism from 1878 until 1890 meant that socialist feminists such as Clara Zetkin and Lily Braun were taboo to the moderates, who in their turn opposed the efforts of the radicals, such as Hedwig Dohm and Helene Stöcker. They, as we have seen, drew much from the arch anti-feminist Nietzsche. Such paradoxes, and the factional splits in the feminist movement in Germany, would continue to hamper progress until the removal of the *Reichsvereinsgesetz* in 1908 resulted in the BDF being flooded by moderates who had hitherto held back from any political activity. The right-wing nature of the German feminist movement after Gertrud Bäumer became its president in 1910 placed it on a path which would lead it very close to collaboration with the National Socialists.

Anti-Semitism was another feature of German cultural and political life which was as pronounced at the end of the century as it was at the beginning. The earlier, harmless view of a nation as a 'people' such as the Saxons or the Prussians became, with the insistence on the German *Volk* as sole constituent of the Reich, a blinkered concept which excluded other nationalities and made the Jews, not even a nation at that time, doubly suspicious and the target of bitter anti-Semitism from such historians as Treitschke. This occurred in spite of the acknowledged cultural debt which the Germans owed to the Jews, dating from the efforts of Moses Mendelssohn onwards. The anti-Semitism portrayed by Franziska zu Reventlow in *Herrn Dames Aufzeichnungen* sounds a warning note for what was to come. It is also significant that many conversions of Jews to Christianity had not always been as sincere as those of Henriette Herz and Rahel Varnhagen earlier in the century. Many Jewish women, such as Fanny Lewald and Hedwig Dohm, found that conversion to Christianity left them in a spiritual limbo, and the result was unfamiliarity with either Judaism or Christianity. What nobody could anticipate was that conversion would not be recognised as a qualification for German nationality under the National Socialists.

What does change by the end of the century is that women are no longer prepared to be the instigators of man's creativity, but instead self-consciously use their writing as a pathway to their own self-knowledge, even if they need a male presence (a husband or lover), or the influence of a male thinker for this to be made manifest. The influence of some women, such as Rahel von Varnhagen, Bettina von Arnim and Malwida von Meysenbug, has remained seminal, though the other women discussed in these pages have not – yet – become sufficiently known to exert such an influence. The effects of two wars, the subsequent division of Germany and, finally, reunification, have interrupted the natural process of influence, but there now appears to be a determined *Putsch* to make up for lost time, as the secondary works amply demonstrate.

INDICATIVE BIBLIOGRAPHY

This bibliography is not exhaustive; where possible, the collected works have been cited, otherwise the main works are cited in every case, and as many secondary sources as exist or as many as was practicable, there being a wide variation in the material available. Articles are not included in the bibliography; relevant details are given in the footnotes to the chapters.

INDIVIDUAL WRITERS

Andreas-Salomé, Lou

Primary Works:

Andreas-Salomé, Lou, (alias 'Henri Lou'), *Im Kampf um Gott*, Berlin, 1885.
——, *Henrik Ibsen's Frauen-Gestalten*, Berlin, 1892.
——, *Friedrich Nietzsche in seinen Werken*, Vienna, 1894.
——, *Ruth*, Stuttgart, 1895.
——, *Fenitschka. Eine Ausschweifung. Zwei Erzählungen*, Stuttgart, 1898.
——, *Menschenkinder. Novellencyklus*, 1899.
——, *Ma*, Stuttgart, 1901.
——, *Im Zwischenland*, Stuttgart and Berlin, 1902.
——, *Die Erotik*, Frankfurt, 1910.
——, *Rainer Maria Rilke*, Leipzig, 1928.
——, *Lebensrückblick. Grundriß einiger Lebenserinnerungen*, ed. by Ernst Pfeiffer, Frankfurt am Main, 1975 [1951].

Secondary Sources:

Binion, Rudolph, *Frau Lou: Nietzsche's Wayward Disciple*, Princeton, 1968.
Koepcke, Cordula, *Lou Andreas-Salomé. Leben, Persönlichkeit, Werk*, Frankfurt am Main, 1986.
Livingstone, Angela, *Lou Andreas-Salomé*, London, 1984.
Mackey, Ilona Schmidt, *Lou Salomé, inspiratrice et interpréte de Nietzsche, Rilke et Freud*, Paris, 1968.
Martin, Biddy, *Woman and Modernity: The (Life)Styles of Lou Andreas-Salomé*, Ithaca and London, 1991.